open your heart

open your heart

12 Weeks of *Daily Devotions*

Martin Shannon
with Carol Showalter

PARACLETE PRESS
BREWSTER, MASSACHUSETTS

3D

Open Your Heart: 12 Weeks of Daily Devotions

2008 First Printing

Copyright © 2008 by Paraclete Press

ISBN: 978-1-55725-580-8

Cover photo of Martin Shannon by Hans Spatzeck-Olsen.
Cover photo of Carol Showalter by Robert Tucker.

Library of Congress Cataloging-in-Publication Data

Shannon, Martin.
  Open your heart : 12 weeks of daily devotions / Martin Shannon, with
    Carol Showalter.
        p. cm.
    Includes bibliographical references.
    ISBN-13: 978-1-55725-580-8
  1. Devotional calendars. I. Showalter, Carol. II. Title.
    BV4811.S53 2008
    242'.2—dc22   2007050152

10 9 8 7 6 5 4 3 2 1

Published by Paraclete Press
Brewster, Massachusetts
www.paracletepress.com
Printed in the United States of America

Contents

Week One The Transparent Heart

Day 1   Hide and Seek

R E A D | Genesis 3:1–13

"[Adam] said, 'I heard the sound of thee in the garden, and I was afraid, because I was naked; and I hid myself.'" (v. 10)

"Amidst all of the instructions about obedience, the exhortations to persevere, and the admonitions against being unfaithful, it might be possible to forget that the way of discipleship is, first and foremost, about a *relationship*. All the methods and teachings and disciplines we can possibly follow are really of no value whatsoever unless, first, like branches attached to the vine, our lives are attached to Jesus Christ. That relationship is the only credible beginning and the only worthy end of the disciple's life."

These words, from the final day's reading of Session 1, make a fitting introduction to the twelve weeks of reflections for Session 2. We ended the daily readings of *Your Whole Life* with this essential reminder: the wholeness of our lives is dependent upon the wholeness of our relationship with God—with the One whose power made us, whose grace redeemed us, and whose love always intends the things that make for our wholeness and well-being. Our relationship with God is the North Star from which we take all the other bearings on our spiritual journey, and without which we are consigned to aimless searching and wandering.

What the Bible makes clear is that our relationship with God was dealt a severe wounding, a *breaking*, from almost the very beginning. In fact, all relationships suffered at the hands of Adam and Eve's rebellious choices. When the writer of Genesis tells us that, at first, the Man and the Woman were "both naked, and were not ashamed" (Genesis 2:25), he is describing so very much more than their physical condition. He is describing the condition of their hearts. Before God and before one another they stood entirely vulnerable and fearlessly transparent. But the joyful fellowship, even intimacy, that God intended for them—and us—to share with him and with one another was sacrificed for the sake of their own self-will and proud independence. Freedom of spirit and openness of heart were replaced with the burden of guilt and the hiddenness of fear.

You are probably reading these words because you already know something about freedom and openness, and you also know something about guilt and hiddenness. And you know which of these makes for a more joyful and whole life. It's just that getting from one to the other is not as easy as we would like. Thankfully, the Genesis story does not end with Adam and Eve's decision to hide from one another and from their Maker. God came to find them. "Where are you?" he kindly (and probably, persistently) calls out to those whom he loves (Genesis 3:8). The only sensible option is to answer. Perhaps reaching a hand out of the bushes, just far enough for it to be seen, is one way we begin to *open our hearts* and find our way back to God and to one another.

REFLECT | *Describe as best you can "where you are" in your relationship with God. How would you describe the level of openness you have with others, with those who are closest to you, and with those in your 3D group?*

Day 2   Open Your Hearts

READ | 2 Corinthians 6:1–13

Our mouth is open to you, Corinthians; our heart is wide. . . . In return—I speak as to children—widen your hearts also. (vv. 11, 13)

One thing that can certainly be said of the apostle Paul is that he was entirely honest and forthright in his relationship with his fellow Christians. His letters reveal a man whose passion for love and for truthfulness inspired every sentence he wrote, and this was never more apparent than when he had something difficult or even unwelcome to say.

There is a sense of estrangement between Paul and the Christians at Corinth as he writes this letter. We do not know all of the details, but of this much we are sure: the problem is severe and divisive, and, unless it is pulled up from the roots, it threatens to choke the very life out of this young church. So, Paul confronts the problem with characteristic directness—lovingly and truthfully.

What an example of wise diplomacy this entire letter is! There are allusions to the trouble, but always they are couched in a framework of positive, loving concern that Paul had toward these, his spiritual children. He knows that a necessary rebuke he has given has caused some of his readers to grow cold and resentful toward him. In their anger, some have questioned his motives and maligned his integrity. Even so, he writes with a sense of confidence that they are all still related to one another in Christ, and that the Holy Spirit of truth will eventually bring insight out of misunderstanding, and reconciliation out of discord. He opens his heart to his readers in the hope that they, in turn, will open their hearts to him and to one another: "our heart is wide—widen your hearts also."

The apostle Paul's approach is an example, and a great encouragement, to those who are looking for something deeper than superficially pleasant and polite relationships. Remember yesterday's reading. Adam and Eve were "designed" by God to live transparently with one another. This means, of course, that there are just as likely to be moments of conflict as moments of concord, just as likely to be moments of anger as moments of affection. But all of these "moments" can be steps toward a deeper, lasting, trusting, open relationship in Christ. Anyone who has once tasted the richness of this kind of fellowship rarely can be satisfied with anything less loving and honest.

In order to experience that kind of fellowship, we really have to open our hearts—"widen" our hearts, as Paul says—to one another. Think of your heart as the doorway into your life. Does it remain closed, or so small and narrow that no one can gain full access to the real you? Or, with a growing confidence in the power of God's love and truth, will you unfasten the bolts and open the way for others to find welcome?

REFLECT | *Does the idea of "opening your heart" appeal to you or frighten you? Why? Think for a moment about the various relationships that you have: which ones are superficial; which ones are deep and meaningful? What makes them so?*

Day 3   One Heart and Soul

READ | Acts 4:32–37

*Now the company of those who believed were of one heart and soul.
. . . (v. 32)*

The book of the Acts of the Apostles records the life of
the first-generation church, its missionary work, its values, its
sufferings, and its growth. But by no means does it present
some kind of utopian dream. Those early Christians knew a
fair share about conflict and dissent, as a complete reading
of this book reveals.

Still, there was no mistaking that something new and
different was taking place in the lives of these new believers,
and that the strongest evidence of their conversion was, in
fact, their relationships with one another. The newborn
church of Jerusalem exemplified the truth of Jesus' words,
spoken to his disciples on the night before he died: "By this
all men will know that you are my disciples, if you have love
for one another" (John 13:35).

The writer's description of this oneness of heart and
soul is intended to give us a taste, to whet our appetite for
the kind of Christianity experienced by those first believers.
Through the centuries, the church has referred to this as
a model of Christian community, one that has formed the
inspiration for Christian communities in every generation.
Don't you find it fascinating that among the very first signs
of the power of God's saving grace in Jesus Christ is the
depth of communion shared by his followers? If the Fall
resulted in our hiding from one another, then the Cross is
meant to bring us back together.

This is the promise, of course, but its fulfillment is not without difficulty. Today's Christian is just as apt to find him or herself living in isolation as did Adam and Eve. Individualism has so permeated the thinking of our time that none of us is exempt from its influence. For example, most of us are uncomfortable with, or even resistant to, any kind of authority over us, especially in spiritual matters. For all intents and purposes, we make ourselves the final court of appeal in all questions of dispute. Allowing others access into our lives, even by simply listening to the way that they see things (or see *us*), is still one of the most difficult tests we face.

The church has traditionally understood that when the writer of Acts says that no one claimed full ownership over his or her possessions, he was writing about more than just material goods. Giving to one another for the sake of the common good—for the sake of love—includes giving our thoughts and our wills, our opinions and our desires, as much as our time and our money. The fact that those first-century Christians were willing to open their hearts to one another in such a radical way is a testimony to the power of the gospel, and a challenge to the Christians of our own generation. You and I are descendents of this early community—we are its inheritors. So, how are we handling what has been passed on to us?

R E F L E C T | *Examine your own heart as honestly as you can. What do you find attractive about this image of Christian community? What do you find intimidating? Why?*

Day 4   A Simple Yes or No

R E A D | Matthew 5:33–38, 6:1

Jesus said, "Let what you say be simply 'Yes' or 'No'—anything more than this comes from evil." (v. 37)

In light of our reflections on what it means to have a transparent heart, here is a text worth pondering again and again. Some have interpreted Jesus' words as an instruction against the making of promises or vows of any kind. But this misses the point. It is not the *making* of promises that Jesus criticizes, but the *breaking* of them. Jesus is drawing a picture of a new kind of righteousness, one that "exceeds that of the scribes and Pharisees" (v. 20). This new righteousness is not the legalistic, hard kind of "rightness" that religious people sometimes display. It is an inner attitude that is without guile, without the desire to conceal or deceive. It is a righteousness that says what it means and means what it says. To the man or woman of integrity, nothing more is needed beyond a simple "yes" or "no." That, it seems, is the point being made here.

Our communication with each other should be so unreserved, so uncalculated, that all we need is a forthright and uncomplicated "yes or no" to express the truth of what we are saying. The problem, of course, is that our words are connected directly with our hearts—"for out of the abundance of the heart the mouth speaks," said Jesus (Matthew 12:34)—and, there, things are not nearly so simple. We cautiously measure our words because we are not so certain about what they will reveal or where they will lead us. We are afraid that we will be misunderstood; we do not entirely understand our own mixed feelings and motives; we do not want to commit to something without leaving ourselves a way out; we might say something that we really do not mean; or, we might say something that we really did mean, but did not mean to say. You see how complicated it all gets.

The answer is not to close our mouths and say nothing at all. The psalmist reveals a better way when he prays: "Search me, O God, and know my heart, try me and know my thoughts, and see if there be any wicked way in me, and lead me in the way everlasting" (Psalm 139:23–24). We do not always know if the "yes or no" of our lips reflects all that is in our hearts, for the heart that we know least is our own. Together with the psalmist, therefore, we depend upon the light of the Holy Spirit to acquaint us with the hidden depths of our mixed-up thoughts and motives.

Opening our hearts to God and to one another requires that we take a certain risk by opening our mouths. We do our best to simply express what we believe to be true, and then God uses—even blesses—our imperfect efforts and adds the light and guidance of the Holy Spirit to our human words and thoughts. He may confirm or correct the courses we are choosing, but in either case, the result is something of a miracle: increased self-understanding and deepened fellowship in Christ. Do not be afraid to seek this simplicity and openness of heart!

REFLECT | *Describe an experience when the words you spoke revealed (perhaps more than you wanted) the hidden thoughts of your heart. What is most difficult for you about making a straightforward commitment to do or not to do something?*

Day 5   The Healing Power of Confession

READ | James 5:13–20

Therefore, confess your sins to one another, and pray for one another, that you may be healed. (v. 16)

James is making a very powerful and a very hopeful connection here. Without claiming to understand exactly how, he is saying that sin and sickness have some kind of association. In some languages, the words for salvation and health actually come from the same root. Theologians have argued about this relationship for centuries, and we are not about to solve this mystery today. But of this much we can be certain—sin that is kept hidden in the dark eventually produces dis-ease and affliction, while sin that is confessed and forgiven eventually leads to peace and wholeness.

Think of a nasty cut caused by a sharp and dirty piece of metal. The temptation may be to quickly stem the bleeding, cover the wound, and get on with the business at hand— whatever leads to the quickest and most painless return to the normal living of the day. But by day's end, the sore is red and tender. Things are anything but normal. A closer examination reveals a dark metal filing, embedded inside the cut. No amount of first-aid cream or bandaging can bring relief. As long as that dirty particle of metal is there, the wound will fester and throb.

Confession for the soul is like the tweezers that reach into the body—sometimes by our own hand, but just as often by the hand of another, take hold of the offending fragment, and remove it from the messy wound. Now, free of infection, and with ever-lessening pain, the body finds that full healing can take place.

This analogy is not perfect, but you can see the similarities. Yes, a good deal of confession can take place directly between the soul and God. The tax collector who prayed in the temple, "God, be merciful to me a sinner" (Luke 18:13), had no need of witnesses in order to know heaven's grace. But, just as often, we need to seek out the presence of Christ in a brother or sister who will listen to our confession and audibly express to us the loving forgiveness of the Great Physician. In certain cases, when sin is particularly grave or sensitive (such as sins of a sexual or very personal nature), we need to seek out the wise and private counsel of a pastor or priest. More often, we can bring our self-inflicted wounds to the fellowship of our sisters and brothers, and there find all the forgiveness and help and healing that we need.

Healing comes in many ways, not the least of which is the relaxation and inner peace that grow out of a clear conscience. A great many of us unnecessarily endure distress and carry burdens that can be relieved through the simple admission to another person that we have done, said, or thought wrongly. Isn't it usually our pride—preserving our good image or fearing what others might think—that keeps us from humbling ourselves to confess before another human being the sin that is crippling us?

REFLECT | *Describe a time when admitting your wrongness to another person brought a sense of relief and joy. What had you "lost" by keeping the sin to yourself; what did you "gain" by confessing it? In what areas of your life do you know you are trying to protect yourself from humbly exposing your sin and need?*

Day 6   The Healing Balm of Forgiveness

READ | Psalm 32

Blessed is he whose transgression is forgiven. . . . (v. 1)

Yesterday we considered the image of an infected wound as one way of describing the effect of sin that goes untreated in the human soul. The first step toward wholeness is to open our hearts to the probing work of the Holy Spirit as God endeavors to pinpoint the source of the problem. If confession is like the sometimes unpleasant tool that reaches in and plucks our sin from the dark recesses of our souls, then forgiveness is the soothing balm that brings relief, comfort, and restoration to the wound it has left.

There are a number of psalms, including Psalm 32, that have traditionally been considered as "penitential" in nature (some others are Psalms 6, 38, 51, and 102). These are essentially prayers of confession, and the crux of their message is that opening our hearts to God includes honestly and humbly acknowledging our offenses. After all, God knows us even better than we know ourselves, and there is nothing about our lives that remains hidden from his sight. The idea that God *sees* everything about us is not meant to force us into fearful hiding (as Adam and Eve attempted to do). Quite to the contrary. God's all-knowing vision of our hearts is meant to bring us back to his side when we have strayed, back to our feet when we have fallen, back to wholeness when we are broken.

The psalmist describes the dismal condition of both his soul and his body when he vainly attempts to cover up his sin and hide his iniquity: I am wasting away; it is as if an unbearably heavy weight clings to my shoulders; my strength has evaporated like the sweat of my brow under the burning sun; all I can do is sigh with discomfort. A dramatic picture, to be sure, but anyone who has experienced even a portion of what he is describing knows full well of what the psalmist is speaking—*guilt.* To the untended soul, the poisonous power of this insidious dis-ease is debilitating and eventually lethal. There is only one antidote, and it comes from heaven itself: "Blessed is he whose transgression is *forgiven!*"

It is as if the psalmist wakes up to his dreadful condition and says, "Why am I living this way? As destructive and inexcusable as my actions (my attitudes, my words, my omissions) have been, there is nothing I have done that has surprised my Maker. So, there is no point in my trying to act as if nothing at all has happened. I will face up to my sin, I will admit it to myself, and I will confess it openly."

No wonder the psalmist begins his song with the word "blessed." He is giving testimony to the joy and freedom that he himself has experienced. The medicine of forgiveness is a guaranteed cure to the sin-sick soul, for its limitless source is the very heart of God himself. The only cost to us is to humble ourselves enough to ask for it.

REFLECT | *Administering the remedy of forgiveness goes both ways—sometimes we must receive it, and sometimes we must give it. Recall an example of both in your life and describe what took place. To whom is it most difficult for you to say, "I am wrong; please forgive me"? Why?*

Day 7 Bearing One Another's Burdens

READ | Galatians 6:1–10

Bear one another's burdens, and so fulfill the law of Christ. (v. 2)

Today we come back to one of the sweetest and most fulfilling fruits of living with a transparent heart—love. Certainly, learning to trust and to open our hearts to one another is not without risk. The story of Adam and Eve reminds us that hiding is "second nature" to us. But it also reminds us that we were made for intimate fellowship with God and one another, and that we will never be fully satisfied, we will never be whole, until we know once again the bond of love that unites us. Can there be any greater sense of fulfillment than what is found in the deep and genuine sharing of pain and joy, the mutual acceptance of one another with all our flaws and failings, the confidence that we can know and be known without any fear of judgment or rejection? Surely, this sense of communion is one of the great gifts God has given the Christian family.

Paul elevates this aspect of our life in Christ to the highest possible value when he writes, "Bear one another's burdens, and so fulfill the law of Christ." We hear an echo of the words of Jesus, teaching us to love God with all our heart, mind, soul, and strength. This is the first and great commandment, he said, and the second is just like it: Love your neighbor as yourself. To bear one another's burdens— to take into our own heart the weight of another's heart—is to become like our Lord himself. To treat another's needs as if they were our own; to be mindful of his or her interests and dreams, as if they were our own; to enjoy another's success as if it were our own—this is the kind of self-sacrificial investment that Jesus made in the lives of his disciples. At its most generous, it was an investment that led him to the most extravagant love of all: "Greater love has no man than this, that a man lay down his life for his friends" (John 15:13). Sometimes this is exactly what opening our heart to others feels like—like laying down our lives. It can be sacrificial and costly. But it can also be rich and rewarding.

Much has been said about the wonders of rapid communication and instant message sending. Computers and cell phones have put us at one another's immediate beck and call. But has all this technology made us any more personally committed to one another? Some have argued that modern technology has actually gotten in the way of genuine contact and personal investment, and that the world has grown increasingly impersonal even though advanced communication has made it ever smaller. In any case, one thing remains certain in every generation: the human heart longs for fellowship . . . genuine, deep, and abiding. Meeting with friends in a weekly group may seem artificial and contrived, but only if we fail to see beneath it the potential for opening our hearts to one another, for reaching out and connecting with someone else's life in a meaningful and life-changing way. There is certainly nothing artificial about that. In fact, ever since Adam and Eve lost that fellowship in the Garden of Eden, God has been about the business of planting new gardens wherever his people gather together. There he intends to grow fruit that will endure forever.

REFLECT | *What does it take for you to be invested in—to be sensitive and responsive to—the lives of others? What does it take for you to allow others to be invested in your life? In what specific way(s) is God asking you to lay down your life this week?*

Week Two Sometimes the Hardest
Person to Forgive is Myself

Day 1   Imperfect . . . and Still Loved

READ | Philippians 3:12–21

Not that I have already obtained this or am already perfect; but I press on to make it my own, because Christ Jesus has made me his own. (v. 12)

Last week, while reflecting on what it means to live with a transparent heart before God and one another, we began to look at the place of confession and forgiveness as building blocks for genuine fellowship in Christ. Communion cannot long endure under the stressful weight of unforgiven sin. Despite knowing this principle, our critical and sometimes hypersensitive natures can still be all too quick to rush to judgment and find fault with others. (Just consider the last time you lost something—whose name did you use when you called out, "_____, where's my _____?"). Just as often, however, we may harbor a deep, underlying, unforgiving attitude toward ourselves. In fact, a super-critical attitude toward others may actually be a symptom of our refusal to accept ourselves as imperfect.

Paul points to his own life to demonstrate both the problem as well as the cure. He was of a religious bent, we would say. As a boy, he was well trained in Jewish Law, and had taken it with great seriousness. He studied for the rabbinical ministry under some of the finest teachers of his day, and was numbered among the elite Pharisaic party. His zeal for righteousness finally led him to defend his Jewish faith with an aggression that knew no bounds. When he heard of the Christians, who seemed to be teaching some dangerous perversion of the Scriptures, he hastened to help those who were trying to stamp out the movement in its infancy (see Acts 9). But, with whom was Paul really fighting?

On the road from Jerusalem to Damascus, Paul met the living Christ, and his life turned from persecutor to disciple. There, under the blinding light of heaven, his eyes were opened to a truth that had, to that point, eluded him. "Since we are justified (made righteous) by faith," he wrote to the Romans, "we have *peace with God* through our Lord Jesus Christ" (5:1). What a wealth of meaning in that verse. It speaks of a settled rest, of a peace that passes understanding, of an utter confidence in and relinquishment to the mercy of God.

By the time Paul wrote to the Christians at Philippi, he had spent years in the service of his Savior. He was a hero in the eyes of those who had come to know the love of God through his ministry. In fact, the whole church knew his reputation as a faithful apostle of the Lord Jesus Christ. Yet, still, after all these accomplishments and at this late point in his life, he is content to say to his readers, "not that I have already attained it, or am already perfect . . ." (v. 12). He recognizes that he still has far to go, that he is still an unfinished sculpture in the hands of God.

What about you? Is being flawed really all right with you? How upset do you get when you fail at something, or when someone criticizes you? Are you striving so much for perfection that you miss the joy of grace? The apostle Paul was certain of one unchanging thing, despite his own imperfections: "Christ Jesus has made me his own." Can any number of defects detach us from the nail-pierced hands of Jesus?

REFLECT | *What about you? How do you feel about your faults, your weaknesses? Is the love of God really a free gift for you, or must you do something to earn it? What connection can you see between the way you see others, and the way you see yourself?*

Day 2   If Any One Does Sin

READ | 1 John 2:1–6

My little children, I am writing this to you so that you may not sin, but if any one does sin, we have an advocate with the Father, Jesus Christ the righteous. (v. 1)

There's that word again—sin. If it seems as if we are spending a lot of time discussing this uncomfortable subject, it is good to remember why we are doing so, because telling a Christian that he or she spends too much time dealing with sin is a little like telling a doctor not to spend so much time dealing with sickness. The fact is, sin is the chief obstacle to personal wholeness and loving fellowship with others. Ignoring it will not make it go away. Better that we face it, head on, identify its symptoms, examine its workings, and determine its causes. Then we can apply directly the only remedy that will cure the pain it causes—the forgiving love of God in Jesus Christ.

The truth is, many Christians find sin embarrassing. We can admit to the big generalization—"Yes, I am a sinner"— but we are less ready to admit to the specific act—"My friend, here is where I sinned against you." The great Bible teacher, F. B. Meyer, explains that this is because Christians have a "defective idea" about what sin really is: they would not hesitate to face up to their sin "if they realized what God's standard of holiness and sinlessness is; if they understood that sin consists in coming *short of his glory* as much as in distinct violation of his will; if they knew that there may be sin in motive as much as in act, and even in lack of love" (F. B. Meyer, *Great Verses Through the Bible*).

We may not even welcome such clarification, since it unmasks some of the thinly veiled excuses we make for ourselves: I was only trying to be helpful; I didn't actually mean to say that; I really wouldn't do anything to hurt you. If we are serious about our life as followers of Jesus Christ, then, sooner or later, just as he did with his own disciples, he will upset all our rationalizations and point out to us what is really stirring in our hearts. And when that happens, we must not mistake the disillusionment we have with ourselves for the displeasure of God. In fact, when my sin is disclosed, it usually turns out that the only person disappointed in me *is* me. Most of my friends already know my weaknesses quite well, and God is most assuredly familiar with every single one of them.

This is why John is so quick to remind his readers of *God's* answer to human sin. Yes, he writes, we should not sin. But, if we do, there is no need for us to defend ourselves, no need to make excuses or to paint a prettier picture than the one that suddenly appears before our eyes. God has provided a faithful advocate, Jesus Christ the only righteous One, and, in the face of our heart's disappointment, he will speak on our behalf. If he forgives us, than we have no choice but to forgive ourselves for being less than what we want to be, less than what we know we should be, and less than what we thought we were.

REFLECT | *What do you find most difficult about receiving forgiveness from God, and from another person? Think of an excuse you made for yourself in the past week. What was the purpose of making that excuse? If you put the excuse aside, with what are you left?*

Day 3   Who is to Condemn?

READ | Romans 8:31–39

Who shall bring any charge against God's elect? It is God who justifies; who is to condemn? (v. 33)

The eighth chapter of Paul's letter to the Romans is undoubtedly one of the most heartening and hopeful texts of the entire Bible. It begins, "There is now no condemnation for those who are in Christ Jesus." No condemnation—why is the apostle so passionate and persistent about assuring his readers of this truth? Clearly he has come to know human nature quite intimately. He knows himself, and he knows his fellow Christians, and, as a result, he knows our penchant for despair and self-reproach.

Isn't our fear of the judgment of others and, even more, the condemnation we level against ourselves, among the foremost causes of self-consciousness and anxiety? Paul seems to be saying, "Relax!"—remember who and what you are by recalling who God is and what he has done for you; do not forget from whence you have come, and for what purpose you were created; never doubt the power of God's love for you or its presence even in the most difficult of circumstances.

Every human life—every life—must endure its times of suffering. It matters not how prosperous and peaceful things may look in the lives of others. Thorns and thistles are now sown into the human condition. There is no escaping their sting (see Genesis 3:18). It is therefore imperative that you know, says Paul to his readers, that you have been claimed by God for his purposes; that he made you, has redeemed you, and is at work in you, even in the most discouraging moments; that he is able to work everything together for your good; and that absolutely nothing can separate you from his love.

The real "condemner" is none other than our old adversary, the devil, who, as Peter writes, goes about like a roaring lion, seeking those whom he may devour (1 Peter 5:8). He is in search of the weak and vulnerable places in our lives, and there he slings forth his fiery darts of accusation and temptation. Especially at those low times of great disappointment or fear, or when we have suffered hurt or embarrassment; and at those high times when we have enjoyed a surprising success or have bathed for a moment in the praise of others—these are the times when we are most at risk before the devil's attacks.

It is important to know that the real purpose of temptations at such hours as these goes beyond getting us to "act sinfully." Hell's deeper aim is to plunge us into condemnation and hopelessness, for that is the most effective condition for dampening our love of God and isolating us from the fellowship of our brothers and sisters. Is there any question now about why Paul's confident words carry such an urgent tone? Our spiritual lives depend upon their truth, and upon our adherence to that truth. You bemoan your imperfections, but who is there to condemn you? You have a Savior, and there is no power imaginable—including your own regrets—that can separate you from him.

REFLECT | *In what areas of your life are you most likely to experience condemnation? (Are they at all related to the areas where you are most likely to judge others?) Which of these verses in Romans 8:31–39 is most important to you? Why?*

Day 4   Having Mercy

READ | Matthew 5:1–11

Blessed are the merciful, for they shall obtain mercy. (v. 7)

There is a biblical phrase that appears numerous times in the Old Testament, describing God as "merciful and gracious, slow to anger, and abounding in steadfast love and faithfulness" (e.g., Exodus 34:6; Psalms 86:15, 103:8). To the Hebrews, mercy was first and foremost an attribute of God himself, a characteristic of the heavenly kingdom. This was especially true in two particular ways: in God's care and provision for his vulnerable creation, and in his forgiveness of sin. In other words, the mercy of God is seen in the compassionate aid he renders to those who are needy or helpless or undeserving. Of course, all of us fall within those categories and, from time to time, we are particularly aware of just how weak and unworthy we are. And though such times usually involve a good deal of grief and discomfort, they can also be the times when we are most aware of God's merciful love. Remember the words of the apostle Paul, who wrote: "While we were still weak, at the right time Christ died for the ungodly. . . . God shows his love for us in that while we were yet sinners Christ died for us" (Romans 5:6, 8). Jesus is the mercy of God in the flesh, and the Cross is the premier instrument by which he helps the helpless and favors the unfavorable.

Is it any wonder, then, that "the merciful" should be among the list of those most blessed in the kingdom of God? If mercy is an attribute of God himself, and Jesus is the expression of God's mercy, then we show ourselves to be citizens of heaven whenever we, too, are merciful—i.e., whenever we give aid to those in need or forgive those in our debt.

What is more, apparently mercy begets mercy—the merciful obtain mercy. It is tempting to think cynically that the thoughtful person gets taken advantage of and the "nice guy" really does finish last. But even in this world we know that the harsh and impatient person usually finds others to be harsh and impatient with him, while the person of compassion, the person who extends understanding and kindness, usually finds others wanting to return the favor. How much more will this be true in the world to come.

In the context of this week's theme—about extending forgiveness even to ourselves—this kind of compassion takes on even further meaning. There is a degree of patience we must learn to have with our own sins and shortcomings. This is not at all the same as excusing ourselves or simply not caring whether or not we do right or wrong in the eyes of God. It has to do with seeing ourselves as God sees us: dependent, weak, and always in need of the love of God. The merciful are those who know that they are walking through life empty-handed and who know, as well, that God has and will continue to provide all that they need. They know the weakness of their own condition and are therefore perfectly prepared to accept the weaknesses of others. Blessed are such people as these.

REFLECT | *Think of a time when someone was particularly understanding and patient with you. What did this feel like? What did it make you want to do or to be? Describe what makes you most impatient with yourself, and with others. Today, who is in need of your mercy?*

Day 5   I Have Calmed My Soul

READ | Psalm 130–131

But I have calmed and quieted my soul, like a child quieted at its mother's breast; like a child that is quieted is my soul. (131:2)

A quiet soul, as peaceful as a contented infant in the loving embrace of its mother—surely this psalmist must have been a parent who witnessed firsthand the hungry cries of a child changing into happy sighs at the breast of its mother. Is this not a fitting image for the kind of rest and delight for which our own souls long? Think for a moment about the many things for which your heart yearns. Isn't an abiding sense of inner peace among the very first things on the list?

Putting these two psalms together gives a complete picture of our own spiritual thirst turning into fullness in the arms of a loving God. But the "conversion" clearly begins with a cry: "Lord, hear my voice!" We do not know the psalmist's particular circumstances—what the "depths" were from which he wailed his prayer—but we can all identify with his tone of voice. There is a sense of acute desperation, even panic in his words.

Turning to God in our need is actually the first step toward healing. It certainly seems straightforward enough, and there are countless examples throughout the Bible. But even with all this evidence before us, including our own past experience, crying to God "out of the depths" actually takes some effort. Where is the first place you turn when you are "in trouble"? Like our spiritual parents in the Garden, we are likely to look first to our own devices to solve even the most insurmountable problems. This is because it is of the very nature of "depths" to be dark and foreboding, to be the places where we lose sight of all light and all hope. The depths make us feel that God is nowhere to be seen, and that he has probably stopped listening. The depths make us feel that we are all on our own.

What infant do you know, however, who is able to feed her own hungry stomach, or clothe her own naked body, or rock her own weary eyes to sleep? No father or mother deserving of the name would ever dream such a thing. The psalmist acknowledges that he stands utterly exposed and defenseless before a holy God. "If you, O God, were to concentrate only upon my sins and shortcomings, then there is nothing further to do. I may as well give up now." The psalmist's hope all turns on a single, tiny, and all-important word—"But . . . there is forgiveness with thee" (v. 4). The light for which he now patiently waits is the mercy of God, and its coming is as sure as the dawn.

There is no depth in a human life that is beyond the reach of God's steadfast love. There is no thirst that he cannot quench, no hunger that he cannot satisfy, and no distress that he cannot calm. We do ourselves severe harm if we ever think that there is anything we have done, thought, or said—anything that we *are*—that cannot be redeemed by heaven's grace. We are only children. Isn't it a bit foolish to expect more from ourselves than even our Heavenly Father does?'"

REFLECT | *In what area of your life do you especially long for contentment? For what "depth" are you tempted to think there is no solution? Why? What is it that God is asking you to believe about himself . . . about yourself?*

Day 6   God Forgets?

READ | Jeremiah 31:27–34
For I will forgive their iniquity, and I will remember their sin no more. (v. 34)

According to the prophet, there seems to be such a thing as divine forgetfulness. How are we to understand such a mystery?

Ironically, some Christians, particularly those who strive inordinately for rightness and perfection, fail to deal constructively with failure. It is of no benefit, of course, to sweep our errors "under the rug," so to speak, to pretend that they are not there or that they do not bother us. Eventually, our subconscious has a way of playing its nasty tricks, by reminding us at particularly vulnerable moments of our past failures. We may not immediately know the cause, but sometimes those self-conscious feelings, those over-reactions and anxieties, those fears and angers that suddenly arise in us are the harassing remnants of unresolved sin. For example, let's say that you lost your temper with a friend, but in your embarrassment you both go on with life as if nothing had happened at all. Sometime later, without any warning, a similar conflict arises, perhaps with someone else, and you find yourself nervous about saying anything at all. Now you are angry *and* fearful. Unconfessed and unforgiven sin has its way of bearing offspring.

As we have seen, the constructive way to deal with sin and failure is to humbly make your confession, receive forgiveness, and then ask God's help so that, as you are working to change your behavior, he is working to change your heart. Then we can move forward, freely and thankfully—cleansed, renewed, and strengthened. Having done with sin means letting go of the accusation, guilt, and despair with which some people flail themselves. (Of course, if some troublesome area of sin persists in our lives, we should seek a minister or priest who can listen to our confession and give us needed counsel and the assurance that God has indeed forgiven us. Pride can be a strong barrier to making such an open confession, but it should only be done with one who is trained and spiritually able to hear it rightly. It is very foolish to make intimate confessions to the wrong people.)

I will forgive their iniquity, and I will remember their sin no more. This is God's attitude toward our sin, once it is confessed and forgiven. It is *gone.* One Christian teacher used to say,

"God says that he will cast our sins into the depth of the sea." With a smile she would add, "Then, I think he puts up a sign that says, 'No Fishing!' " If God himself has "forgotten" our wrongdoing, if God himself has "thrown it away," then who are we to rehearse our failures, reiterate our weaknesses, and fret about our imperfections? What we call remorse is not the same as what the Bible calls repentance—the former is the seed of discouragement and heaviness, while the latter gives growth to freedom and change.

What is the difference between "ignoring" and "forgetting" your sin? What about the sins of others—is there any connection between what you remember about others' offenses and what you remember about your own?

Day 7   Repentance, the Key

READ | Luke 18:9–14

I tell you, this man went down to his house justified rather than the other; for every one who exalts himself will be humbled, but he who humbles himself will be exalted. (v. 14)

In many respects, this story summarizes some of the central elements in the teachings of Jesus. The story of the Pharisee and the tax collector praying in the temple goes to the heart of the gospel, the "good news," for it explains the principal reason why God came to us in the flesh—Jesus said: "Those who are well have no need of a physician, but those who are sick; I came not to call the righteous, but sinners" (Mark 2:17).

Before we judge the Pharisee too harshly for his pride and self-confidence, let us be sure that we understand what Jesus was saying about him. (Someone has said that there is no difference between the Pharisee's saying, "Thank you, God, that I am not like that tax collector," and our saying, "Thank you, God, that I am not like that Pharisee.") The truth is that the Pharisee did, in fact, live a more righteous life than the tax collector. His praying, fasting, and tithing were all according to biblical law and were faithful to Jewish tradition. He was not lying about his uprightness. In a sense, he had good reason to boast.

But it was not the Pharisee's moral rectitude that Jesus found defective. The heart of his problem is contained in the description of his prayer: "The Pharisee stood and prayed thus *with himself*" (v. 11). It was not that the Pharisee did not have some genuine things of which to be proud—it was that he did not need God. To his mind, his soul had no need of a physician, no need of a savior. Even in his prayer he was carrying on a conversation only with himself!

The tax collector, on the other hand, could barely bring himself to even approach God, much less speak to him. Jesus says that he stood at a distance with his head bowed and his eyes fixed upon the ground. He brought no list of accomplishments or good deeds, no record of successes or testimonies to his faithfulness. Apparently he did not even notice the Pharisee as he whispered: "God, be merciful to me, a sinner." There is no question as to the destitute condition of this man's soul. He presented no excuses, no desperate explanations, no promises of improvement. His only plea was for mercy.

Of the two men, said Jesus, it was this man who returned home justified. One meaning of the word "justify" is "to be pronounced free of guilt." The difference between the state in which these two men left the temple is this: one went away forgiven and free, while the other went away still bound in the shackles of his own self-sufficiency. So long as he remained blind to his own need, he would always be blind to the light of God's love.

We conclude this week's reflections on forgiveness—especially forgiving ourselves—with this graphic reminder of Jesus' perspective on sin. It is clearly not the same as our own. For while we are prone to wander back and forth between the two extremes of either excusing ourselves or condemning ourselves, God aims straight down the middle . . . and forgives.

REFLECT | *In what ways do you identify with the Pharisee? with the tax collector? This week, what, if anything, has changed about your understanding of sin and forgiveness?*

Week Three The Hidden Bitter
Root Of Jealousy

Day 1   Who Will Be First?

READ | Mark 9:33–37

They were silent, for on the way they had discussed with one another who was the greatest. (v. 34)

In the last two weeks, we have been discussing the indispensable place of confession and repentance for the sake of our own wholeness, as well as our relationships with others. The brokenness we have inherited since the Fall has left us all spiritually ill—too weak and willful in our relationship with God, and too untrusting and unloving in our relationships with others. Through his Son, God has done, and continues to do his part for restoring us to the fullness of health and fellowship and, as long as we have breath, it is for us to work with him toward those same ends. "Work out your own salvation with fear and trembling," wrote the apostle Paul, "for God is at work in you" (Philippians 2:12–13).

I know a man who suffered a heart attack some years ago. The cause was a blocked artery that prevented blood from delivering the vital oxygen necessary to feed the muscle of his heart. He is alive and well, but periodically he goes through a series of tests in order to determine if any new blockages are forming. He tells me that the procedures are mildly uncomfortable, but nothing whatsoever in comparison with the pain he felt on that day when he thought he might die. These regular examinations are what assure him that he may never have to face another day like that one.

In the coming weeks, we will be addressing more specifically some of those sins that can choke our spiritual hearts and cause such painful brokenness in the Body of

Christ. These are the pesky and destructive "foxes" that spoil the vineyards of the Lord (Song of Solomon 2:15)—things like anger, resentment, self-pity, fear, and, this week's nuisance, jealousy. We open our hearts to God and to one another so that we can honestly, even courageously, examine these sins for what they really are, and find their curative treatment in the loving forgiveness and power of God. So, let us begin.

There is a story about an old saint, an ascetic, who lived in the desert, and denied himself every form of carnal pleasure. The devil tried to tempt him with all sorts of pictures and allurements, but the man of God was too firmly fixed in his devotion to be swayed by them. Then the devil whispered in his ear, "Did you hear that your old friend, brother Ambrose, has been made bishop?" And across the saintly face, a scowl of envy and jealousy signaled that the devil had hit his mark!

As disciples of Jesus, we must face our personal jealousies. Even the first disciples expressed their fair share of this divisive sin, and apparently they did so in full view of their Master. How refreshing to know that they actually spoke openly with one another about the kinds of things that we only entertain in our thoughts. Jealousy seems to be one of those sins that are particularly difficult for us to confess, perhaps because, by doing so, we are admitting that we are lacking in some way. Nevertheless, the human soul is, by reason of its fall from original purity, tainted with jealousy. Some people have a greater struggle with it than others. But we all experience it from time to time. So the first thing to do is to recognize the "good news" of sin, which is that, like the twelve disciples, we *all* have the same question on our mind: who will be first?

REFLECT | *In what circumstances or with what people do you get jealous? What signs do you recognize that tell you that you are jealous? Think back to your childhood—who did you most want to surpass? Now who is it? Is there any connection?*

Day 2   The Sin of Lucifer

READ | Isaiah 14:12–20

You said in your heart, "I will ascend to heaven; above the stars of God I will set my throne on high . . . but you are brought down to Sheol." (vv. 13, 15)

Christian tradition has long taught that this passage in Isaiah refers to none other than the devil himself, Lucifer, the Day Star and son of the Dawn (v. 12). The prophet describes a glorious and shining angel who once stood at the right hand of God, but who, nevertheless, was not content with his creaturely status. "I will ascend above the stars of God," he ambitiously declared. "I will set my throne on high . . . I will make myself like the Most High." His fate, however, was to be cut down to the ground and cast into the depths of the Pit.

The tangled mystery of free will and sin's origins is too knotted for us to make any straight lines of it all. But this much the Bible makes clear—one of God's first angelic messengers fell from the heights of heaven because he wanted to become *like* God, *better* than God. Is it any surprise, therefore, that he would tempt God's first earthly children by suggesting the same desire? The serpent said to the woman: You will not die if you eat the fruit of this tree that

God has told you not to eat. He is only saying that because he knows that if you do eat it, "your eyes will be opened, and you will be like God" (Genesis 3:5). *Like* God . . . maybe even *better* than God!

And so it was that, by succumbing to the same deadly desire as did the devil—the jealous desire to rise above the limitations that God himself had set in place—our first parents sinned and fell from the light and from fellowship with God. Human nature has ever been subject to this subtle and powerful temptation to *be* God, to rule over others, to be preferred above all others, to be subject to no one, including God. It is the devil's own sin, tragically passed on to the children of men.

Certainly you and I are subject to the same temptation. Do you recognize it—perhaps when others are praised or advance beyond you; or, when you absolutely must make that new purchase like so-and-so has; or, when your best friend is put in charge of your committee? Some of our jealous reactions are petty and even humorous. "Keeping up with the Joneses" (better yet, passing them by) can get pretty ridiculous. But, we do well to remember that jealousy got its start as an act of bitter mutiny against the loving reign of God, and its flames have been stoked in the pit of hell ever since. Left unchecked (which means, unrecognized, unconfessed and unforgiven), it has caused, and can still cause, colossal damage to our own souls and to the Body of Christ.

REFLECT | *Where do you recognize jealousy's activity in your own life? One sign of jealousy can be dissatisfaction, restlessness, or ingratitude. How do you compensate for not getting what you want?*

Day 3   The Root of Bitterness

R E A D | Hebrews 12:7–17

See to it that no one fail to obtain the grace of God; that no "root of bitterness" spring up and cause trouble. (v. 15)

The letter to the Hebrews was written to a group of Christians who, because of suffering and difficulty, were tempted to renounce their faith in Christ and return to the old covenant. Again and again, the writer reminds them that God has fulfilled all of his promises in the person of his Son, and that what they stand to lose by going back is actually the answer to all of their longings. So, press on, he says. Countless others have gone before and are now watching as you make your own way to heaven. Do not turn back. After all, you have the example of Jesus Christ himself, who endured more pain and hostility than you can imagine. Now it is time for you to endure, and the trials you face are meant to strengthen, not to destroy, your faith. Stand and walk uprightly.

Then this cheerleader of the faith says something rather interesting and supremely practical: "Strive for peace with all men." The enemy of such peace he likens to a "root of bitterness" that suddenly springs up and causes all manner of trouble and conflict. All the time that they are facing trouble from without, they must be mindful that the only thing that can really destroy their faith and their fellowship is the corruptive root that arises from within . . . and jealousy is just such a bitter root.

The author's readers would be familiar with the story of Esau, who, he says, "sold his birthright for a single meal" (v. 16). If you recall, Esau craved the meal of his brother, Jacob, and greedily agreed to give over his birthright in exchange for it. (Jacob does not come out of this story looking so good, either.) Thus, says the writer of Genesis, "Esau despised his birthright" (see Genesis 25:29–34).

In your own cravings, warns the writer to these Hebrew Christians, do not succumb to the temptation to give away what is eternally important for the sake of an instant gratification that will soon pass away. The birthright of every Christian is the love of God in Jesus Christ, and that particular love that calls us by name belongs to no one else. Jesus loved us so much that he would have died for one of us alone! Such is the story we have in the parable of the lost sheep, where the Shepherd "left the ninety and nine in the wilderness" to go in search of the one sheep that was lost. Is not the bequest of heaven priceless? And will we jealously trade it in because we must have the "bowl of pottage" that is immediately before our eyes?

REFLECT | *Why is jealousy likened to "bitterness"? What do they have in common with one another? Is there some "root of bitterness" caused by jealousy that threatens to choke off your own spiritual life? What can you do about it? What are the "bowls of pottage" that tempt you most?*

Day 4 Sibling Rivalry

READ | Luke 15:11–32
There was a man who had two sons. . . . (v. 11)

The opening words of this parable tell you right away that there is going to be trouble! Two sons, one father. The question may never be put in exactly this form, but it is in every child's mind: will there be enough of Dad to go around?

Clearly the three parables contained in Luke 15 are making the point that God loves all his children so much, and so individually, that he will search high and low to find whichever one is lost, and will rejoice exceedingly, together with all of heaven, whenever the lost is found. Along those lines, Jesus easily could have ended the story of the prodigal son at the party thrown by his father. The point has been made—our Heavenly Father will leave us to our willful devices and foolish choices, but he will always be watching and waiting for our repentant return. And when we do come home, there will be no rejection, no reprisals, only loving welcome and merry celebration. We rightly treasure this picture of God as the waiting and forgiving Father who accepts us in all our unacceptability.

But Jesus does not end the story there. He has not yet told us about the second son, the eldest son, and, when he does, it is understandable if we are left to wonder who it is that is really "lost" in this family.

Years ago, a friend asked a retreat group to read this story and to write down the character with whom they most identified. He assumed that most everyone would name the prodigal, because they would recognize in his shame and in his repentance the testimonies of their own conversions back to God. To my friend's surprise, however, almost half the group said that they most identified with the elder brother, whose faithful work for his father went unrecognized and unrewarded. Plainly and simply, they thought, the elder son got a raw deal. It turned out that each of them had, in their relationships, some past experience when they felt that someone important to them had "gotten away with something" while, all the while, they had remained "good, true, loyal, and faithful."

Any of us with brothers and sisters, or sons and daughters, or very close friends, knows the tell-tail signs of sibling rivalry. Most all of us have experienced it, in our childhood and perhaps even as adults. We have competed for attention, approval, and favor, and when our "adversary" seems to have won out, with hardly any effort at all ("Dad/ Mom simply liked you best, and there was nothing I could do about it"), we may have tried other ways to win praise, or to make up to ourselves for what we felt was lacking.

The thing is, it seems quite apparent that the father in Jesus' story loved *both* his sons deeply and steadfastly. And neither one of them could do anything to deter that love. Unfortunately, however, jealousy knows no logic and submits itself to no amount of reason. When it thinks it has been slighted, it cannot be talked out of its reactions. The only effective solution is to confess it . . . and then to join the party.

REFLECT | *With which of the characters in the parable do you identify? What have been jealousy's effects in your own sibling relationships? How easy/difficult is it for you to rejoice in someone else's good fortune?*

Day 5   Is Life Fair?

READ | Matthew 20:1–16

These last worked only one hour, and you have made them equal to us who have borne the burden of the day and the scorching heat. (v. 12)

"It isn't fair!" How often have you said or thought those words? In some cases, you may have been absolutely right. There is such a thing, of course, as righteous anger against injustice and exploitation. The Bible, and especially the prophets' message, makes it perfectly clear that God sees everything and that his wrath is set against all injustice and unrighteousness. Truth to tell, most of us do not really burn with holy indignation at unfairness unless it affects us personally! What may seem like perfectly justifiable and righteous ire may actually be nothing more than jealousy in disguise. Of one thing we may be certain—how we are treated by others matters to us. Having said that, let us look at this parable of Jesus.

Many of the stories Jesus told were about the characteristics of the Kingdom of God, and this parable is among them. Like any good teacher, he used familiar images in order to explain unfamiliar ideas. The parables of the Kingdom were designed to introduce his listeners to a whole new "world" that did not necessarily operate according to all of the rules of this world. Through many of his stories, Jesus was turning their view of things upside down. That was certainly the case in this parable. Consider the main points:

In need of laborers, the householder goes out early in the morning and hires a group of men to work in his fields, and he promises to pay them a certain wage for the day. Later in the morning, he finds others without work and hires them also, promising simply to pay them "what is *right*" (this is an important phrase in the story). He repeats the same thing at noon, then again at three o'clock in the afternoon and finally again at five o'clock. By the end of the workday he has hired four groups of laborers, the last of which only worked for one hour. This is the group he pays first, and they receive exactly what he had promised the early-morning group. You can easily see why those who had worked for a full twelve hours would think, "Ah, he is going to give us more." But, the householder pays them only what they had agreed to—in fact, everyone receives the same wage, no matter how long they have worked—and that's when things get messy. "Unfair!" they cry, and it is safe to say that we would, too.

But, what is "fair," what is "right," from God's point of view? This is what the parable is really about—God's magnanimous favor and kindness. His limitless love is the measure of what is "fair" and "right," not our limited judgments. "Do you begrudge my generosity?" asked the householder. Can God not freely give his love in equal measure to all of his children, regardless of their worthiness or unworthiness? The truth is, that when jealousy penetrates our hearts, we do begrudge God's generosity to others. Jealousy actually blinds us to God's point of view. When we feel, for whatever reason, that we are "owed" something by God or by others, then jealousy is quick to accuse, "Unfair!" when payment is not forthcoming.

Even after saying all this, it is probably safe to say that we are still uncomfortable with this story. Why is that?

Day 6 If You Have Bitter Jealousy

READ | James 3:13–4:12

But if you have bitter jealousy and selfish ambition in your hearts, do not boast and be false to the truth. (3:14)

The letter of James is filled with practical directions for how to live in the world in faithfulness to God's word and the values of his kingdom. "Be doers of the word and not hearers only," it exhorts (1:22). So the author tackles some fairly dicey issues: how we speak to one another, what we ought to do with our wealth, our hypocritical words and actions, and the pride and ambition that cause divisions among us. Here is an interesting commentary on the passage we are considering today. It has to do with the problem of jealousy with regard to our ideas and opinions:

"True wisdom displays itself in a good life, particularly in 'gentleness' to the opinions and even the faults of one's neighbors. If anyone forgets this and is so absorbed in a sense of the sole correctness of his own opinions and a resulting sense of superiority as to feel bitter jealousy of his rivals and selfish ambition to be recognized as an exclusive leader, then when such a man claims wisdom, he is a liar." (Burton Scott Easton, *The Interpreter's Bible*, Vol. 12)

Remember, James is addressing some very down-to-earth issues, examining them from a very heavenly perspective. He sees rifts and rivalry in the Body of Christ and pinpoints "jealousy and selfish ambition" as one of the causes, especially with regard to claiming the superiority of one's own ideas. This, he says, is quite the opposite of that wisdom and openness that makes for peace.

Christian fellowship is certainly marred, if not destroyed, when we jealously maintain the correctness of our own points of view, and cling to the superiority of our own opinions. Even when our "facts" are objectively correct, it is possible that our *self*-righteous attitudes offend and hurt others. Consider some of the arguments that we have with one another. Usually, not long into the quarrel, the facts become of less importance than winning the battle. What we feel is at stake is more than the value of our opinion—it is the value of *me*. This is when "jealousy and selfish ambition" begin to lead the charge, and what began as a skirmish escalates into outright combat. By that point, we are actually fighting to raise ourselves above the other, perhaps in order to feel better about ourselves, but almost always at someone else's expense.

What is the solution? What you are doing through these twelve weeks is actually an essential part of it. Opening your heart to God and to one another—in humble honesty about your own needs, weaknesses, and sins—nourishes love for one another and actually helps us grow more comfortable with simply being wrong. The better we know that we are loved, by God and by others, the less we have to defend ourselves. Less is at stake. We can be gentle and merciful with others because they have been gentle and merciful with us. This is one way that we learn humility, which is one of the strongest weapons there is against jealousy.

REFLECT | *Think for a moment about how you feel about your own opinions and ideas. How do you feel when others agree with them? when they disagree with them? Locate the places where you are ambitious. What is it that is motivating you to "get ahead"?*

Day 7   It Was Out of Envy

READ | Matthew 27:11–23

For [Pilate] knew that it was out of envy that they had delivered him up. (v. 18)

Jealousy springs from a bitter root, and its fruits are also bitter. This week we have discussed jealousy's "origins"—its destructive power in the heart of one of God's angels, the inspiration it was in the fall of Adam and Eve—as well as some of its expressions—sibling rivalry, accusations of unfairness, quarreling, and ambition. We conclude the week's reflections by considering one of jealousy's most bitter fruits: the crucifixion of Jesus.

Sometimes conviction of sin, and the longing to be different that results from such conviction, is aroused within us when we become aware of the hurt it has caused someone we love. The sudden realization that a seemingly harmless, or at least justifiable, word or action on our part has actually inflicted pain upon another person gives us pause. It had not been our intention to wound, nevertheless we did. At such times, "what did I do?" is perhaps less of an important question than, "*why* did I do it?" It may very well be that the "why" was more injurious than the "what."

If jealousy had a personality, it would be that it likes to sneak around and go unnoticed and unrecognized, even disguising itself as something noble and righteous. The crowd that delivered Jesus over to be crucified seems to have been convinced that it was acting with the most religious of intentions. "This man has blasphemed against God, opposed the emperor, and disrespected the high priest; he deserves to be punished," they reasoned. But even Pontius Pilate knew better. The bloodlust of the chief priests and elders of the people had to stem from something far more malicious than simply upholding the law. Pilate knew that "envy" is what drove the crowd to cry out, "Crucify him!"

Human jealousy was—and *is*—one of the things that nailed Jesus to the cross. It can be both conniving as it schemes and vicious as it acts, and, left unchecked, it will satisfy itself with nothing less than the elimination of its competitors. The Book of Proverbs states, "Wrath is cruel, anger is overwhelming; but who can stand before jealousy?" (27:4). It is, writes the poet, "as cruel as the grave" (Song of Solomon 8:6). Thus, we see the most graphic example of its effects in the brutal murder of our Lord—"it was out of envy that they delivered him up."

What comes, naturally, is a sobering realization when circumstances cause us to face the jealousy that lives in our own hearts. This is why humbly opening our hearts to the scrutiny of close friends, our brothers and sisters in Christ, and to the convicting and cleansing work of the Holy Spirit, is so necessary in order to pull it out by its tangled roots. Jealousy, writes the apostle Paul, is one of the earmark "works of the flesh" (Galatians 5:20); love is the "fruit of the Spirit" (v. 22). Is there any question as to which one we want growing and blossoming in our own hearts?

REFLECT | *What are some of the "disguises" that jealousy takes in your own life? Think back upon this week—when were you jealous of someone? What did you do when you realized it?*

Week Four The Modern-Day Idol

Day 1   The Resurrected Christ— The Center of our Lives

READ | Colossians 3:1–17

Put to death, therefore what is earthly in you: fornication, impurity, passion, evil desire, and covetousness, which is idolatry. (v. 5)

The letter to the Colossians is one of the apostle Paul's most upbeat and encouraging messages. At times he seems electrified with delight at the thought of what God has done for us in Christ, and by the hope that we now enjoy through the resurrection to live an entirely new and fruitful life. He explains that, in a spiritual sense, we all died and were buried with Christ and that, when he rose victorious from the tomb we all rose with him! This is the best news imaginable, because it contains the absolute guarantee that we can live according to a different power and standard than what the world has to offer. Since you have been resurrected with Christ, he urges, then aim for the things of heaven. Put to death what is earthly in you and put on what is divine. Make the center of your life the Lord Jesus Christ.

If you know something about God's covenant with the children of Israel, and their deliverance from slavery in Egypt at his mighty hand, then Paul's teaching has a certain familiar ring to it. Upon Mount Sinai, God set forth his law, instructing his people about how they were to live now that they were free. The first of those commandments was: "I am the Lord your God who brought you out of the land of Egypt, out of the house of bondage. *You shall have no other gods before me*" (Exodus 20:2–3). The most basic requirement of their new life was to put God first, above all other "gods."

Both the Old and the New Testaments are clear, therefore—the worship of "idols" is not simply the practice of pagan religions; it is the chief temptation of all God's people. And Paul gives us a clue as to its meaning when he says that "covetousness" is idolatry.

Covetousness, the dictionary tells us, is the state of having an inordinate desire for that which belongs to another. Whenever we love with an excessive, unlawful desire to own for ourselves, we are coveting. It stands to reason, therefore, that we are putting the thing that we covet in the place of God; we are making it a rival "god" in our hearts. God alone is to be the center of our affections, and when he is not, we are committing idolatry.

Idolatry, therefore, is the worship of something or someone in the place of God. *Anything* we place before the love of God is an idol—it could be our possessions, our reputation or status, another person, our job, our family, even our own "spirituality." We pin our hopes and affections on these persons or things because of how they make us feel, and what they attain for us. Ultimately, idolatry is nothing more nor less than ordinary self-love.

Put it to death, Paul insists. For the sake of putting Christ first and having no other lords before the Lord your God, put idolatry to death. This is the focus of this week's readings, for in order to eradicate idolatry from our lives we must first identify what the idols are that we have enthroned in our hearts. Open your heart once again, and let us begin the search.

REFLECT | *Even before you ask the Holy Spirit's guidance, what are the things you suspect might be idols in your life? Describe what it feels like when you are covetous.*

Day 2   Wisdom Turned to Foolishness

READ | 1 Kings 11:1–13

And the Lord was angry with Solomon, because his heart had turned away from the Lord, the God of Israel, who had appeared to him twice, and had commanded him concerning this thing, that he should not go after other gods; but he did not keep what the Lord commanded. (vv. 9–10)

The reign of King Solomon was inaugurated with great hope and expectation. The first ten chapters of the First Book of Kings is an almost festive record of Solomon's good deeds and achievements. It had been the desire of his father, David, to build a temple for the Lord in Jerusalem, but it was Solomon who actually completed the deed. He loved the Lord, and when God asked him what the one thing was that he most desired, mindful of the burden he bore as the new king of Israel, Solomon prayed for an "understanding mind to govern thy people" (1 Kings 3:9). He was greatly respected for his wisdom, and widely known for his wealth and for the prosperity of his kingdom. But history records that Solomon's glory was not to last, and its darkening came at his own hand.

Solomon's ruin is traced to two fateful decisions on his part. First, the writer tells us, Solomon "loved many foreign women," taking into marriage many of the princesses of neighboring countries, in order to insure peace with those kingdoms. This was a case of human wisdom overriding the express command of God (see verse 2). Relying upon the logic of the day rather than upon the Lord of the universe, Solomon chose to disobey God's express will. This, in turn, led him to his second choice: under the influence of his foreign wives, he began to build altars, to burn incense, and to make sacrifices to their gods. Solomon *clung* to these wives in love (v. 2), and then he followed them as they led him away from the Lord his God.

> The poet Alexander Pope wrote:
> Vice is a monster of so frightful mien,
> As to be hated needs but to be seen.
> Yet seen too oft, familiar with her face,
> We first endure, then pity, then embrace.
> (*Essay on Man*, 1733–1734)

Removing God from the center of our lives is almost never done with a single, dramatic decision. The "vice" that leads us away from heaven usually presents itself in very reasonable form, and, over time, it becomes a comfortable companion. As was true of Solomon, our desire to be successful, to be at peace, to enlarge our circle of friendship, can lead us first to excuse the things we know to be wrong, and, ultimately, to practice them. When we excuse sin in others around us, because we do not want the conflict of standing for the truth we know and love, our own vision becomes blurred and our consciences numbed. Then, that which we first endure, we may eventually "pity, then embrace." Idolatry breeds idolatry, and soon the ways of God are all but forgotten. In Solomon's case, had he remained faithful and obedient to the Lord his God, he never would have begun that vicious cycle of decline in the first place.

REFLECT | *Identify some places in your life where you allow your human reason to discount the simple command of God. Where do you excuse others in order to avoid conflict?*

Day 3 A Mother's Idolatry and Its Fruit

R E A D | Genesis 27

Then Rebekah took the best garments of Esau her older son, which were with her in the house, and put them on Jacob her younger son. (v. 15)

The Bible is unblinking in the portraits it paints of its "heroes." No matter how much we look up to them, there is no glossing over of the weaknesses and failings of these men and women of faith. There is no question that we have as much to learn from their faults as from their faith.

The matriarch Rebekah had a favorite son. So, apparently, did her husband, Isaac, though that fact does not seem to figure so largely in the story. But Rebekah definitely preferred Jacob. Not content to let God raise Jacob above his brother, not even considering whether or not such elevation was God's will at all, Rebekah instigated a deceptive scheme in order to win (really, to steal) a blessing that rightfully belonged to Esau. (Although the men were twins, Esau was firstborn, a position that in those days gave him a distinct advantage when the father bestowed his paternal blessing.) The plan was successful. Isaac was deceived and gave his blessing to the second-born, Jacob. But that was not the end of the story. "Now Esau hated Jacob because of the blessing with which his father had blessed him," and planned to kill his brother in revenge. Again Rebekah intervened, fearing that she would lose both her sons if one should kill the other.

The point, of course, is that Rebekah's interference in the lives of her sons, and her obvious preference of one over the other, did much to cause friction, hatred, and alienation between these two brothers. Without doubt, they bore their own responsibility for the rivalry, but Rebekah's hand was definitely soiled with her sin of idolatry and control. As is true of so many well-meaning parents, her "help" often did more harm than good, because it was really motivated by selfish desires. It was not so much love for Jacob that compelled her to help him get ahead, as it was love for herself. Remember what idolatry actually is—putting something or someone before God, *for our own sake.*

God intervened and redeemed this situation, as he so often does. Esau came to know great blessing in his life, and Jacob (who was to become the father of the twelve tribes of Israel) was purged of his ambition through a long series of difficulties and sacrifices. Still, we can learn from their mother's mistakes. Manipulating others, especially our families, for our own selfish purposes, is never an acceptable means of parenting, though it is a very common one. It is one form of idolatry, for it reveals that we do not trust God with our children's lives as much as we may think we do. But God loves our children more than we do, and with a love that is entirely free of personal interest and ambition. He knows what is best, and our own scheming and control can only add confusion, pain, and delay in the working out of his purposes.

REFLECT | *Most of the manipulation we do with our families (or with others) is quite subtle. Where do you recognize it in your own life? What steps can you take to trust your family to God's will for them?*

Day 4　A Father's Idolatry and Its Fruit

READ | Genesis 37

Now Israel loved Joseph more than any other of his children, because he was the son of his old age; and he made him a long robe with sleeves. (v. 3)

Rebekah is not the only parent in the Bible whose preferential treatment of one of her children resulted in a good deal of pain and suffering. One might have expected that her son Jacob would have learned from his mother's example, but, then again, how many of us do? The presence of idolatry within our family relationships is neither an easy nor a comfortable thing to face. So the Bible gives us these vivid examples from among God's own favored people. From the records of their lives perhaps we can recognize some of the signs of trouble in our own.

It turns out that Jacob, the favored son of Rebekah, visited upon his own son some of the same preferential attitude he had received from his mother, not so much in the form of control (as was the case with Rebekah) as in outright favoritism. Not surprisingly, Jacob's preference for the young Joseph led to bitter jealousy and enmity with his older brothers, so much so, in fact, that they actually plotted to kill him. (Joseph, of course, did nothing to endear himself to his brothers when he "ratted" them out to their father, nor when he revealed his dream to them. Some things never change!)

The writer of Genesis clearly identifies the reason for Jacob's favoritism: Joseph was the son of "his old age" (v. 3)—something to be grateful for, but also something that had much more to do with Jacob than with Joseph. Can you see that in loving Joseph, Jacob was actually "loving himself," and that the superior attitude that Joseph had toward his brothers was the unfortunate result?

If they are honest with themselves, most parents will admit that one or two of their children "please" them more than the other(s). No matter how much effort is put into treating them all "equally," parental affection is not apportioned by a mathematical formula. This is because, like Jacob, we bring into our parenting the experiences and emotions that we ourselves had as children. It has ever been thus. Some of those experiences and emotions are still active, and they are still informing our attitudes and decisions. For example, some of you who read these lines may have felt yourself to be among the unfavored, and some have spent years striving fruitlessly to gain that preferred place. Others may have basked in the favored position.

In later years, God's dealings in the lives of Jacob and Joseph eventually changed both men. In Joseph's case, God allowed great and prolonged hardship to come in order to mature him and cleanse him from the effect of Jacob's idolatry. And Jacob suffered greatly at the erroneous report that Joseph had been killed in the desert. In both cases, it was the gradual maturing brought on by trial and testing that purified their love for one another, for the rest of the family, and for their God. There is no shame in admitting that our relationships, especially with the ones we love most, are tainted with self-interest and self-love. This is one of the areas of greatest need for all of us, and only the healing power of Jesus Christ can make of our relationships what they are meant to be.

REFLECT | *Look back on your childhood: what place did you have in your family? How does the way you were treated inform the way you treat others? If you are a parent, what decisions are you making about parenting that are drawn from your own experience as a child?*

Day 5   Who Is First?

READ | 1 Samuel 2:22–31 and 4:1–18
Thus the Lord has said, "Why then . . . honor your sons above me . . . ? (vv. 27, 29)

Raising children—training them in "the way they should go" (Proverbs 22:6)—is challenging all the time, can be frightening some of the time, and is always rewarding when a young soul begins to be formed in the ways of God. It can also be heartbreaking when that soul casts aside (if only for a time) the values and ideals that were planted within it in its youth. The story of Eli and of his sons is an example of the latter, and of a father's own unintentional role in the sadness. We have considered the ruinous effects of idolatry in the family when it takes the shape of favoritism and preferential treatment. It is important that we consider one further sign of idolatry's presence in family life.

Eli was a priest. Together with his sons, he was entrusted with the sacred duty of overseeing the prayers and sacrifices offered in the house of God. The writer of 1 Samuel tells us from the start that "the sons of Eli were worthless men who had no regard for the Lord" (2:12). How did they come to be in such a state, rejecting what their father surely had taught them? The message of the "man of God," who came to Eli in his old age, tells us succinctly that Eli, too, disregarded the Lord by honoring his own sons ahead of God. Here is how one writer describes the condition of Eli and his sons:

"There is always a difference between sentimentality in the handling of children and the sound preparation which is necessary for a life of service. So often the home is nothing but a cell of soft selfishness. Children do not learn within it the meaning of sacrifice and devotion and service. Parents, in their struggle to make their children better off, fail to make them better. Unconsciously they betray their own true ambitions. Anyone connected with education quickly recognizes how many children are spoiled by their parents' inverted pride. Materialistic standards of success control too many parental hopes, and consequently bring ruin upon distinguished family traditions. Eli was weak when he allowed Hophni and Phinehas to defame their office. He was content with the preferment their position gave them, instead of demanding from them any adequate discharge of their responsibilities" (John C. Schroeder, *The Interpreter's Bible*, Vol. 2).

In the case of Eli's idolatry, it was not that he preferred one of his children to the other; it was that he preferred both of his sons to God. Even while carrying out all of his religious duties, Eli was actually serving himself, and the bitter fruit of his idolatry was borne in the lives of his children. The conclusion of both their lives and their ministry was tragic.

It is essential that we honestly ask ourselves what we are really conveying to our children—by the way we live our own lives, by the things we really love and by the aims we really live for. Children, as you know, are highly perceptive.

Intuitively they can tell the difference, especially over the years, between what we say and what we really think. In the end, it is our own heart attitudes that form them much more than do our words. What is the message that our children are receiving from us? Is God first in our own lives? Or, by our own idolatry, are we subtly teaching them that it is all right to put ourselves first?

R E F L E C T | *This form of idolatry in family life can be very subtle and easily mistaken for genuine love, which is the sacred privilege and duty of every parent. What are you conveying to your children (if you are a parent) or to others around you, by the things you really love and live for?*

Day 6 Idolatry—Avoiding Truth

R E A D | 2 Timothy 3

But as for you, continue in what you have learned and have firmly believed. (v. 14)

Today's reading divides itself into two related sections— first, a bleak description of "the last days" (which the writer understood to include the time in which he lived), and second, an exhortation to live faithfully in the face of such difficult times.

The apostle Paul describes the last days as a time of great "stress" (v. 1). We all know something about stress in our personal lives, but Paul is saying that this type of stress will permeate all of society and that its essential cause will be unrestrained human sin. His list of offenses against God and neighbor is staggering, and seems to get worse as it goes on. The moribund condition of these "lovers of pleasure rather than lovers of God" reminds one of a disturbing story by Oscar Wilde, *The Portrait of Dorian Gray*. Wilde writes of a young man who gives himself increasingly to a life of utter self-pleasing, seeking to satisfy his own desires no matter the cost to those around him. Strangely, however, through the years he continues to appear young, strong, and healthy, as if his self-indulgence were preserving his vitality. All the time, however, a portrait of himself (which he kept carefully hidden away) grew increasingly grotesque, the painted face reflecting the spiraling decline of his soul toward complete disintegration and ruin. In the closing scene of the motion picture, Dorian destroys the portrait, only to find himself now appearing with all of its accumulated ugliness before he dies.

Paul himself is painting a portrait of the effects of sin in the world, of self-love gone rampant. This is idolatry that knows no limit. The condition of the human soul is not readily visible to us, but perhaps if we could see from God's point of view what sin does to us, we might be more willing to undergo the momentary pain of self-denial or the discipline of self-control in order to be changed and healed.

The second half of this chapter suggests that we can paint an entirely different picture of our lives, using the pigments of God's word. Paul is so bold as to present to his spiritual son, Timothy, a portrait of himself, of a life lived in faith, love, and steadfastness—and, yes, with persecutions and sufferings. There is no question but that the heart of the Christian life is the bearing of one's cross just as our Lord did. Paul essentially says that as we continue faithfully in "what we have learned," our experiences of self-denial and sacrifice will make room in our hearts for God's truth to do its re-forming work. This is the testimony of his very own life. If the last days will be filled with those who give themselves entirely over to their own wills and pleasures, and thereby "go on from bad to worse" (v. 13), they must also be filled with those who give themselves entirely over to God, and thereby become "changed into *his* likeness, from one degree of glory to another" (2 Corinthians 3:18). This is what Paul is urging Timothy to do. For, in the end, the only successful remedy for idolatry is an all-consuming love for God.

REFLECT | *What are the particular areas in your life where you know you have difficulty preferring God's ways to your own desires? What is the area where you are particularly concerned that you could become "ugly" if you do not change? What can you say about the value of self-denial in your own experience?*

Day 7   Idolatry and Insincerity

READ | Galatians 2
For before certain men came from James, [Peter] ate with the Gentiles; but when they came he drew back and separated himself, fearing the circumcision party. (v. 12)

Today's reading should encourage all of us who have a problem in the "good image" department, that is, wanting people always to approve of us. This chapter gives us a little insight into the spiritual struggles of two of the most distinguished Christians of all time—the apostles Peter and Paul. Despite all he had been through, Peter (or Cephas, as Paul calls him here) was still plagued by the desire to be approved of by others. Lest we judge him too harshly, we should remember that this seems to be a very common human characteristic. It becomes a real problem, however, when the approval of others means more to us than the approval of God himself.

Peter and the other apostles had gone on record with their conviction that God did not require Gentiles to be circumcised in order to be Christians, but there were some in the early church who did not fully agree with this, fearing that the traditions of the Jews would be lost. These were the so-called "Judaizers" who wanted all Christians to become Jews first.

Paul tells us that on a certain occasion, Peter (a Jewish Christian himself) was freely sharing a meal with the Gentile Christians of Antioch. When some Jewish Christians came from Jerusalem, Peter, fearing their disapproval, withdrew from eating at the table. Worse still, writes Paul, his actions led others to draw away as well, "so that even Barnabas was carried away by their insincerity" (v. 13). For the sake of looking good in the eyes of some, Peter turned his back on others.

The desire, even the genuine need, for the approval of others is common to us all. Paul confronted Peter, however, because obtaining such approval had become so important that he was willing to lay aside his own convictions and sacrifice some of his own friends in order to get it. This is another form of idolatry—of putting something or someone before God—because it says that what we think we *need* is of more value to us than what we *believe*. Furthermore, as in Peter's case, it sends a message to others, especially to those who may respect us or look to our example of faith. Regardless of what we say, are we telling others by our actions that there is nothing more paramount than the good opinion of others? Are we guilty of putting on an insincere face in order to be accepted? Are we sometimes guilty of saying behind someone's back what we would not say to his or her face? Or do we avoid doing or saying certain things in the presence of someone we know might not approve?

As we have seen this week, the modern idol takes many shapes, and all of them are formed of the same basic material—"me first." The wholeness God desires for us, and the unity he desires within the fellowships we share, can be fully realized only as we clear the shelves of our hearts of all the various idols we keep there. Someone once said that our god is whatever we love the most. Idolatry clearly identifies that god as "I." So, if we are to have no other gods before the Lord our God, then "I" must be taken down from the throne, and this is precisely what life in Jesus Christ is designed to do.

R E F L E C T | *Think of a time (even recently) when the desire for approval caused you to be insincere. In what other areas of your life do you put yourself before God? Why?*

Week Five Self-Righteousness

Day 1   What's Wrong with Being Right?

READ | Luke 15:1–7

I tell you there will be more joy in heaven over one sinner who repents than over ninety-nine righteous persons who need no repentance.
(v. 7)

During our reflections on the subject of forgiving ourselves, we considered Jesus' parable of the Pharisee and the tax collector who went to the temple to pray (Week Two, Day 7). Did you notice to whom Jesus addressed this story? Luke tells us that he was speaking especially to those who "trusted in themselves that they were righteous" (Luke 18:9). *Self*-righteousness—the idea that our own efforts, noble intentions, and good deeds make us worthy of God's favor— is one of those sins that actually prevent us from knowing the depth of God's mercy as well as the gift of others' love. While few of us would easily admit it, and we may not display it as obviously as did the murmuring Pharisees and scribes, the notion that we are "sufficient" unto ourselves (or, at least that we *should* be sufficient unto ourselves) subtly permeates much of our thinking.

This week, we will spend some time considering self-righteousness, looking at the ways in which we depend upon ourselves for our own salvation. We will also consider the often misunderstood opposite of self-righteousness— humility. The psalmist wrote: "As a father pities his children, so the Lord pities those who fear him. For he knows our frame; he remembers that we are dust. As for man, his days are like grass; he flourishes like a flower of the field; for the wind passes over it, and it is gone, and its place knows it no more. But the steadfast love of the Lord is from everlasting to everlasting upon those who fear him, and *his righteousness* to children's children." (Psalm 103:14–17)

God "remembers" that we are dust, even if we forget from time to time. He is intimately aware of how feebly we stand and how perversely we wander, so his own expectations of our goodness and abilities are far lower than our own. Humility, which is the only genuine and lasting answer to self-righteousness, is about lowering our own expectations for ourselves, and raising them for God. As St. Augustine said, "O man, realize that you are man; all of your humility consists in knowing yourself."

Truly knowing ourselves, that is, accepting ourselves as deficient, is usually a problem in one of two ways: either we have such a high opinion of ourselves that we are blind to our faults and shortcomings, or we have such a low opinion of ourselves that our defects and failings are all we can see. In either case, *accepting* our fallen condition—embracing our own weakness and fallibility as ordinary sinners—is one way that we open our hearts to the grace of God. Repentance has little to do with scolding ourselves for tripping and falling. It has much more to do with allowing ourselves to be found and picked up by the love of God. Self-righteousness says, "I'm all right. I usually don't fall like this. Just give me a little more time and I can get up and find my way back." Or it says, "Just let me lie here. It's miserable, but I'm used to it. Maybe someday I'll catch up." But repentance calls out, "Here I am, over here," as we turn our faces away from ourselves and toward our Good Shepherd who comes to save us.

REFLECT | *With which side of self-righteousness do you most identify? What comes to mind when you think of the word "humility"? Is this a positive concept or a negative one? Why?*

Day 2 Whatever Was Gain to Me

READ | Philippians 3:1–14

I count everything as loss because of the surpassing worth of knowing Christ Jesus my Lord. (v. 8)

Paul's letter to the Philippians has been called the "Epistle of Joy," and a complete read of it will clearly reveal why. "Rejoice in the Lord always," he writes, "and again I will say, Rejoice" (4:4). Paul's words to this young church exude love for God, and a secure trust in his purposes, even when (*especially* when) circumstances are at their most difficult. Above all, Paul wants his own life, as well as the lives of his readers, to revolve entirely around Jesus Christ. He wants all other competitors for our affections, all other sources for our confidences, to take a far-distant second to our love for and hope in the Lord. What is more, he is absolutely certain that this is possible, not least of all because of his own experience of Christ's love for him.

Apparently, the Christians of Philippi have been hearing from some who suggest that there is more that they should be doing in order to be saved. Confidence in grace, they are being told, is not sufficient. Paul is indignant at the suggestion and presents the example of his own life as testimony to the fact that putting any "confidence in the flesh"—i.e., ourselves—is of no value whatsoever, and that the only glory we should know is the glory we have in Christ Jesus. Paul is making a blow at the most common self-righteous expression of all, pride.

If anyone has a reason to boast, writes Paul, it is he. His fine family lineage, his exceptional education, his moral accomplishments, and especially his religious fidelity and zeal, all combine to give him more than sufficient reason to be proud. Self-righteousness says, "These are the things that define me; these are the things that make me a person of value; and, some of these things actually make me more valuable than others." But the apostle knew that this could never be true; since he had come to know Christ Jesus his Lord, his value could never again be measured by his lineage or his accomplishments. When he met Jesus face to face on the road to Damascus, all these things seemed to fall away into nothingness. There, he was confronted by a Truth so lucid and undeniable that his own opinions and ideas fell to the ground. He was confronted by a Holiness so pure that all his own goodness shown tarnished and defiled. He was confronted by a Life so brilliant that he was blinded to everything but its Source. No wonder that he said to the Philippians, "From here on, what is before me—*Who* is before me—is worth everything. What is behind me is worth nothing."

The problem with self-righteousness is that it negates the grace of God; it diminishes the value of Jesus' death and resurrection. While self-righteous pride seeks to promote its own meager accomplishments and to rely upon them for a sense of security and self-confidence, humility looks elsewhere, away from its puny self, to find meaning and purpose. Humility says, "In the end, these things that I have made, and that have made me, do not matter at all. In fact, they are like so much soot. What predominantly matters is that Jesus Christ is in my life, and I am in his. He is worth everything to me, because I am worth everything to him."

REFLECT | *Identify the sources of your own pride. Be honest—what are the things that make you feel that you are valuable, acceptable, even superior to others? What is the difference between being "proud" and being "grateful"?*

Day 3 The Listening Heart

READ | Proverbs 12:15–19

The way of a fool is right in his own eyes, but a wise man listens to advice. (12:15)

The writer of the Book of Proverbs was apparently well acquainted with human nature. His ability to go straight to the heart of a matter, to identify the source of a problem and to give clear counsel as to the solution, show him to be someone who knew himself and others quite well. Much of what he writes has to do with wisdom, which may be understood as the capacity to live a life of integrity, love, and understanding; a life that begins, he says, with faith in God—"the fear of the Lord is the beginning of wisdom" (Proverbs 9:10). Obtaining such wisdom, however, is not a matter of study and learning; it is a matter of *listening.* The teaching of the Scriptures, said one of the Church Fathers, requires "an attentive ear."

Benedict of Nursia, the sixth-century monk whose work has defined much of Western monasticism for the past 1500 years, wrote a "rule" (a guidebook, really) that set forth the basic principles and instructions for a community's life and health. In it, he gives wise directions for everything from personal spirituality and discipline (prayer, Scripture reading, eating, and sleeping) to communal practices and traditions (greeting guests, observing Lent, manual labor). It is seventy-two chapters long, and it begins with this single word: *Listen*—"Listen, my son, to your master's precepts, and incline the ear of your heart" (*Rule of Benedict*, Prologue).

It sounds, does it not, as if Benedict had read the Book of Proverbs? "My son, if you receive my words and treasure up my commandments with you, making your ear attentive to wisdom and inclining your heart to understanding . . ." (2:1–2). "Listen to advice and accept instruction, that you may gain wisdom for the future" (19:20). "A wise son hears his father's instruction, but a scoffer does not listen to rebuke" (13:1).

The command to "listen" is about more than opening one's ears. It is about opening one's heart—making room within ourselves for the words of another because we know that our own words are not enough to help and to guide our lives. It is about being ready to receive a word of counsel or insight or correction from outside ourselves. This is never more difficult than when that word may be unexpected, unbidden, or even unwelcome. The "fool" rejects such advances out of hand. "I see things quite clearly on my own," he says. Foolishness and self-righteousness are siblings, as are wisdom and humility. The command to "listen" is really an exhortation to be humble, because it asks us to set aside the confidence we naturally place in our own view of things for the sake of hearing the voice of God, through whatever instrument it comes. The writer of Proverbs applied this principle to the making of a wise and faithful soul. Benedict applied this principle to the making of a strong and loving community. How does it apply to you?

REFLECT | *Through what voice(s) has God been speaking to you lately? What do you know to be the greatest obstacles to your own listening? What "words" have been most unwelcome to you this past week?*

Day 4   Praising the One True God

READ | Psalm 100

Know ye that the Lord he is God: it is he that hath made us, and not we ourselves; we are his people, and the sheep of his pasture. (v. 3, KJV)

The psalms have always played a substantial role in the worship and prayer of Christ's church. This is because they find their source in the hearts and experiences of God's covenanted people. The Book of Psalms was the prayer book of the Hebrew people, and, as such, its verses of song point us again and again to the Source and End of our lives. They tell us that the things that we see and feel and think are not the whole story, that behind and above and within our lives there is always the presence of our Maker and Redeemer. The intention of these prayers is to give glory to God both because of and regardless of the circumstances from which they are sung. They remind us that, in *all* times and places, "the Lord, he is God!" This is the jubilant shout of praise that cries out above all other noises.

This is why the psalms may actually be a helpful weapon in our fight against self-righteousness. For instance, consider the words of psalm 100. Look at the number of succinct commands to praise God that appear in so few verses: make a joyful noise, serve the Lord, come into his presence, enter his gates with thanksgiving, give thanks to him, bless his name! And all these imperative calls, all these activities, revolve around the one central and more interior entreaty to "know that the Lord, he is God." Just consider how much we could benefit from living according to that truth, every day. It is not that we do not believe that the statement is true; it is that we find it so difficult to be living all the time according to the wonder of it. And the psalmist gives us a hint as to why that might be.

There are two legitimate readings of the Hebrew in verse 3: "It is he that made us, *and we are his*," or, "It is he that hath made us, *and not we ourselves*." We have been talking about the very human (and very sinful) penchant for self-reliance, for making ourselves the answer to our own needs, and thereby "boasting" when things go well or "despairing" when they do not. Either reading of this verse (and both together) is a corrective to such self-righteous thinking. God is our Maker. Therefore, we belong to him and to him alone. Our lives are not of our own making. Can any one of us breathe into our nostrils the breath of life? Nor are our lives our own, to do with what we please. God has a loving plan for us, and whatever circumstances of success or failure we may experience, they all have as their ultimate aim the fulfillment of his intentions for our lives. Neither boasting nor despairing will make us humble. Both are signs that we have lost sight of who *we* are in the eyes of God, and therefore who *God* should be in our eyes. The humble are those who place all self-made plans—all successes and failures—under the reign of God's own purposes, because they know that, in every way, they have been made by God and belong to God.

REFLECT | *In the past week, when has your "boasting" or "despairing" blinded you to the presence of God in your life? Many of us are taught to take pride in being "self-made" women or men. How does this idea fit, if at all, in the Kingdom of God?*

Day 5   When Evidence is Ignored

READ | Jeremiah 2:20–37

Yet in spite of all these things you say, "I am innocent." (v. 35)

God recruited the prophet Jeremiah for an altogether unpleasant task. Because of its rebellion against the ways of God, the kingdom of Judah was on the threshold of its own destruction. Eventually, that threshold was brazenly crossed and, as a result, God's judgment descended upon the nation in the brutal form of its own enemies. But not before the prophet had a chance to repeatedly give warning about the severity of Judah's faithlessness and disobedience.

The prophet likened the nation to an unfaithful and adulterous wife. God himself was to be her husband, but she refused to give herself to him. Instead, she lustfully ran after other lovers (other gods), degrading herself in their service and staining herself with her shame before the eyes of heaven. It is a graphic and sordid picture of spiritual infidelity and apostasy. Still, despite the disturbing image, despite all the evidence set before her, Judah refused to acknowledge her guilt. Astonishingly, she said, "I am innocent" (v. 35). Jeremiah was chagrined: "How can you say, 'I am not defiled?' " (v. 23).

A good question. How is it that any of us can look squarely at the evidence of our own wrongdoing—the hurt we have inflicted on another, the failures of our own commitments, the lies we use to excuse our attitudes or actions—and still maintain that we are blameless? The prophet set forth a spiritual principle of the kingdom of God. God is willing and desirous to forgive sin, and even the most abhorrent of sins can be cleansed by his mercy. What defies his love, however, is the stubborn refusal to acknowledge our need of it. Even greater in God's eyes than all her sins of unfaithfulness was Judah's denial of her impoverished condition. "I will bring you to judgment," says God, "for saying, 'I have not sinned.'" (v. 35).

This is similar to the charge that Jesus laid before the scribes and the Pharisees. In their case, their outward actions might lead one to believe (and *did* lead them to believe) that they really were not sinners at heart. You are like freshly painted mausoleums, Jesus said to them, all good looking and attractive on the outside, "but within you are full of hypocrisy and iniquity" (Matthew 23:28). They were self-deceived. Their blindness to the presence of their own sin blinded them also to the presence of God's love. The one is a prerequisite for the other.

The apostle John wrote, "If we say we have no sin, we deceive ourselves and the truth is not in us" (1 John 1:8). Obstinate self-defense—the epitome of self-righteousness—is opposed to the forgiving grace of Christ. It is a prison house that keeps our hearts closed, locked up from the approach of God who, when he comes with convicting truth in one hand, always brings loving mercy in the other.

REFLECT | *Lately, where has God been working to convict you of your sin? How well are you receiving him? In what areas of your life are you the most defensive? In other words, what truth are you most resistant to hearing about yourself? Why?*

Day 6 True Righteousness

READ | Matthew 5:1–20

For I tell you, unless your righteousness exceeds that of the scribes and Pharisees you will never enter the kingdom of heaven. (v. 20)

By now we are getting the point. It is becoming clear that the Christian life is not meant to be a fierce and determined striving after perfection. Its clarion cry is certainly not, "I've got to be right at all costs." The cross that Jesus calls us to bear will most assuredly bring its crucifying hardships, but these are quite different from those that we inflict upon ourselves by anxiously clinging to the sufficiency of our own lives. The life of Christ's disciples is the "up and down" experience of real people who are happily aware that they have not yet arrived, but are glad to be on the way!

Scholars tell us that the main characteristic of the Pharisaic party was their rigorous adherence to the law. They inseparably linked the precision of their belief and behavior to their spiritual fitness in the eyes of God, and they were genuinely serious about observing correct religious ritual in every way. A second characteristic of the Pharisees was their respect for the traditions of the elders and their conformity to conventions passed down to them from the past. Thus, they were disturbed by an untrained teacher such as Jesus, who came saying things in a new way, and did not cite from the ancient teachers or rabbinic tradition. Instead, he claimed to be speaking on behalf of God himself and, based upon their conviction that no mere mortal could make such a claim, the Pharisees ridiculed and rejected him.

On the one hand, such an approach to faith seems initially reasonable, even commendable. But, says Jesus, it is not that this kind of righteousness is inherently wrong; it is that it is not *enough*. Jesus was actually requiring *more* than what the Pharisees were giving. The great early church teacher and pastor John Chrysostom said that "wherever the Holy Spirit is present, people of clay are turned into people of gold." The problem with the Pharisees was that they thought they were people of gold already, and that their own righteousness made them so. They thought that it was actually possible to adhere to God's laws in every way, and thus to enter the kingdom.

We should not be too quick to judge them. The temptation is common to us all to believe that our abilities and gifts and good will make us acceptable to God, if not superior to others. Reading the Beatitudes may be just the right corrective to such thinking, for they remind us just how *impossible* are God's standards. Meekness, purity of heart, mercy, righteousness—how is one to attain these divine characteristics on one's own? It is impossible to do so. And that is precisely the point. It *is* impossible to live the Christian life by one's own strength. Our hearts are not strong and agile enough to run such a course successfully. We need *more* than the righteousness of the Pharisees. The end of self-righteousness comes when we fall into the arms of our only Strength and Help. "In his days," wrote the prophet

Jeremiah, "Judah will be saved, and Israel will dwell securely. And this is the name by which he will be called: 'The Lord is our righteousness' " (Jeremiah 23:6).

REFLECT | *What Pharisaical attitudes do you recognize in yourself? Be specific. Which of the Beatitudes is the most appealing to you? which do you long for the most? which seems the most impossible for you? For which personal merits or achievements is God asking you to lay aside your claim for being acceptable?*

Day 7   He Came for the Un-righteous

READ | Matthew 9:1–13

For I came not to call the righteous, but sinners. (v. 13)

In a sense, we end the week where we began. On Day 1 we said that "*accepting* our fallen condition—embracing our own weakness and fallibility as ordinary sinners—is one way that we open our hearts to the grace of God." The fallen, weak, and fallible are precisely those for whom Jesus came. We are in good company!

Another way of putting it is this: Jesus came for those who are *wrong* and know it. His sacrifice is meaningless to those who believe that they are perfectly fine the way they are. Without an awareness of sin and need, there is no need of help and no desire for salvation. The sick seek out a physician; the wounded look for healing.

The joyful news of the gospel is that it is safe to face our sin—what we are, what we have done, what we have left undone—because we have a Savior. From him there is absolutely no condemnation. None whatsoever! Not our righteousness, but our *lack* of righteousness is what draws God's mercy and grace. Our wrongness appeals to his righteousness. Our inadequacy to make it on our own without him evokes his plenitude of grace, strength, and help in time of need.

Someone has said that unless we recognize our pain and bring it to speech, we are doomed to live without hope. People who are numb to their pain are also blind to their hope. What does that say to us who know our pain, our failure, or our need? It means that we experience hope, for we meet the One who touches us at the very point of our pain. He touches our wounds from our past, and heals them. He touches our guilt, and gives forgiveness. He touches our traumas, and sets us free from their oppression. And, perhaps more than we can know, he touches our hearts, and step by step converts us and brings us to greater wholeness. It would be foolish indeed to think that we had to provide all this healing, forgiveness, and freedom for ourselves. If you are in need of any of these—*because* you are in need of any of these—Jesus the Savior came for you.

R E F L E C T | *Where is it that you feel you simply cannot change? In what particular area of your life have you come to the end of hope in yourself? In what area do you have new hope?*

Week Six Who Me, Angry?

Day 1　*Be* Angry?

READ　|　Ephesians 4:22–32

Be angry but do not sin; do not let the sun go down on your anger, and give no opportunity to the devil. (vv. 26–27)

The overarching theme of these twelve weeks has to do with the deepening and strengthening of our relationship with God and with one another. If we are serious about following Jesus, then this actually will be the "theme" of our entire lives, for the life of discipleship is a lifelong journey of learning and changing—learning the ways of God and changing our own ways. As such, it is about so very much more than changing our behavior. God intends for the work of the Holy Spirit in our lives, and our cooperation with that work, to re-make us in the image of his Son and our Savior, Jesus Christ, not so that we can *act* like him, but so that we can *be* like him. We open our hearts to God and to one another so that this work can be done, so that by the light of the Holy Spirit and the help of friends, we can locate those dark and broken places that cripple our stride and weaken our resolve. Our feet will walk more securely in step with our Lord as our hearts come to beat more evenly in rhythm with his own.

The apostle Paul is referring to this transforming work of the Spirit when he writes to the Christians of Ephesus, urging them to put off the "old nature" of deceitfulness and corruption, and to live according the "new nature" of true righteousness and holiness (the likeness of God himself). To help them in this endeavor, Paul identifies some of the telltale signs of the old nature's crippling and destructive work. Among them, he points to anger. One of the things that Paul says about anger, however, is somewhat unexpected—*Be* angry, but do not sin. *Be* angry? This seems odd. What is being suggested here? You may have noticed that the instructions the Bible gives at this point are all given within the context of one overriding directive: put away falsehood and speak the truth with your neighbor (v. 25). Being honest, being truth-full, is the reason for which being angry is entirely normal—because it is *real.* Our misguided attempts to repress or deny our angry reactions are one way in which we lie to ourselves and to others. A "good Christian," we say, does not get angry. Paul apparently takes exception to that statement.

Like all other human emotions, anger is a tightly woven thread in the tapestry of our humanity, and it cannot simply be detached without unraveling many other emotions with it. (Often, the people who suppress their angry feelings are also the ones who find it difficult to express other feelings as well, such as affection, grief, or zeal). If you are angry, Paul writes, then *be* angry. The most deadly and dangerous thing to do is to push it down and pretend that it is not there. For then, like a root fire, anger travels underground until it finds another outlet and bursts out on some unsuspecting target. Sometimes our overreactions, our unreasonable hurts and lost tempers, have at their source some unacknowledged, and therefore unresolved, anger from the distant or recent past. This is why Paul says, "do not sin; do not let the sun go down on your anger." Facing one's anger, admitting and sometimes even expressing it, is actually the constructive way toward resolving it.

REFLECT | *What do you think about anger? What experience(s) have you had recently when you were surprised at how angry you felt? What do you think was the source of your strong feelings?*

Day 2 　 An Angry Savior?

READ | John 2:13–23
And making a whip of cords, he drove them all, with the sheep and oxen, out of the temple; and he poured out the coins of the moneychangers and overturned their tables. (v. 15)

Before we go any further, perhaps we do well to be reminded that anger is something with which God himself is thoroughly familiar. Yes, we might say, God is obviously the only one who can "be angry" and never sin, but from that we should not conclude that somehow God is "too good" to be angry, as if the anger and the mercy of God cannot live in the same divine heart. God's anger is most definitely *never* separated from his love, just as our anger is virtually *always* connected with our self-love. But, does it not help us to face our own anger if we know that God, our Maker and Redeemer, also "gets angry"? Perhaps one of the reasons that we find anger to be such an unacceptable emotion is that our view of God himself, and of his Son, is incomplete.

If, as the Bible tells us, we have been made in the image and likeness of God (Genesis 1:27), then the entire range of human emotions must, in some way, reflect the very character of God. They are broken and blurred reflections, to be sure, but to deny any of them is to repudiate one possible connection that we have with our Creator. Even our anger must remain open and available for God to remake and to use for his own glory. Jesus' harsh treatment of the greedy merchants in the temple tells us that there is divine purpose to the anger that is set against evil and injustice. God's anger is against all that destroys, warps, or abuses his people, whom he made in free, untrammeled love. As imperfect as our own expression of such indignation might be, it is no reason to deny or stifle it. The gospel does not instruct us to become repressed, artificially "good" people. At times we may even have some of God's righteous wrath within us!

At any rate, we do not need to be afraid of feeling. Emotions—all emotions—are an integral part of our created nature. What we should fear, however, is to be blind to whatever is true, about God or about ourselves. And anger is something that is "true" about us both. The issue is not whether or not we get angry (we all do); the issue is whether or not our anger has, as its source, the love of God or the love of ourselves. Being a disciple of Jesus Christ means that we are on the road to learning the difference.

R E F L E C T | *Which is more familiar to you—the idea that God is loving or that God is angry? Why? How does this influence the way that you view yourself or the choices that you make about what to do with your own feelings?*

Day 3　How Much Anger Lives in Your Heart?

READ | Colossians 3:1–17

But now, put them all away: anger, wrath, malice, slander, and foul talk from your mouth. (v. 8)

This week we are reflecting on one of those common and quite understandable human emotions that can, nevertheless, cause us a great deal of difficulty in our relationship with God and with one another. Once we have acknowledged anger's presence in our own hearts—because we have heard its expression from our own lips—how are we to deal honestly with it? Several generations ago, a famous pastor preached a sermon entitled "The Expulsive Power of a Great Affection." Using biblical examples, he argued that when a believer is possessed by a great love for God, that love expels from the heart all negative and harmful things. The pure of heart are those whose hearts are filled to capacity with only one thing— love for God and neighbor. There is no more room in such a heart for anything else. Love has expelled it all.

This is a wonderful concept, to be sure, and opening our hearts to this kind of miraculous makeover is exactly what the life of discipleship is about. But this holy transformation takes place within very ordinary circumstances and among very ordinary fellow sinners. The desire to have our hearts renewed—filled with love—grows and strengthens because we experience how *unloving* we are to the people with whom we live and work and pray each day. This is the world in which we learn love.

Paul points out to the Christians of Colossae some of the things that they allow to occupy space in their hearts and crowd out the Spirit of God. Among those unwelcome (but often entertained) inhabitants is anger and all of its nasty children: malicious feelings, slanderous talk, resentment, impatience, lying, and unforgiveness. These are all indisputable signs that love does not yet fill every room in the house.

Once again, it is for this reason that honestly facing our anger is so imperative. The prophet Jeremiah said that "the heart is deceitful above all things, and desperately corrupt; who can understand it?" (Jeremiah 17:9). Our most inward desires and motivations are usually hid from our own sight, especially when they are entirely opposed to what we know God intends for our lives. How are we to know what lives in us, therefore, if we do not listen carefully to what comes out of us? Our angry reactions to others are among the outward signals that there is something amiss in our lives, that love is lacking and that faith is weak.

REFLECT | *What kinds of circumstances or people most often make you angry? Why? What practical step is God asking of you in order to make more room in your own heart for love?*

Day 4 The Anger of Man

READ | James 1:19–27
For the anger of man does not work the righteousness of God. (v. 20)

There are two important points about anger in this reading from the Letter of James. The first is that, as forceful as anger may be, we actually do have some control over it.

Everyone, says James, must be "slow to anger." There exists a space of time between the cause and the expression of anger, and that space should not be too short. There are times when we are consciously aware of that brief moment of choice, when the initial feelings of anger begin to arise, and we can either take them to God or give vent to them upon others. With practice, the apostle seems to be saying, we can enlarge that moment. We can choose not to fly off the handle.

For some of us, this is a much harder battle than for others. Anger is such a powerful and unpredictable emotion that some of us deny its existence even while others of us give free reign to its destructive forces. François Fénelon, a French archbishop of the late seventeenth century, gave this sage advice through one of his letters: "A heated imagination, vehement feeling, a world of argument, and a flow of words are really useless. The practical thing is to act in a spirit of detachment, doing what one can by God's light, and being content with such success as he gives" (*The Royal Way of the Cross*, p. 133). This is what James is talking about when he counsels us to be slow to anger.

When he writes that heated arguments and violent emotion are "really useless," Fénelon's counsel is also touching upon the second important feature of these verses from James—anger rarely accomplishes the goal for which we aim, nor solves the problem that lies before us. For a brief moment, anger may give us the illusion that we are in control of a certain situation; it may give us a sense of strength and confidence, and it may even intimidate others into doing as we wish, but the long-term result is really nil. "The anger of man," writes James, "does not work [read "accomplish"] the righteousness of God." There is a divine anger that can accomplish divine purposes—consider Jesus chasing the money changers from the temple (as we read from John), or the judgment of God against sin and death (as we will read in Jonah). But rarely is human anger so selflessly motivated or constructively expressed. Through our anger we are usually attempting to control unwelcome circumstances or to shape the attitudes and actions of others to our own liking—in other words, our aim is to get our own way. The anger of man has little to do with love, and far more to do with power.

James gives an interesting piece of his own advice about how such anger might be averted in the first place: "Let every man be quick to hear." There is that compelling charge again—*listen.* Love demands that we be more ready to listen to the other, than to make the other listen to us; and that we listen more intensely to the other's voice than to the demanding cries of our own anger and hurt and fear. For, in the end, anger is usually the heavy instrument of pride, and pride always says, "Listen to *me.*" Listening to the other person, therefore, is sometimes the most practical and effective way of making pride put down its weapons.

REFLECT | *Think about a recent example of your own anger—what is it that you were trying to accomplish? If it was against another person, what were you trying to get them to do? What makes it so difficult for you to listen when you are angry?*

Day 5　Do You Do Well to be Angry?

READ | Jonah 4

But it displeased Jonah exceedingly, and he was angry. (v. 1)

Since we have introduced the connection between anger and getting our own way—a connection, by the way, that most of us successfully made at a very, very young age!—let us consider a colorful illustration. Jonah is a delightful and thoroughly human biblical figure. In spite of his flaws, or, more likely, because of them, we feel a genuine kinship with this rebellious and angry character. We know, perhaps, the lengths to which *we* are willing to go in order to avoid those unwelcome tasks that we find so thoroughly disagreeable.

The prophet Jonah took what seemed an effective means of escape in order to avoid the unpleasant mission of proclaiming God's judgment upon Nineveh. It was not that he minded Nineveh's destruction. On the contrary, he would welcome it. He simply did not want to be the one who had to announce the city's terrible fate to its citizens. Most of us are familiar with the story—he tried to flee from God by taking a ship to Tarshish (it is not clear why Jonah thought that God would not be in Tarshish!); during a storm, he was thrown into the sea by the ship's crew; God sent a mighty fish to swallow him and bring him back to shore; there, God gave him his assignment once again and, this time, Jonah consented. The part we are less familiar with is what happened *after* Jonah announced to Nineveh that it was about to be destroyed—the people believed him; they repented and changed their ways; and God withdrew his judgment. Now Jonah really thought he had something to be angry about! He had walked about the city proclaiming its destruction and, instead blessing came. Embarrassed and disappointed, Jonah went off to a corner to sulk. "I knew this would happen," he angrily complained.

Chapter four of this remarkable book is a gem, because it shows a man at his petty worst in conversation (honest conversation, we might add) with his Creator. The remarkable thing is that God took no offense at Jonah's antics. Instead, he engaged his prophet in a reasonable conversation, like a patient father to his stubborn son, in order to make him see the foolishness of his ways. Jonah's anger, truthfully displayed, became God's opportunity to show forth his mercy and to teach his child a lasting lesson of faith.

A thorough reading of the prophets (and of the psalms, as well) will reveal many of these kinds of honest conversations—even arguments—between God and his servants. The key to having the argument settled is found, first, in our willingness to be completely honest, and then, in our willingness to listen. There are some people who maintain a constant grudge against God, who have grown comfortable in their anger against him for any number of reasons. The stories of Jonah and of these other men and women of faith tell us that God understands such intense feelings, and is always ready to listen to them. But such stories also tell us that we, too, may have some listening to do in order to see our anger for what it really is. Opening our hearts to God means handing him our most ugly feelings as well as our most beautiful. Becoming convinced that God is right and that we are wrong can be one of the most delightful and liberating experiences of the Christian life.

REFLECT | *Where do you recognize yourself in the story of Jonah? What "argument" are you having with God these days? What anger do you have against him that you have not yet told him or that has not yet been resolved?*

Day 6 Anger's Fearful Roots

READ | Isaiah 31:1–9

Woe to those who go down to Egypt for help and rely on horses who trust in chariots because they are many and in horsemen because they are very strong. (v. 1)

Let me tell you a story. Today I walked my dog around the block and through the woods just as I usually do each day. She is familiar with every turn, every tree, every lawn, and every person she meets along the way. The route we take is through "her" world, and she always walks it with the carefree spirit of a soul that is altogether at peace with her surroundings. At least, most of the time. Today we were nearing the end of our walk when we turned a corner and met something, someone, utterly unfamiliar. It was actually a person she knew quite well, but today this person was hunched over a wheelbarrow, digging out some dirt with a small shovel that scraped menacingly against the sides of the old metal box.

The dog reacted instantly. She stopped dead in her tracks, spread her legs, lowered her head, raised her fur and began to bark at the top of her lungs. For a few moments there was nothing either of us could do to make her stop. No amount of scolding or soothing, no amount of calling her by name or trying to distract her attention, was able to calm her down. For those moments, until she finally recognized her friend—and, with tail wagging, ran to get a hug—she was wholly given over to her fear, and to the fury that arose from it.

We said earlier that anger is very often a helpful signal that something is amiss in our hearts. For this reason, we need to pay attention when we feel angry, because our reactions may be telling us something more. The saying goes that "the best defense is a good offense," which goes a long way toward explaining that altogether human (and animal) connection between fear and anger. Oft times, our most angry reactions, especially those sudden and unreasonable outbursts that take us (and others) by surprise, are nothing more than the burning flares we send up when we are in trouble.

The prophet is rebuking God's people because, in the fear of their enemies, they are turning for help to the strength of flesh—in this case, to Egypt and its seemingly invincible army—rather than to the Lord. Anger is among those "horsemen of Egypt" that makes us think we are strong and invincible when what we really feel is weak and defenseless. In the hope of safety we lay hold of anger, but such times as these are meant to point us to the only source of reliable help that we have, the Lord of hosts. Sometimes the answer to our angry feelings is to trust the Lord with our own well-being, and the well-being of those whom we love. No other power is sufficient, and especially not the imaginary power that arises out of our own anger. "Impotent rage," is what a friend called it once; it barks loudly and makes a big display, but all the time its heart is racing and it is shaking in its boots.

REFLECT | *What connection do you make between the things that make you angriest and the things that make you fearful? Describe a specific example. In what areas of your life do you have the most difficulty trusting God?*

Day 7   Sharp Contention!

READ | Acts 15:22–41

And there arose a sharp contention, so that they separated from each other; Barnabas took Mark with him and sailed away to Cyprus, but Paul chose Silas and departed, being commended by the brethren to the grace of the Lord. (vv. 39–40)

Anyone who argues that the early church was always harmonious and unified has not read the entire New Testament. In fact, we read of controversy even in the lives of the twelve original disciples. It is a sad, but no less authentic, fact of human relationships that from time to time we are hurt with one another and we get angry, and that from time to time, we may actually turn our backs on one another. In the case of Paul and Barnabas, these two pillars of the church, their dispute over the fitness of John (called Mark) as a missionary companion led them to go their separate ways. Apparently the young and inexperienced Mark had abandoned the team once already (vv. 37–38), and Paul was not willing to trust him on their next journey. Barnabas, on the other hand, was prepared to give Mark another chance. One can see both sides of the argument (which also makes one wonder if God did not use the anger of these two men in order to actually advance the gospel—for now there were two teams instead of one!).

The letters of Paul reveal a man of obvious fiery disposition and single-minded focus, while the Acts of the Apostles portrays Barnabas as a man of great generosity and thoughtfulness. Even the new name given him by the apostles means "son of encouragement" (see Acts 4:36–7). So, the new church of Christ is being served by two men with very different personalities and very different opinions about the best course of action to be taken. Should there not be room in the Body of Christ for both?

Though it is never made explicit, it would seem that Paul and Barnabas eventually reconciled. At least we know from Paul's second letter to Timothy that he not only came to accept Mark, but also to recommend him for his faithful service (4:11). Among the lessons to be drawn from the Bible's forthright presentation of this "sharp contention" is that conflict *does* happen in the Body of Christ and that it can also be resolved.

Paul and Barnabas' argument appears to have been quite volatile. One can only imagine how angry the words must have been in order to turn these two friends and co-workers away from one another. Nevertheless, the things we have discussed this week remind us that such enmity can only be resolved if it is faced directly. Yes, above all we are to love one another. But, as Paul writes to the Romans, love must be "genuine" (12:9). Love for God and neighbor cannot be faked. Its strength and endurance are dependent upon the honesty with which we face those things that would weaken or destroy it. Genuine love comes at a cost.

REFLECT | *How are you facing your real feelings about someone with whom you differ? How can you allow God to help you to resolve those feelings?*

Week Seven Woe Is Me: The Crushing Weight Of Self-Pity

Day 1　Whose Arms are Strong Enough?

READ | Isaiah 53

He was despised and rejected by men; a man of sorrows and acquainted with grief. . . . Surely he has borne our griefs and carried our sorrows. (vv. 3, 4)

"I've tripped up and fallen so many times, I just don't know if I can keep at this. Obviously I'm no good at it. I don't think I've got what it takes. It's all just too much for me." Halfway through these twelve weeks it would be surprising indeed if these words, in some form or another, have not already passed through your lips (or, at least through your mind) many times already. Sometimes the journey of the disciple of Christ seems endlessly uphill. Rather than our step growing lighter and quicker, our clumsy feet seem to find absolutely every pothole and every stone along the way. "This is abundant life?" we ask. "This is where following Jesus gets me?"

Failure—there is not a one of us who has not known its bitter taste or been bruised by its heavy stroke. It is a most unwelcome guest for, when it comes into our homes, it usually brings its gloomy companions, disappointment and discouragement. The question before us this week is not about whether or not failure will come through our door. Failure will visit often. He is the first cousin to our fallen human condition and he will always know our address. The question is, how long will we entertain its nasty cohorts? How long will we live with discouragement and entertain despondency? How long will we let them sit at our table?

This week, at the mid-point of these reflections, we turn to the subject of self-pity. We do this, keeping in mind that, like any other sin (and, so long as it diverts us from love for God and for others, it is, most definitely, sin), it need not, it *cannot*, have the last word in our lives. The griefs that pierce our hearts, due either to those circumstances quite beyond our control or to those of our own making, are intimately known to God. He knows better than we, that we are not strong enough to bear them alone. Remember the story of Adam and Eve; God never intended them to "go it alone." They were created to be dependent upon their Maker. Only by their own misguided choices did they and their children come to believe that everything depended upon them.

Some people seem to have a natural penchant for hopefulness and trust. For most of us, however, these are qualities that must be learned, and those lessons begin by returning to the most basic truth of all—God loves us. We have a Savior, One whose arms are more than strong enough to lift us, together with all the sorrows and disappointments that sit heavily upon our own shoulders. Jesus is both the Lamb, who knows the roughness of the journey, as well as the Good Shepherd, who is never far from our bleating cries. Refusing to give in to the insidious temptation that we are "on our own" is the beginning of learning hope. Looking to the love of God rather than to our own unloveliness is the beginning of learning faith. Relying upon the help of God rather than upon our own feeble efforts is the beginning of learning joy.

REFLECT | *Name specifically those places in your life where you are discouraged this week. Now consider the ways in which you can (must) look to God for his help in these places. What is it that you most hope for in your life? What are the ways in which God is answering that desire?*

Day 2   Repentance or Self-pity?

READ | 2 Corinthians 7:2–10

For godly grief produces a repentance that leads to salvation and brings no regret, but worldly grief produces death. (v. 10)

Before we delve further into our discussion of self-pity, we do well to make an important distinction about its meaning. Paul's words to the Christians in Corinth may be helpful.

The apostle knew a good deal about the comfort of God, because he also knew a good deal about affliction and failure. We know that in his service of the gospel, Paul endured many trials and many hardships. Later in this letter, he offered a fairly thorough list to his readers (see 11:23–29). Through these events, Paul learned again and again the priceless lessons of perseverance and hope. God had been his comforter, sometimes through the hearts and hands of his companions, sometimes in the midst of his darkest and most lonely hours. Paul also knew the comfort of God's forgiving love. The conviction that cut into his heart on that day when he met Christ on the road to Damascus (Acts 9:1–19) caused him a burning sorrow that he would remember and speak of for the rest of his life. His face-to-face encounter with

Jesus caused him a painful grief before it brought him to an enduring joy. For this reason, he understood well what the Corinthians were feeling.

In this letter Paul refers to an earlier letter by which he had severely reprimanded the church in Corinth for some serious sin. Titus brings word to Paul, while he is working in Macedonia, that the letter was received, that it caused a good deal of distress and sorrow, but that it also resulted in the Corinthians' repentance followed by a renewed zeal for the gospel. This, writes Paul, is the "*godly grief* that produces repentance that leads to salvation" (v. 10).

There is a vast difference, says Paul, between "godly grief" and "worldly grief," and that difference is seen most clearly in their exceedingly different results—the first brings salvation while the latter brings death! By "godly grief" Paul is apparently describing repentance, the same response to the conviction of the Holy Spirit that he himself experienced at his conversion. It is "godly" because Paul allowed it to actually open his heart to the love of God and make him responsive to the truth of the gospel. The end result was Paul's salvation, and all the joyful benefits that came with it.

Apparently, something similar happened with the Corinthians. The apostle's message had cut them to the quick, but the grief it caused compelled them only to change their ways and to renew their zeal for God. By "worldly grief," however, Paul means something entirely different, for the world knows only how to help itself, and when its own help fails, there is nowhere else to look for comfort. This is a sadness that actually turns us away from God, closes our hearts to his love, and leaves us alone with our remorse. There is nothing at all "godly" about such grief.

Pain will always compel us to look for relief. The question will always be: to whom will we look? "Godly grief" produces repentance—it draws our vision away from ourselves, toward the only Savior who is able to save. "Worldly grief" produces regret—it drags our vision inward, where we look in vain for the help we need and despair at our lack of it. The fruit of the first is joy. The fruit of the second is self-pity.

R E F L E C T | *In what area(s) of your life are you now experiencing repentance? In what area(s) are you experiencing remorse? How do you know the difference?*

Day 3 Lord, Where Have You Gone?

R E A D | Psalm 77

Has [the Lord's] steadfast love forever ceased? Are his promises at an end for all time? Has God forgotten to be gracious? (vv. 8–9)

So, what are some of the signs of self-pity, and what are some of the tools we can use in order to come free of its stifling grip? Recognizing that self-pity has us by the throat is certainly the first step toward getting loose. Then there are some other steps we can take to keep it at bay. For some insight, we turn first to the psalms.

One early pastor of the church compared the book of psalms to a garden wherein one can find growing every possible variety of human emotion: love, hate, anger, fear, joy, praise, hope, sorrow, and self-pity, among others. Another said that the psalms are like mirrors—we can look into any one of them, and, at any given time, we can see our own emotions looking back at us. For example, there is a whole category of psalms that have been called "psalms of lament," and this is one of them. It is easy to see why. Do you "see yourself" in any one of the psalmist's complaints: things are so painful that I have nothing to say; I can't get any sleep; when I think about God I only feel worse; where is God, anyway; has he forgotten all about me; I used to know that God loved me, but not any more; I'm trying my best, but it's just no good?

By the time he "cries aloud," this poet's self-pity has ripened into a full-grown case of hopelessness and accusation against the goodness and mercy of God. As with any of us in such a state, this soul is in danger of losing all desire to be faithful and all determination to be obedient to God and to his will. Self-pity saps the heart of all energy when it convinces it to believe the worst lie of all—that God doesn't care and that, in fact, he never has.

The psalmist makes no attempt to hide or to diminish the depth of his lamentation. In fact, the reason we have it recorded in the Bible in the first place is that the writer presents it as a genuine prayer of the heart. Bringing our true feelings to God is actually the first step toward sorting them all out. The safest place for us to laugh or cry, to grieve or rejoice, even to rant and rave, is before the face of God. "Look at me and tell me what you are feeling," seems to be God's constant invitation to his sons and daughters. Doing so, even in anger, is one way that we begin to turn our eyes heavenward.

Reading the entire psalm reveals to us that there is also a second step toward our recovery. Having poured out all his grievances, the psalmist appears to stop and remind himself that they do not tell the *whole* story of his relationship with God. "I will call to mind the deeds of the Lord," he says. "I will remember thy wonders of old. I will meditate on all thy work and muse on thy mighty deeds" (vv. 11–12). Having gathered all the thorns that he could possibly find in this garden of despair, the psalmist now starts picking some fragrant flowers, and their sweet scent begins to renew his hope. Remembering the things that God has done for us in the past is a most effective way to fight present despondency. The pathway of our lives is plentifully covered with commemorative signs of God's faithfulness, and no amount of grief today can remove these marks of God's lovingkindness.

REFLECT | *If God were actually sitting in a seat across from you, what would you most want to say to him today? Recount for yourself at least six good things that God has done in your life in the last year; in the last week; in the last day.*

Day 4 Child, What Are You Doing Here?

READ | 1 Kings 19:1–18

And there he came to a cave, and lodged there; and behold, the word of the Lord came to him, and said to him, "What are you doing here, Elijah?" (v. 9)

We know the prophet Elijah to be one of God's most faithful servants and zealous defenders. Many of the stories we read of him are filled with intense activity and drama, and it seems in keeping with the rest of his colorful life that, at its close, he should be taken to heaven in a fiery whirlwind! (2 Kings 2:11–12). But, did you know that this great man of faith and courage was also given to bouts of discouragement and despair? Today's reading, from the history of Israel's monarchy, describes Elijah in his most dispirited condition, and it does so with a bit of humor as well.

The end of the previous chapter left Elijah enjoying the sweet taste of victory over the pagan prophets of Baal (see 18:17–46). Before the eyes of all his enemies, God had vindicated Elijah by answering his prayer: first, he sent fire from heaven to consume a thoroughly waterlogged offering, and then he sent rain to end a long season of drought. In every way, Elijah was shown to be a true prophet, and this only raised the ire of his most bitter enemy, Jezebel the queen. This is where we pick up the story.

Elijah quickly abandons faith for fear when he hears the threats of the queen. Having just stared down an entire nation, what does this man of faith do in the face of Jezebel's fumings? He runs away. Into the wilderness he flees, and there, discouraged and full of self-pity, he simply gives up: "That's enough. Now, Lord, just take away my life" (v. 4). God does no such thing, however. Instead, he feeds him and sends him on his way.

Elijah's next step is a cave, far off in Horeb. But in this place, before he can say anything at all, God puts to him this question: "What are you doing here, Elijah?" The rest of the story tells us that Elijah really has no good answer. Thinking that he has been abandoned ("I, even only I am left," v. 10), Elijah discovers that there are thousands of others who are keeping faith with God (v. 18). With a "still, small voice," God quiets Elijah's complaints and calms his trembling heart. Reassuring Elijah that the cause is not lost, God sends him back to Israel to finish his work.

The wilderness and the cave—are these not apt images for a "place" we might call self-pity? One is dry, the other is dark; one is expansively large and dangerous, the other is oppressively small and confining; in one it seems you cannot hear the sound of your own voice, while in the other it seems your own voice is all that you can hear. In both of these dreary places, God comes to us. We may run to them when we are afraid and discouraged, but we can be certain that God will get there first. "Child, what are you doing here?" he will ask. And our answers will make no more sense than did Elijah's.

Remember that kind and probing question the next time you find yourself feeling downcast, defeated, or sorry for yourself. Answer it as best you can, and then listen for what God will say to you. "Go, return," was God's message to Elijah. God still had much that he intended to do through his faithful servant, and others were still waiting to benefit from his work. So Elijah "departed from there" (v. 19), and returned.

REFLECT | *To what places do you run to "hide" when you are feeling sorry for yourself? What are you doing there? Notice how Elijah's discouragement followed immediately on the heels of his success. What lessons can you draw from this?*

Day 5　Lord, Don't You Care?

READ ｜ Luke 10:38–42

Lord, do you not care that my sister has left me to serve alone? (v. 40)

Mary and Martha and their brother, Lazarus, were friends as well as followers of Jesus. The Gospel of John tells us, "Now Jesus loved Martha and her sister and Lazarus" (11:5), and, from the tears that Jesus shed at Lazarus' tomb and in the presence of Mary and Martha, we can infer that Jesus held these friends dear in his heart. So it must always have been a joy for these three to host Jesus in their home, and it would appear that they did so more than once. The first occasion, however, seems to be this one recorded in Luke's Gospel.

No doubt, when Jesus came, others came with him. All of the twelve? Quite likely. In any case, there was enough work to do that "Martha was distracted with much serving." You can imagine the scene, can you not? Jesus and the disciples are gathered at the table. Lazarus is asking questions of this young and fascinating rabbi, because he has already received news about some of his wise words and miraculous deeds. Mary, who may have brought the water so that these weary travelers could wash their feet, stands politely at the entry to the room. Before long, however, she forgets her other duties and gradually begins to move closer. Every word of Jesus' seems to draw her. She ends up sitting at his feet.

Meanwhile, Martha is at work preparing the meal. After all, it seems that she is the one who has invited all the guests. She awaits Mary's return so that they can share the duties, but her sister never comes. A bit of irritation grows to genuine annoyance when, looking into the room, she realizes that Mary has no intention of returning to the kitchen. Martha is on her own to do all the work. She returns to the kitchen, but all the time her troubled feelings are churning: "This isn't right; this isn't fair. Why should I have to do all the work? Why isn't my sister helping me? Even the rabbi would agree with me." So she turns, and makes her appeal for him to correct her sister. And, in doing so, Martha is led to break all the rules of proper etiquette by complaining to her guest about how much *she* had to do to feed him! This story is a high-definition picture of the dance of jealousy and self-pity.

The answer to Martha's (and our) predicament is actually presented in the story itself—"one thing is needful" (v. 42). The eyes of self-pity are prone to wander about the rooms of our lives and fix upon anyone else who seems to have it better than we do. Self-pity whispers: "This isn't right; this isn't fair. Why should I have it so hard? Why should she have it so good? Even God would agree with me." You and I know this to be true, because we have heard this whispering voice ourselves, and we have agreed with it. All the time we are having this sort of conversation with ourselves, however, the Lord, who himself is the "one thing needful," waits for our wandering eyes to make their way toward him. Fixing the eyes of our hearts upon Jesus is the only lasting remedy for the kind of feeling sorry for ourselves that springs from jealousy. Everything else can be taken away from us (v. 42).

REFLECT | *What unfair duties or responsibilities do you bear that sometimes (all the time?) cause you to feel sorry for yourself?*

What is the "good portion" that Jesus is inviting you to receive from his hand today? When you feel sorry for yourself, what are the specific ways in which you can turn your eyes to Jesus?

Day 6 A Hope That Lifts the Soul

READ | Psalm 42

Why are you cast down, O my soul, and why are you disquieted within me? Hope in God; for I shall again praise him, my help and my God. (v. 5)

Alexander Maclaren, the great nineteenth-century English Baptist preacher, says about Psalm 42, "The whole psalm reads like the sob of a wounded heart. The writer of it is shut out from the Temple of his God, from the holy soil of his native land. One can see him sitting solitary yonder in the lonely wilderness . . . with a longing, wistful gaze, yearning across the narrow valley and the rushing stream that lay between him and the land of God's chosen people, and his eye resting perhaps on the mountain top that looked down upon Jerusalem. . . . He was depressed because he was shut out from the tokens of God's presence [the Temple]; and *because he was depressed, he shut himself out from the reality of the Presence*" (Alexander Maclaren, *Psalms for Sighs*, italics mine).

Maclaren makes an interesting point. On the one hand, it is quite understandable that the psalmist should be "cast down" under the burden of his sad circumstances. He could remember the days when he made his way to Jerusalem and the beautiful temple of the Lord with singing and dancing.

Now, separated from the home he loved, he felt like a deer without water, and his soul languished. On the other hand, *because* he languished, he turned his face from God, and, for a time, he shut the gates of his own heart to God's entry.

Have you noticed this insidious thing about the fiend called self-pity? it provokes us to do the very thing that will keep it nourished and strong. We *feel* that God is not present, or that God does not love us, or that we are too pitiful to be loved. The strength of these feelings convinces us that what they are saying is true. So we end up turning away from God, and our hearts become even more discouraged. The psalmist's prayer provides an escape from this vicious circle: "My soul is cast down within me, *therefore* I remember thee" (v. 5). Wise to self-pity's sneaky ways, he gives his heart a good talking-to: "Listen, my heart. What are you doing down there? The things that you are telling me are just not true. God is not like that. You are telling me that he does not love me, but I know better."

An older and wiser friend met me on the road once, when I was in a particularly bad way. Discouraged and lost, I told him that I was confessing to God repeatedly how faithless and fearful I felt. But it seemed all for naught, and I was tiring of it. "Have you talked with God recently about the things he has done for you?" asked my friend. My silence was answer enough. "Because," he said thoughtfully, "I think one act of thanking God for his goodness is worth more than a dozen confessions of your own sin." I don't know how the theologians would parse that sentence, but I do know that encounter started my own journey back to the face of God. Like the psalmist, I found solace and then joy by "remembering" God.

REFLECT | *What has God done for you in the last week? Name the places where he is present in your life, and in the lives of those you love. What do you need to say to your own soul today to help it turn its eyes toward heaven?*

Day 7 　 Go Forward!

READ | Exodus 14:5–31
Fear not, stand firm, and see the salvation of the Lord, which he will work for you today. (v. 13)

One final thing must be said about this week's subject— sometimes feeling sorry for ourselves is the understandable, if unfortunate, result of being faced with circumstances quite beyond our own control. Sometimes, the "overwhelming odds" of life's pressures simply get us down. The endless tasks of caring for home and family, the demands of the job, conflicts with those we love most, financial strains and worries for the future—these sometimes swell up like a stormy sea and overcome us with their billowing waves. We understand the plight of the lonely Breton fisherman who prayed: "Lord, be good to me; the sea is so wide, and my boat is so small."

The story of God's deliverance of the people of Israel has, for centuries, been a source of consolation and promise. (In some Christian traditions, the account is read on the eve of every Easter, reminding the listener that, when he divided the Red Sea, God was just getting warmed up to open the Garden Tomb.) The people's hope for a clean escape from slavery was distinctly thwarted as Pharaoh's army charged them from behind and the sea loomed up ahead. And, from within, there arose the worst enemy of all: Fear, panic, self-pity, accusation, and anger—the whole discouraging gang got together to make its malicious attack. "We should have stayed in Egypt," the people cried. "What are *you* doing to us, Moses, and what were we thinking to have ever followed you?" I'm sure we all know the desperate tone in their voices.

We also know how the story ends, but how *did* the people get from one side to the other? "Go forward," God told them through the mouth of Moses. As hopelessly impossible as the situation appears, go forward. The Lord will do the fighting, while you turn your face forward. The Lord will make a way, while you take another trembling step forward. The Lord will work for you today, while you work to set your sight forward.

Only after they had completed their journey across the sea did the children of Israel get the full view of what had happened behind them. From the far shore they could now see all the signs of God's deliverance, whereas before, from the midst of their troubles, all they could see were the signs of their own impending doom. And, when they saw the great work that the Lord had done, "they believed in the Lord and in his servant Moses." The tone of their voices was then utterly changed and raised in the praise of their Deliverer. If you have time today, you should read their song in the first half of the next chapter of Exodus, where you will find these words: "Thou hast led in thy steadfast love the people whom thou hast redeemed, thou hast guided them by thy strength to thy holy abode." How did the people get from one side to the other?—God led them . . . and they went forward.

REFLECT | *Where are the voices coming from that are telling you to give up? What are they saying? Where are the voices coming from that are telling you to keep going forward? What are they saying? Which voices are you going to listen to?*

Week Eight The Irresistible Strength Of A Forgiving Heart

Day 1   Overcome Evil With Good

R E A D | Romans 12:1–21

Repay no one evil for evil, but take thought for what is noble in the sight of all. (v. 17)

In many respects, Paul's letter to the Romans is his most theological work. Through the first eleven chapters he sets forth both a reasonable as well as a passionate argument for faith in Jesus Christ. He traces God's work through creation and in the covenant with Abraham and the people of Israel; he demonstrates the character of belief in God's promises, and makes the case that all those promises have been fulfilled in Christ; he explains the overwhelming power of sin and describes its defeat under the even more overwhelming power of the Cross. "O the depth of the riches and wisdom and knowledge of God!" Paul concludes. "To him be glory for ever. Amen" (11:33, 36). With that exclamation, he begins to apply the things we believe to the ways that we live. *Therefore,* he says, given all the strength and beauty of God's mercies, you can be living lives of strength and beauty yourselves (12:1–2). For the remaining four chapters of his letter, his words are decidedly pointed and practical, and, not surprisingly, he opens by making the case for loving one another.

God's love, as we know, takes very concrete forms ("the Word became *flesh*")—it has far less to do with our feelings than with our actions. Perhaps in no case is this more evident than in that internal conflict we all know between the need to forgive and the desire for revenge. The cliché goes: "Don't get mad—get even!" We human beings have an uncanny ability to tenaciously remember wrongs that have been done to us. Often the heated conflicts that arise between wives and husbands, or among children, or with friends, are actually stoked by the embers of hurts that we have quietly, steadily, and sometimes quite unconsciously fanned over time. When opportunities to "even the score" come along, our supply of wounded feelings and angry reactions is at the ready, and we fling out our vengeful thoughts from it like so many hot sparks fly from the fire. What's more, our vindictiveness comes in a whole range of shapes and sizes: angry words, humorous remarks, hurtful actions, lapses of memory, and stubborn refusals, just to name a few. What is more, we sometimes visit these reactions upon innocent bystanders who just happen to "walk into our path." Something they say or do hits a nerve in us and brings down upon their own blameless heads the vengeance that we were really saving for someone else.

The apostle Paul writes that the only "burning coals" we should be heaping on anyone's head should be deeds of love and mercy (v. 20). He says that true nobility of heart is found in forgiveness rather than in reprisal, and that the truly strong are those who overcome evil before they are overcome by it. In the end, he says, only God is in a position to justly vindicate the aggrieved or persecuted soul, because God is the only one who is just in the first place. Putting our own hand to vengeance is not only contrary to the law of love, but it usurps the place of God himself.

This week, we will reflect further on what the Scriptures teach us about the destructive power of human vindictiveness, and how it is overcome by the healing power of divine love.

REFLECT | *Think about the events of the past week. Even if you did not act upon them, what desires did you have to "get even" with someone? When you do act upon them (in thought or in deed), what different shapes does your own vindictiveness take?*

Day 2 A Hurt for a Hurt

READ | Matthew 5:38–48

But I say to you, Love your enemies and pray for those who persecute you, so that you may be sons of your Father who is in heaven. (vv. 44–45)

Most of us wholly consent to the ideal of total love for absolutely everyone, including our enemies. We believe this to be a basic Christian principle that is in every way consistent with the gospel. But the ideal quickly succumbs to the severe blow of a real offense—a real harmful word, a real slight, or a real attack. The loud crack made by some concrete hostility thrown against us drowns out the sound of all our good intentions. Then, our hurt feelings scream out, pushing aside all our convictions with their shrill demands to be avenged. Is love for our enemies really possible?

Let us first agree that, as impossible as these instructions may seem (and this could be said for the entire Sermon on the Mount), Jesus does not waste his breath giving directions that cannot somehow be followed. In fact, "directions" may be a helpful way to look at what Jesus is teaching, for directions are designed to successfully guide us from one place to another. How do we move, in this case over some fairly rocky and uneven ground, from our starting point—

seeking revenge—to our destination—love? And what are the turns we have to make along the way?

We can begin with the realization that you and I were once God's enemies and that the way he "won us over" to his side was with love. The Bible says that, while we were *still* enemies, while we were *yet* sinners, Christ died for us (see Romans 5:6–11). God did not wait for us to come around before he sent his Son. Love often has to be sent one way before it can ever come the other.

Second, love for one's enemies is not the reason but the sign that we are children of our Father who is in heaven. Our inheritance as children of God is not only the forgiveness of our own sins, but also the God-given ability to forgive the sins of others. By the Holy Spirit's help, it is now a divine trait received from God that we hold in common with our most direct "blood relative"—Jesus himself. Once, when defending the Christian faith, the early church teacher Tertullian fixed upon one distinctive mark. "All people love their friends," he said, "but only Christians love their enemies."

Third, such forgiving love is rarely, if ever, effortless. Love is a very tangible and often difficult series of choices and actions. Among its practical expressions, says Jesus, is prayer—"pray for those who persecute you." By these instructions, Jesus is asking no more of his followers than he would do himself, even while suffering the most evil of offenses against him: "Father, forgive them, for they know not what they do" (Luke 23:34). Long before any sentiments of love may arise in our hearts, our lips can still love when they say, "Father, forgive us our sins as we forgive those who sin against us" (Matthew 6:12).

Someone has said that our enemies can be our greatest teachers, because their actions more quickly unveil some of the secret things that are in our hearts than would ever emerge in the presence of friends. Once those "secret things" do emerge—the hurt, the anger, the vengeful feelings— Jesus gives us directions for how to move from our hearts to his own. It is the way of love.

REFLECT | *Name one "enemy" you have today. What tangible steps of forgiveness and love is God asking you to take? Will you?*

Day 3 Revenge: The Weakest Alternative

READ | Genesis 4:1–16
And if you do not do well, sin is couching at the door; its desire is for you, but you must master it. (v. 7)

In case there was any question about the seriousness of vindictiveness and its consequences, we have the tragic tale of Cain and Abel. The Bible presents their story as almost the immediate aftermath of the "fall" of their parents, Adam and Eve. Whereas God, from the first day of creation, had intended life for his sons and daughters, the terrible result of their rebellion was the complete opposite. They had been warned that death would follow their proud act, so the church has always understood our mortality to be interwoven with our fallen condition. Still, both life and death were to remain in the hands of God. It was for God alone to give, and to take away. What is uniquely horrific about the story of Cain and Abel, therefore, is that it is about life and death being seized by the hands of sinful humanity. It is the story of the first murder.

While the events that led to Cain's violent act are somewhat obscure (why did God "have regard" for his brother's offering, but not for his?), the immediate causes are quite clear: Cain became jealous of his brother; that jealousy evolved into bitter anger and resentment; then, when the opportunity presented itself, Cain got his revenge. Of course, he more than evened the score; his deed went far beyond "an eye for an eye." Nevertheless, the principle of revenge is at work. Convinced that Abel had wronged him by taking something that was rightfully his—that is, God's approval—Cain plotted and succeeded in wronging Abel in return, by taking something from him—his life.

Violence, even if it is only acted out in one's imagination, is so often the fruit of vindictive feelings, but it does not have to be. Cain had opportunity to stop the downward spiral of his own thoughts and actions, but, quite simply, he did not choose to do so. In his conversation with Cain, God portrayed sin as being like a beast laying in wait at the door for its victims. It is strong, but it can be mastered.

Like all sin, it takes more strength to *resist* the temptation for revenge than it takes to *give in* to it. This is true of most any act of self-discipline or self-denial, as well. True strength lies in mastering our darker motivations, not in giving unrestrained vent to them. God accepted, and no doubt understood, the fact of Cain's anger and jealousy, but he sternly warned him not to let these monsters consume his better judgment.

Interestingly, the weakling of vindictiveness disguises itself as a means to power. We are tempted to think that, if we could only get even, we would feel "stronger." We think that whatever has been "taken" from us has left us weak (i.e., we lose an argument), when, in fact, our greatest weakness is our inability to stop the craving to get it back (i.e., to win). For example, how many arguments have you rewound in your mind, so that you could insert just the right word or phrase that would win the day and show your opponent just how shrewd you are? That's vindictiveness at work. Now, try to stop having those imaginary fights. Which is easier?

REFLECT | *What conversations or events are you playing out in your own mind these days? How do phrases like "give in," "let go," and "give up" make you feel? Why? What is the most effective means of "mastering" your vindictiveness?*

Day 4   Who is the Final Winner?

READ | Genesis 39
But the Lord was with Joseph and showed him steadfast love. (v. 21)

Today, we turn to one of the most classic examples of revenge in the Bible. After reading the story of Joseph and Potiphar's wife, no one should think that the Scriptures are anything but candid in their portrayals of twisted values, sexual desire, and vengeful deception. This story has all the drama and intrigue of a soap opera. It also contains an important lesson.

It is, of course, the story of unrequited passion and of the revenge that springs from it.

Vengeance borne of humiliation will always turn attraction into hatred. Consider the effects of something like gossip or backbiting. (Does the fact that we hardly use these words anymore say something about how common they have become?) The angry pain caused by such remarks has been the cause of countless estranged friendships and broken families. With her own proud and lustful advances spurned by Joseph, Potiphar's wife planned her retaliation, and succeeded. It appears that vindictiveness wins the day . . . but only the day. The spotlight moves elsewhere, and from this point on, we hear nothing more of Potiphar's wife. It seems that she only had a bit part to play and on a much bigger stage than she imagined. From the perspective of heaven, she gets away with nothing at all.

Remember that Joseph was already the victim of his brothers' vengeful betrayal. His enslavement in Egypt was already that direct result of jealousy and vindictive scheming (see Genesis 37). But, what his brothers (and Potiphar's wife) had planned for Joseph's undoing, God planned to use for Joseph's making. Following their eventual reconciliation, Joseph said to them, "You meant evil against me; but God meant it for good, to bring it about that many people should be kept alive, as they are today" (Genesis 50:20). The Psalms tell us: "His feet were hurt with fetters, his neck was put in a collar of iron; until what he had said came to pass the word of the LORD tested him" (105:17). From God's perspective, it was "the word of the Lord" that was at work in Joseph, so that even his brothers' cruel and unfair treatment could be transformed into the means for his blessing and maturing.

This is not to say that evil and malice are in any way defensible. There are things that have happened in some of our lives that should never be overlooked or excused. But God is the only just and perfect vindicator, and, though his ways seem dark and slow, he is the Master of bringing good out of evil. And there is no sweeter "revenge" than that. Joseph's enslavement to Potiphar led to his imprisonment, which led to his employment by Pharaoh, which eventually led to the salvation of his entire family and the formation of the Hebrew people. Suppose he had escaped from Egypt and returned to exact his own vengeance upon his brothers. Or, once he was invested with the authority of Pharaoh himself, suppose he had executed his brothers in justifiable retribution for their spitefulness to him.

Aside from the fact that revenge should always be left to God, exacting retribution from another may actually frustrate the deeper purposes of God in our lives. When we reach our hand out to vengeance, we may be deflecting God's hand reaching out to us.

REFLECT | *With what unfair circumstances in your own life is God asking you to trust him? Give an example of at least one event in your own life when God "turned evil into good." Who do you need to forgive today in order not to put your hand to vengeance?*

Day 5   Whose Words Shall Prevail?

READ | Mark 6:7–29

*And Herodias had a grudge against [John] and wanted to kill him.
(v. 19)*

John the Baptist was like the prophet Elijah of old:
bold in his dedication to the will of God and fearless in
his confrontation with power and corruption. With the
single-minded intention of being true to his God, he did
not hesitate to call all people—both low and high alike—
to account for their actions. His cry for repentance, as he
announced the coming of God's kingdom, was heard in the
wilderness and in the palace. In John's eyes, God's standards
were for *everyone.*

Herod the king had unlawfully married his brother's
wife, Herodias, after divorcing his own. Faithful to his own
convictions, and heedless of his own safety, John cried out
against this, and brought down upon his head the vengeful
wrath of Herodias, who, Luke understates, "had a grudge
against him and wanted to kill him" (v. 19). As we noted
in other readings, and in the life of Jesus himself, the
work of a prophet was always dangerous, especially when
it required them to speak God's word to those who were
more interested in power than in the truth. In such cases,
the prophet's only protection was God himself. In John's
case, the woman he offended accomplished her plans to
silence him, when Herod, drunk and inflated with vanity,
promised the sultry Salome whatever she asked, "even
half of my kingdom." The kingdom is not what Herodias
wanted. It was revenge.

It is helpful to look at these events through two sets of eyes, Herodias' and John's. From Herodias' point of view, John had overstepped himself by addressing criticism against one as important and superior as she. She found his remarks offensive to the extreme.

"What right does he have to speak to me in such a way?" she undoubtedly complained to her husband. Her interest, of course, was not in what was true, but in what was expedient. In other words, anything that would reinforce the manner in which she lived her life was to be welcomed, while whatever called it into question was to be rejected (along with whoever it was that asked the question!).

John, on the other hand, was more interested in truth than in power. He dressed and ate like the poor man that he was and made the wilderness his home. He loved God, and was intensely committed to proclaiming a message that would cut out the diseased growth of Israel and help restore a strong and healthy people of faith. "Repent!" he cried, "The kingdom of heaven is at hand." It was neither an easy nor necessarily a reassuring message to give, but it stirred everyone who heard it: some went to be baptized by him in the Jordan, confessing their sins; others mocked and waited to see him get into trouble.

Herodias' commitment to power made her untruthful, while John's commitment to truth made him powerful. In the end, she took a life, while he gave one. Her act of vengeance was designed to protect her superior image and to maintain her grasp of power. His act of submission was freely given for the sake of God's word, and the only image he needed to protect was but a reflection of that Word. "He must increase, but I must decrease," he once said in reference to Jesus (John 3:30). Herodias sought to prevail over John, and used the means of deceit and revenge in order to do so. John never sought to prevail in anything, but only to be faithful, and the means at hand were love for and obedience to his God. Two perspectives on life were moving two hearts in two extremely different directions. Which way are you going?

REFLECT | *Which way are you going? Which way do you want to go? How will you get there?*

Day 6　A New Commandment

READ | 1 Thessalonians 5
See that none of you repays evil for evil, but always seek to do good to one another and to all. (v. 15)

On the very night of his betrayal and arrest, you remember, Jesus shared a meal with his disciples in the Upper Room (see John 13:1–12). In preparation for supper, in an act of unconditional love and humility, he washed all of the disciples' feet, including Judas'. Knowing full well what was soon to take place, and that the catalyst for all those horrid events would be the hypocritical kiss of his friend, Jesus bent to the ground, poured water on Judas' feet, and dried them with his own hands. Then, after the meal and after Judas had gone out from among them, as if to explain the entire meaning of his life and ministry, he charged the remaining few with these profound words: "A new commandment I give to you, that you love one another;

even as I have loved you, that you also love one another. By this all men will know that you are my disciples, if you have love for one another" (John 13:34–35).

You will pardon the pun if I say that Paul puts feet on this commandment when he writes his letter to the Christians in Thessalonica. As always, his words reveal his uncanny ability to soar to the heavens with his theology, and then plummet to earth with his most practical advice. "See that none of you repays evil for evil, but always seek to do good to one another and to all" (v. 15). There it is again, the same direction he gave to the Christians in Rome (Romans 12:17).

Do you notice that the Bible's instruction is to do more than simply resist the temptation to get even? As difficult as that is, it is only the beginning: it is only the first half of the divine duty with which we have been entrusted. Withholding evil in the face of evil is a start. Doing good in the face of evil is what it means to follow Jesus. In this case the saying is true—the best defense *is* a good offense. The most effective way we fend off the desire for revenge is by feeding the desire to love.

We live in an evil world where people do bad things to other people. They lie and cheat and hurt one another by their words and by their actions. They do evil to one another, and no more vehemently than when evil has been done to them. Sometimes we have been the perpetrators, and sometimes we have been the victims. It all becomes a vicious cycle of wrongdoing if someone does not stop and then turn around and go in the opposite direction. That is what Paul is talking about here. That is what Jesus is demonstrating to his disciples—an entirely different way to live.

Love compels us to run to the cross of Christ when evil is done to us. There, we gaze upon One who when reviled did not revile back; who did not complain to his accusers, but prayed for them; who could have brought down the wrath of heaven upon his tormentors, but instead poured out for them the love of God. How can we stay long at that cross, and still desire to wreak vengeance upon those who, for reasons we do not understand (and which they do not fully understand either), seek to do us harm? We do not have to repay evil with evil. For once we start down that course, what real difference is there between ourselves and those whom we call "evil"? The strength of love is ours to wield at any time, because it was put into our hands by the Lord of love himself. Let those who seek to follow Christ learn his way of love and leave the judgment with God!

REFLECT | *What are the weapons of vengeance that God wants you to put down today? What are the tools of love that he wants you to take up? What "good" thing can you do today for someone who has done you "evil"?*

Day 7   Worthy to Suffer Dishonor

READ | Acts 5:12–42

Then they left the presence of the council, rejoicing that they were counted worthy to suffer dishonor for the Name. (v. 41)

As their penalty for preaching the gospel and healing the sick, the apostles were arrested and thrown into prison. It would not be the last time. On this occasion, they were miraculously released by an angel, and instructed to again stand and teach "the words of this Life" in the temple. Seized a second time, they were carried before the Council where, after declaring that they "must obey God rather than men," they were beaten and charged not to speak in the name of Jesus and released. Twenty-four hours of serving God, doing good, witnessing miracles, and preaching the gospel—in return for which they received a sleepless night, imprisonment, threats of death, beatings, and warnings to stop. What a deal!

There is something noble going on here that appeals to us all. And nothing is nobler than the reaction of these men to their unjust treatment at the hands of others. They returned home, and then returned to their mission, *rejoicing*, not because their enemies had been defeated, not because their honor had been vindicated, and not because hundreds had been converted to faith in Christ that day. They rejoiced because they had been treated just as their Lord had been treated.

As we finish this week's thoughts about our innate, human desire to get even, let this lesson carry our minds and hearts to a higher plane. God's honor is at stake, and some are called to suffer *dis*honor for the sake of serving him. Not everyone. Not even every Christian. But some are called to bear that burden, to carry that part of the cross for the sake of the whole Body of Christ. The apostles counted it an honor. Do we?

Perhaps it would help us to once again accept the reality that following Jesus comes at a price. We cannot expect to be faithful disciples of Christ and to live a pain-free life in this world. For this world is still hostile to the things of

God, and the spirit of this world is antithetical to the spirit of God. Those who follow Jesus *will* suffer some degree, some form of hurt, rejection, and persecution. It may be slight, or it may be severe. What is more, we may visit it, even unintentionally, upon one another. Those, perhaps, are the times when the pain is most bitter. In any case, we have a decision to make about how we will respond to it. This week's reflections have given us an alternative to the vengeful ways that we might choose most naturally. They are a reminder that we can choose the "still more excellent way" of love (1 Corinthians 12:31).

REFLECT | *What is it costing you this week to follow Jesus Christ? How can you turn that "price" into a "prayer" of praise and thanksgiving to God?*

When I Fall I Shall Rise

Day 1   Delivered!

READ | Psalm 34

I sought the Lord, and he answered me, and delivered me from all my fears. (v. 4)

David is singing a song of hope and confidence in the Lord, giving joyful testimony to the goodness and power of God, and doing so with every bit as much intensity as we have already encountered in other psalms of grief and complaint. (Remember, the psalms are the prayer book of the human heart, in all its variable conditions!) On this day, he has something very tangible for which to praise his God—God protected and delivered him from the hands of his enemies (see 1 Samuel 21:10–22:1). After days of living in fear for his life, he now enjoyed the fresh taste of freedom and safety once again. This was a new day, and he would praise God for it.

As we travel this remarkable journey of discipleship, we too need days of new beginnings, and they do not need to be as dramatic as David's in order to bring praise to our lips. Any path we pursue in the name of our Lord can become wearisome or troubling over time, especially one that requires discipline and self-denial. Sometimes we slip or stumble along the way, and sometimes we trip over our own wobbly feet, straight into the hands of our old "enemies." We falter, we fall, and we fail. What then?

The prophet Micah, like all the prophets, carried a heavy load of responsibility in the service of God and, from time to time, he fell down under the weight of it. Then it was that he declared: "But as for me, I will look to the Lord,

I will wait for the God of my salvation; my God will hear me. Rejoice not over me, O my enemy; when I fall, I shall rise; when I sit in darkness, the Lord will be a light to me" (Micah 7:7–8). *When* I fall, he said, not *if* I fall. For just such times, what are the psalmist and the prophet telling us to do?

First, remember the Lord's help in the past. When the dark, old "enemies" hover over you, call back to your mind those blessed days you have already enjoyed, when light and hope pierced through the shadow and you knew that God was near at hand. You know that such moments are in your memory somewhere; it's just that you have forgotten them. They are like the seed sown by the roadside that the birds of the air (the frets and cares and demands of the day) came along and plucked away, to keep them from taking root. Remembering God's love is like re-gathering those precious seeds and re-planting them in your heart. They may not make the current troubles disappear, but they will most assuredly give you a different perspective on them. David "blessed the Lord" because the Lord blessed David—he answered, delivered, heard, saved, kept, and redeemed David. This truth could not be denied. Present failings may conceal past victories, but they can never erase them.

Second, forget your failings in the past. Do you remember the apostle Paul's declaration about "forgetting what lies behind and straining forward to what lies ahead"? It was said with the same assurance in God's help that inspired Micah to say confidently, "when I fall, I *shall* rise." This day is a new day. Past failures, mistakes, disobediences belong where you left them—in the past. What is it about this penchant we have for forgetting God's help and remembering our own failings? Today is a day to reverse that perverse routine. "Look to him and be radiant." He has delivered us in the past, and he will free us in this present.

REFLECT | *List at least a half dozen testimonies you have to the love and power of God working on your behalf. Why do you think our own failings come to mind so much more often than God's blessings?*

Day 2   The Source of our Joy

READ | Luke 10:1–20

Nevertheless, do not rejoice in this, that the spirits are subject to you; but rejoice that your names are written in heaven. (v. 20)

This may seem a rather strange story to be discussing at this point on our journey. We are in the midst of some serious work, endeavoring to do something that we believe is both in God's name and in our best interest and, all along, trying to keep our "eyes on the prize." The hope of success (or the fear of failure) is actually one of the things that keeps us going, is it not? Yes, but Jesus is also waving a big caution flag about it.

As desirable and "good" as it is, our view of success is not the same as Jesus' view. In the kingdom of God, success actually is not a compelling enough goal to pursue. Jesus hears the delight of his disciples as they list off all their success stories, but he knows the true nature of success; he knows both its brevity as well as its potential dangers.

We have all witnessed what "success" at its extreme can do to a person. We see it sometimes in public figures when they allow the adulation of the crowd to blind them to the realities of life. Becoming intoxicated by such praise and recognition, they then become addicted to it, and live only for more and more approval. Like any addiction, other than a pure love for God, the blind craving for success has the power to destroy, to take the soul out of a person. This can happen in the realm of spiritual things just as easily as the world of material things. Consider those successful spiritual leaders, for example, who allowed their God-given success to "go to their heads" and plunged forward disastrously to their own ruin and the scandalizing of those who followed them. Today's "successes," like all our works, reminds the psalmist, "pass away like smoke" (Psalm 102:3).

Of course, these are extreme examples and, for most of us, out of our league. But, so too is the example of Jesus and his miracle-working disciples. The principle, however, applies to us all. Jesus is saying that the true object of our rejoicing should never be something as fleeting as success. We can be rightfully grateful for our achievements, and we should be thrilled when we "hit the targets" that have been set before us. But, says Jesus, there is a deeper and more lasting joy to be found elsewhere, and that is not dependent upon what we have done or failed to do. Neither our successes nor our failures are the things that define us and ultimately give our lives meaning.

Having our names written in heaven—inscribed with the indelible ink of Jesus' blood—means that God knows us, and that our true citizenship is in his kingdom. This calls for a rejoicing that can never be dampened or taken away.

Yes, we have been called, as were the first disciples, to do great things for God. But the only lasting source of our joy is the great thing he has done for us. We move on from past and present failures, and we move beyond past and present successes. In the end, all of them are only stepping-stones to our true goal, and He awaits our coming.

R E F L E C T | *How much does the desire to be "successful" motivate your life? How much does the fear of "failure" motivate your life? How can you come to see both your successes and your failures from God's point of view?*

Day 3   The Poverty of Job

R E A D | Job 1:1–2:10
Naked I came from my mother's womb, and naked shall I return; the Lord gave, and the Lord has taken away; blessed be the name of the Lord. (1:21)

"There was a man in the land of Uz, whose name was Job"—and thus the sometimes disturbing but always fascinating story of Job begins. He could be anyone, really—anyone who enjoyed the pleasures of family and business, home and friends, anyone who knew enough peace and good health to be content, anyone who endeavored to build a good life for themselves and for their children. Job could also be anyone for whom a single instant of time changed everything. In that "single instant" Job lost his children, his livelihood, and then his health. What he did not lose, however, was his faith, or his God.

This is not to say that Job did not struggle or complain or fight. In fact, the rest of the book of Job is the record of his struggles as heard from his own lips and described by his three so-called "comforters." Job was a man of faith, to be sure, and he confessed that faith when he blessed the name of the Lord, even after his home and his heart had been emptied of their treasures. This could not have been an easy statement of faith to declare. But, as we read on, we find that Job also had a good deal of faith in himself, in his own goodness and faithfulness and uprightness. His friends were of little help. Badgering him about his own sin and guilt, essentially saying that, somehow, it was Job's sin that had brought this calamity upon him, they missed the point altogether. They kept trying to convince Job that he must have done *something* to deserve such suffering. All the time, Job defended his integrity and his good intentions. Neither he nor his friends had the eyes to see under the surface to what the real issues were.

Like a good mystery writer, the author takes us behind the scenes and lets us eavesdrop on a conversation that Job and his friends never hear. At the very beginning of the story he pulls aside the curtain and says to his readers: "In order to understand what happens to Job when he loses everything, you have to see what happened before that day. You have to see what was going on in heaven in order to see clearly what is going on in Job." And from that little peek, we know at least two things.

First, we know that Job is never, *never* forgotten by God. The dreadful events visited upon Job are tools of the devil himself, but, even so, God has set a limit upon the devil's harassment. Job is one of heaven's own sons, and God will not allow any power over Job's life to supersede his own. Every bit of Job's suffering, as was every bit of his prosperity, is in the hands of God. Second, we know that Job's sin did not cause his suffering, but neither did his faith deliver him from it. In the end (as we will see tomorrow) God saved Job and restored his good fortunes. Until that point, the story reveals a man who knew himself to be impoverished in every way but one—in himself. In other words, up to this point in his life, he had more faith in the strength of his own faith than he had in the strength of his God.

Both our risings and our fallings are intimately known to God, and he will have a purpose for both. The fact that we cannot see or understand that purpose has nothing to do with its ultimate accomplishment. Sometimes our faith is weak, barely breathing, but this in no way weakens the God in whom we place that faith. The richness of his love and power cannot be diminished by our poverty. "Blessed be the name of the Lord."

REFLECT | *Consider some of your own losses and sufferings. Looking back on them, what can you now see about the ways in which God was at work? How can this help you as you consider your present disappointments or pains?*

Day 4   Knowing God / Knowing Yourself

READ | Job 40:1–9; 42:1–17

I had heard of thee by the hearing of the ear, but now my eye sees thee; therefore I despise myself and repent in dust and ashes. (vv. 5b–6)

God appears only twice in the story of Job, at the beginning, behind the scenes, and then again at the end, speaking directly to Job in the presence of his friends. In between, we imagine God listening in to the questioning and debating that is going on, waiting for just the right opportunity to inject himself into the conversation. That moment comes when all of Job's defenses come to an end, all his accusations against God cease, and all his arguments have been made. There is nothing more to say. Then, the silence is broken and Job is confronted by a new Voice coming out of the whirlwind: "Who is this that darkens counsel by words without knowledge? Gird up your loins like a man, I will question you, and you shall declare to me" (38:2–3). In other words: "I have been patiently listening to all your so-called wisdom, your allegations against me, your arguments and claims. Now, it is time for me to speak, and I have a few questions for you."

From time to time, God puts us in our place, not vindictively, not meanly, but always firmly. The questions he put to Job were all designed to remind his beloved child that God was God, and that Job was not. In the midst of his suffering, Job spent his breath defending his innocence and integrity against the counsel of his friends. In doing so, he was actually accusing God of being capricious and unjust. He was claiming that he had the proper view of things, that his own knowledge and righteousness were sufficient to see him through his troubles. As imperfect as they were, Job's friends were telling him to be quiet and listen, but they finally stopped speaking to him, says the writer, "because he was righteous in his own eyes" (32:1).

It was, so to speak, "his own eyes" that Job was having trouble with. His vision of God and of himself were both severely impaired, but he did not know it. So God set out to correct his eyesight. The sufferings of Job are almost unimaginable. But, as we discussed yesterday, they took place always under God's strong and wise supervision and were used by God for a good and loving purpose. Job could perceive none of this, in part because he was so busy telling everyone what he thought was going on.

I am not sure that Job ever really expected that God would listen to all his ranting, or that God would have something to say in response. I am not sure that we expect it either. But once God does enter the conversation—through the voice of his Spirit, of friends, of the circumstances themselves—everything changes. We come to realize that many things we thought we knew about God, we really did not know at all, and that we really knew even less about ourselves. As with the difference between seeing a blurry picture and meeting the real person, we, like Job, are dumbstruck by the difference. And that is what opens the way to new insights, to a renewed vision of God, and, really, to an entirely new life.

REFLECT | *What have you discovered about yourself in recent weeks, that has also revealed to you something more about God? How about the other way around? In what area of your life is God asking you to be still and to listen?*

Day 5 Failure: The Soil of Salvation

READ | Psalm 51

Create in me a clean heart, O God, and put a new and right spirit within me. (v. 10)

The heading for this psalm reads: "A Psalm of David, when Nathan the prophet came to him, after he had gone in to Bathsheba." This tells us immediately that these timeless words grew out of the most shameful episode in David's life (2 Samuel 11 and 12). His disobedience and lust led him to an adulterous liaison with Bathsheba, the wife of Uriah. When David found that she was carrying his child, he plotted to have Uriah killed in battle, to cover up his sin. Then David took Bathsheba for his own wife. Not a very pretty picture of the king who is called "a man after God's own heart."

But God was not finished with his servant. He sent the prophet Nathan to confront David with his deceit and cruelty. "You are the man!" must have been chilling words to David's ears. More important, they were heart-rending words to his soul. David repented and the 51st psalm was his prayer.

For generations, both this story and this psalm have been vivid reminders that God does not give up on his frail and wayward children. David remains a hero of the faith, as much because of his failings as because of his victories. He and all those other biblical figures, whose flaws have been recorded for all time to read, are presented to us as examples of God's faithfulness and deliverance *in the midst* of defeat, *despite* defeat, *because* of defeat. In fact, the entire Bible is an account of how God has been dealing with failure ever since time began. There is a medieval Christmas carol that actually gives thanks to God that Adam and Eve ate of the forbidden tree because, had they not, we would never have known the Savior. This is a poetic way of saying that God is so just and merciful, so powerful and so gracious, that he is able to bring forth the best from the ashes of the worst. If the worst had not happened, we may never have known God's best.

Failure, therefore, should never become the breeder of more failure, nor relapse the occasion for giving up. We must remember that our adversary's real intention through temptation is not to cause us to fall into sin, but to prevent us from getting back up to hope.

The momentary pleasure we derive from our indulgence is scarcely as destructive as the devastating sense of condemnation, guilt, and despair that follows. This is when David's prayer comes in handy. Humbled and chastened under the weight of our own failings, we go as quickly as we can to the throne of a holy and loving Savior, not to be excused but pardoned. "Once again, O God, I am in need of your saving grace," we pray.

David lived many more years following that fateful spring. They were years of more blessing and more trials, more victories and more failures. Through them all, David remained "a man after God's own heart." Under his reign the land of promise was secured, and from his house came forth the seed of salvation. What amazing things the Gardener can grow from such desolate soil!

REFLECT | *When have you let failure or relapse become the occasion for giving up? The prophet Jeremiah wrote that God's mercies "are new every morning" (Lamentations 3:23). For what "old" area in your life must you remember that promise and begin again, today?*

Day 6 A New Creation

READ | John 8:1–11

Neither do I condemn you; go, and do not sin again. (v. 11)

Speaking of "new mercies every morning"—here is a story for the heavy-hearted soul. Try to imagine for a moment what it must have been like for this poor woman to be cornered by a mob of men and dragged into the presence of Jesus. The sheer embarrassment must have been excruciating, not to mention the fear that must have gripped her by the throat. Death was only a few stone-throws away. Since she had actually "been caught in adultery" (why and how, one wonders), there was no question of her guilt— nor of the required punishment. What is worse is that, in the eyes of these sanctimonious scribes and Pharisees, she was simply a means to an end. Her sin and shame meant nothing to them. Neither did her life. She stood in the midst of them as nothing more than an object lesson, a trap to be sprung on this so-called prophet and rabbi.

Was the woman tempted to think that Jesus did not care either, as he bent over and scribbled in the sand? Did he even look at her before he turned his eyes to the ground? And what was he writing? What could be more important than the crisis at hand? The silence that followed must have been the deepest and longest she had ever known. What would he answer to their question? What would he say about her?

We usually read this story as a lesson against self-righteousness and judgmental attitudes toward others. As the apostle Paul asked the Romans, "Who is in a position to condemn?" Certainly none of these men. Certainly none of us. But all the time this showdown is taking place, this poor woman is standing there with only her sin and guilt for company. Eventually, under the weight of their own shame and unease, all these men turn away and leave her alone. Alone, that is, but for One other, who is stooping and writing in the dirt once again.

I wonder, sometimes, if the confusion she felt then, alone in Jesus' presence, was not even greater than what she felt when she was surrounded by her accusers. She knew clearly what they thought about her. I wonder if she was more worried about what he thought. They all turned away and left, but what if he did, too? All that mattered now was what he would do, or say . . . but he was still writing in the dust . . . and she was waiting.

I like to think that Jesus was mimicking his Father as he hunched over the earth that day.

In the Garden, his Father had first formed man of the dust of the earth, and certainly that meant that he had gotten his hands dirty. He had created something from nothing and then, out of grains of sand, he had sculpted his own image, and breathed into his likeness the breath of life. I like to think that with his finger working in the dust and with the word he was about to speak into the silence, Jesus was doing some creating of his own, some re-creating. And behold, it was very good.

"Therefore, if any one is in Christ, he is a new creation; the old has passed away, behold, the new has come." (2 Corinthians 5:17)

REFLECT | *Wait . . . listen. What is Jesus saying to you?*

Day 7 Do Not Lose Heart

READ | Luke 18:1–8

And he told them a parable to the effect that they ought always to pray and not lose heart. (v. 1)

We all know the frustration and discouragement that comes with unanswered prayer. "I'm praying, but I don't know if God is listening." "I've been praying about that for years, and nothing is any different." "I don't think there's much point in my praying about that any more." Have you ever noticed how the teachings of Jesus seem to anticipate our problems and confusions? Almost as if he answers a question before we even ask it? The story of the unjust judge and the importunate widow is just such a teaching.

Of course, Jesus is not telling us that God is like this callous, selfish judge (though he may be telling us that this is what we sometimes think of God). What he is doing, however, is presenting such an extreme example of heartlessness that making any comparison with God whatsoever is actually laughable. "If even this judge— who has such disdain for God and who doesn't care one whit about people—if even he will finally listen to a poor widow's persistent pleadings, how much more will God, who has nothing but compassion and justice in his heart, answer the cries of his children."

Jesus must have known how prone we are to discouragement when we do not see the answers to our prayers *when* we want to see them. He must have known our penchant for giving up and giving in. According to

John's Gospel, many of his disciples (there were more than the central "twelve") "drew back and no longer went along with him" when his message either struck too close to home or when its demands grew too difficult (John 6:66). There is little difference between that and turning away from God because we think he is no longer listening, no longer caring.

"Losing heart" is a common, though dangerous, occurrence in the Christian's life. The challenges we face can be debilitating, and the failures we suffer can be demoralizing. Jesus never takes them for granted, nor underestimates the potential they have for wearing down our resolve. What he asks of us, however, is that we neither stop nor wander away when we are in the midst of such circumstances, that we not give up on him when we are tempted to believe the hellish lie that he has given up on us; that we instead believe him when he tells us that God loves us and hears our prayers. "Keep asking," he is saying, for when your voice is lost to prayer, then your heart cannot be far behind.

REFLECT | *In what area of your life have you "lost heart," or given up? Where is God asking you to believe him more than you believe yourself? What prayer can you pray to help you do that?*

Week Ten Fear: Faith In The Wrong Person

Day 1   No Spirit of Fear

READ | 2 Timothy 1

For God did not give us a spirit of timidity, but a spirit of power and love and self-control. (v. 7)

Timothy was a young leader in the church and a colleague of the apostle Paul. It is clear from these letters, and from the other times that Paul mentions him in correspondence, that Timothy was a valued co-worker who, personally as well as professionally, meant a great deal to his mentor. The King James Version of the Bible translates verse 7 like this: "For God hath not given us the *spirit of fear*, but of power and love and of a sound mind." Paul was apparently writing to Timothy, in part, to encourage him to remain faithful to God's call in the face of trial and danger.

Fear takes many forms. On the one hand, fear is a useful reaction to have in sudden times of peril, and it can avert us from foolish risks or careless decisions. Fear can be an early and effective signal, warning us to flee from approaching harm and to seek protection. But, fear can also be a dark shadow that clouds our vision and prevents us from seeing things as they really are. When it becomes panic or depression, fear can become so debilitating that it actually prevents us from reacting, or acting. Then, "paralyzed with fear" can be an apt description for the soul as well as for the body. When fear whispers (or screams) that there is no place to run, then giving up appears as the only alternative.

When you stop to think about it, then, fear is really a form of unbelief. It acts as if, in any particular threatening situation, God is absent or unable to help. Fear does not recognize the irresistible power and the limitless love that God's presence brings in times of need. It sees only the danger. Put another way, fear is a form of belief, but in the wrong thing or person. We say that we trust God, and to a great extent we do. But, frightening situations usually reveal to us the things that we are really counting on, because they let us down. They show us the things we really believe to be the source of our strength, because those sources run dry. I am afraid because none of the things I depend upon are dependable enough to help and protect me—least of all, myself. I am afraid because I know I haven't the ability to be my own strength and protection. I feel helpless . . . and then I feel afraid.

But fear is not meant to have the last word. As a tool it is quite useful, but as a master it is inept and oppressive. As a tool it leads us to safety, but as a master it only turns us away from God. Remember the response of Adam when God came searching for him in the Garden: "I was afraid of thee . . . and I hid myself" (Genesis 3:10).

The truth is that we do not have to live in fear. Yes, fear lives in us all, but "God hath not given us the spirit of fear, but of power (his power), and of love (living in his love) and of a sound mind (seeing things for what they really are)." This week, we will discuss some of the fears that are most common to us all. Naming them gets us halfway toward overcoming them, because often fear is actually the hidden force that lies behind many of our more obviously misdirected words and actions. (Remember what we observed earlier about the best defense being a good offense?) We have also added a prayer at the conclusion of each of this week's reflections. If one of fear's deceptive tricks is to lead us away from God, then prayer is just the thing we need to send us in the opposite direction.

> O God, who has been a refuge and strength through all generations, be my refuge today in every time and circumstance of need. Be my guide through all that is dark and doubtful. Be my guard against all that threatens my spirit's welfare. Be my strength in time of testing. Gladden my heart with thy peace; through Jesus Christ my Lord. Amen.
> (John Baillie, 1886–1960,
> *Oxford Book of Prayer*, 123, adapt.)

R E F L E C T　|　*What are some of your present fears? How do you know when you are afraid? What are the signs?*

Day 2　Fear of Others

R E A D　|　John 20:19–31
The doors being shut where the disciples were, for fear of the Jews, Jesus came and stood among them and said to them, "Peace be with you." (v. 19)

If any group of people ever had legitimate cause to be afraid, the disciples were that group. Their Leader had been arrested, maligned, beaten, and, finally, crucified as an enemy of the state and the temple. The disciples were known associates of this criminal—they believed and preached the same message that he had taught, and they were commissioned by him to carry on with the cause. There was every reason for them to assume that, if discovered and seized, they would face from their captors the same treatment as their Lord. So, "for fear" of these men, they gathered secretly and hid behind closed doors.

The anxieties we suffer for fear of what others might do to us, or say about us, or think of us, may not include the fear of death, but they can still cause us to "shut the door of our hearts," lest our true selves be discovered. The prospect of being vulnerable and transparent with others can be very threatening, even when we know rationally that no one means us any harm. We have inherited from our forebears an innate fear of being known, especially with all our flaws and defects. "If he/she really knew . . . what I am like . . ," we fearfully wonder. Then we usually keep the door shut.

But neither the doors of the house nor the doors of our heart can shut out the Risen Jesus: neither can they shut us in from him. The latches were fixed, says the Gospel writer, and still Jesus came and stood among his beloved. The sight of his face and the sound of his voice must have driven away all their fears. "Peace be with you," he said, with his pierced hands outstretched and his wounded side displayed.

These fearful few went on to turn the world upside-down with their bravery and love. Of the Twelve, only John died an old man of natural causes. All the rest met and welcomed a martyr's death, bright reflections of their Lord's own unquenchable flame. From such inauspicious beginnings—a tiny huddle of frightened souls trembling behind closed doors—Jesus brought forth his church, and all of hell itself cannot prevail against it.

"Peace be with you," Jesus says to you and me. He gently comes and passes effortlessly through all the barriers we set up as he makes his way into the midst of our hearts. And he brings others with him—friends and family, sisters and brothers in Christ, people known and unknown, kind and unkind. Unlike our Lord, however, they have to use the door, and it is left to us to either open it or to leave it shut. If we lift the latches and give them a chance to come in, we will find that any fears we have of them are quickly dispelled by Jesus' presence. But this takes some time and practice. Opening our hearts to others—letting them see the blemishes on our souls, the weaknesses in our character, even the fears that compel us to keep them out in the first place—this is done with one little decision at a time. In the end, we will find that nothing they can ever do, or say, or think can really harm us. Like the apostles, we may find that the peace of Jesus is more than enough protection.

> Christ with me, Christ before me, Christ behind me,
> Christ within me, Christ beneath me, Christ above me,
> Christ on my right, Christ on my left. . . .
> Christ in the heart of everyone who thinks of me,
> Christ in the mouth of everyone who speaks to me,
> Christ in every eye that sees me,
> Christ in every ear that hears me.
> —*Canticle of St. Patrick*
> (Phyllis Tickle, *The Divine Hours: Prayers for Summertime*, 312)

REFLECT | *What are you most afraid of someone else doing to you, or saying about you, or thinking of you? What are some of the fearful barriers you use to shut out other people? What one person can you let further in today? How?*

Day 3　Fear of Conflict

READ | Psalm 27

Though a host encamp against me, my heart shall not fear. (v. 3)

Often our fear of others has to do with our fear of conflict. In other words, it is not so much the other person we fear, as it is the hurt and other disturbing sensations we experience when we are at odds with one another. Quarrels and discord arouse some of the emotions and attitudes within us that we most want to keep still—anger, self-righteousness, helplessness, uncertainty, and even hatred. In the face of conflict we fear that we are likely to be harmed, perhaps as much by what arises from within us as by what comes at us from outside us. In any case, we fear conflict and the potential it brings for injuring us. As we have seen, however, conflict has always been a fellow-traveler on the road of discipleship, and there is no real way to avoid his company, no matter how much we may try to steer clear of him.

David, as we know, was a soldier as well as a king. In fact, it was because he knew so much warfare and bloodshed that God prohibited him from building the Temple in Jerusalem (1 Chronicles 22:8). What David did build, however, was a kingdom, dedicated to the worship of God and to the fulfillment of his purposes. In that endeavor, and despite his flaws, David never wavered. So when we read the 27th psalm, we are reading the words of a man who was willing to face conflict, even risk his own destruction, for the sake of something greater and more lasting than himself. In order to do the will of God, David was willing to accept conflict as a part of his life, so long as he knew that God would be his salvation.

A word of caution is in order here—this has nothing to do with the presumptuous notion that "God is on *my* side and therefore *I* will prevail." Some of us think of a fight (or even spoil for a fight) as an opportunity to win and, by winning, to feel even stronger about ourselves. The source of David's confidence was not his own rightness but rather the loving protection of God. His interest was in doing God's will, and the only way that could be accomplished was by God's strength, not his own. He sings his song of assurance in praise of God's protection and deliverance: "He will hide me in his shelter in the day of trouble; he will conceal me under the cover of his tent, he will set me high upon a rock" (v. 5). There is nothing whatsoever in these words in praise of David's own might or valor. His ability to face conflict is firmly rooted in the Lord, who is "the stronghold" of his life.

When our paths cross with the unwelcome company of conflict, to whose strength do we turn for our defense? When those situations arise that threaten our security, our peace of mind, or the lives and welfare of those we love, do we "wait for the Lord," or do we muster up our own might and count on our own abilities to win the battle? If we do the latter, then we are consigned to the fears that accompany such misplaced trust. In contrast to trusting in the "mighty fortress" of God, Martin Luther wrote: "Did we in our own strength confide, our striving would be losing." If we do the former, however, if we cry aloud to the Lord and seek his face, then we can take courage in the face of conflict, and we can know the joyful melody of David's song.

Almighty God, who sees that we have no power of ourselves to help ourselves: Keep us, both outwardly in our bodies and inwardly in our souls, that we may be defended from all adversities which may happen to the body and from all evil thoughts which may assault and hurt the soul; through Jesus Christ our Lord. Amen.

—*Gregorian Sacramentary*

(John Wallace Suter Jr., ed., *The Book of English Collects,* 77)

REFLECT | *What situations are you facing right now that are beyond your own strength? With whom are you most afraid to be in conflict? Why?*

Day 4   Fear of Death

READ | Hebrews 2

Since therefore the children share in flesh and blood, he himself likewise partook of the same nature, that through death he might destroy him who has the power of death, that is, the devil, and deliver all those who through fear of death were subject to lifelong bondage. (vv. 14–15)

John Wesley was brought up in a strict, devout home. His father was a clergyman of the Church of England, and his mother, Susanna, was also the child of a clergyman. The entire family, for generations, had been trained in the Bible and in the spiritual life. John writes, however, that he was ceaselessly plagued by one anxious thought—the fear of dying. Other fears he was able to conquer, but not this one, at least not until the night he found his heart "strangely warmed" at the thought that God's love and his Son's redemptive death on the cross was for him, for John. Following that hour, when he knew Christ to be his only Lord and his only Savior, Wesley noticed one thing in particular—he no longer feared death. And when the fear of death came knocking upon his door, he forbade its entry by hurling in its face his trust in the Risen Christ.

According to the writer of Hebrews, the fear of death is the subjugator of all humanity. We all live under its foreboding shadow. For some, the very idea of dying—of being no more, cut off from loved ones and from the joys of life, to face an unknown eternity—can be terrifying. No wonder the world, by exalting youthfulness and mastering sickness, spends so much time and energy creating the illusion that we can live forever. The alternative is simply too fearful for us.

Christians have never been taught to treat death lightly, or to pretend that it is anything other than the mortal enemy of life. It is clear from Scripture that death had no place in God's good creation until it entered the world through sin. This puts death and the devil in league with one another, and many of us have experienced the darkness it brings— when it steals from us someone we love, or breaks into our lives with no warning, leaving no time to prepare. At such disruptively devastating times, all romantic notions of death being "just another step on the journey" quickly take a back seat to the utter sense of helplessness and to the raw anger and fear that takes hold of us.

Reconciling ourselves to death's inevitability with more than weak resignation or quiet bitterness requires that our hearts be reconciled with the Lord of both life and death.

He died in order to conquer death, and his rising again is the evidence of his success. Facing death, our own or someone else's, with courage and humility, requires that, in the midst of our honest grief and struggle to understand, we also trust and believe.

Someone has said that the best way to prepare to die is to die daily—for the sake of Christ to take up our own crosses and to follow him. In his great chapter of exultation in the Resurrection of Christ, the apostle Paul says of his own life, "I die every day!" (1 Corinthians 15:31). For Jesus, the cross was no surprise; it was the completion of an entire life lived, not to do his own will, but the will of his Father who sent him (John 6:38). Perhaps this is the secret to defeating our fear of death—by giving up our lives more and more along the way. Then, by the time we arrive at death's door, it will hold no surprises for us and we need not be afraid of it. It really will be "just another step along the journey."

Save us while waking, Lord, and guard us while sleeping, that when we awake we may watch with Christ, and when we sleep we may rest in peace. Amen.
(An antiphon for night prayer)

REFLECT | *Describe what your own fear of death feels like. What was your most recent experience of death? How did you face it?*

Day 5   Fear of Want

R E A D | Matthew 6:19–34

Therefore I tell you, do not be anxious about your life, what you shall eat, or what you shall drink, nor about your body, what you shall put on. . . . Do not be anxious about tomorrow, for tomorrow will be anxious for itself. (vv. 26 and 34a)

What one of us does not know the anxiety of worrying about the future? Especially prone to these fears are those who bear primary responsibility for the care of others, for children or parents or spouse. "What will we do?" "How will we make it?" "What if we don't have enough?" "Who will take care of me?" You can add your own particular anxious question.

Jesus teaches that the lasting answer to our anxiety will never be found by scurrying about, restlessly searching for everything we think we need, and then hoarding it up in some stockpile. This, he warns, will give us only a false sense of security, for such stockpiles are deceivingly small when compared to enormous need, and regularly susceptible to decay and ruin. Jesus does not advocate our being foolishly naïve about the future, either, as if life held no risks and we would face no failures. He talks about the dangers of fear and anxiety precisely because he knows the fleeting and perishable nature of this life, and he knows that we have not yet learned how to live it with peace and confidence. From whence is such peace and confidence to come—that is the question he is answering.

First, Jesus says, take a lesson from the things that you see around you. Consider the created world itself. The apostle

Paul said that God's invisible nature can be perceived in the things that he has made, that what can be known about God and his ways is made plain by creation (Romans 1:19–20). I sometimes envy those who live closer to the earth than I. I know that I miss much of the wisdom it has to offer. But I can still hear it in the words of Jesus. "Consider the lilies." "Look at the birds." "Touch the grass." If, as the Creator, God can clothe and feed and provide for all that *they* need, how very much more, as your Father, can and will he supply the things *you* require. God is neither blind to our need nor miserly in his giving. Jesus is telling his listeners that if they would be more trusting in God they would be less anxious for themselves. One or the other—fear or belief—will take up the majority of space in the human heart, and the choice will be ours.

Speaking of the human heart, however, Jesus gives a second instruction for overcoming anxiety: make it your first aim, above everything else you seek, to seek the kingdom of God. The reason we suffer so much anxiety about our futures is that the priorities of our hearts are upside-down. They are listed in the wrong order. It is a natural phenomenon of living that when we are faced with a demanding and seemingly insurmountable task, other less important tasks get set aside, even forgotten for a time. They become of less importance until the primary obligation confronting us has been accomplished. Our anxieties about the things of earth will diminish the more we focus on the things of heaven. Jesus says that there simply isn't enough room in our hearts for both.

A PRAYER

O God, facing all that is before us, we know not whether we will live or die, but this we know: that all things are ordered and sure in heaven. Everything is planned with unerring wisdom and unbounded love by you, our God, for you are love. Grant us in all things to see your hand; through Jesus Christ our Lord. Amen.

(Rev. C. Simeon, 1759, adapt.)

REFLECT | *What are the things that make you most anxious about the future? For what one particular anxiety will you trust God today?*

Day 6   Fear of Humiliation

READ | Exodus 4:1–17

But Moses said to the Lord, "Oh, my Lord, I am not eloquent, either heretofore or since thou hast spoken to thy servant; but I am slow of speech and of tongue." (v. 10)

Today we approach a subject that can be somewhat sensitive. But bear with me for a moment and see if this does not make sense. Moses resisted God's call upon his life because he was afraid. Biblical scholars tell us that Moses' reference to being "slow of speech and of tongue" may have had to do either with his fear of speaking in public (a *very* common anxiety!), or to some kind of impediment in his speech. In either case, Moses was clearly self-conscious about this weakness and wanted nothing to do with an assignment that required him to do the very thing that he was worst at doing. During his argument with God, for a brief time, it seems that Moses feared being humiliated in the eyes of men more than he feared God. God was even willing to make a compromise in order to secure Moses' agreement. (We can all be grateful that God is not as quick as we are to move on when he meets resistance.)

In and of itself, humiliation is not something any of us seek. It can even be devastating. How many of us suffer wounds inflicted by the demeaning actions of others or by degrading events out of our own control? It is because of experiences like these, experiences that strike at our very dignity and sense of security, that Jesus came to heal us and make us whole. But the humiliations we receive at the hand of a loving God are designed to strike at something else, something deadly, something that separates us from God and from others. It is not our dignity as children of heaven that God is after—it is our pride as children of earth.

Humbling ourselves of our own free choice is an extremely difficult thing to do—and it's impossible to do without mixed motives. The very act of "trying to be humble" before others betrays a lack of genuine humility, because humility, by its very definition, is entirely un*self*conscious! This is why we need what comes from outside us to humble us, to humiliate us. In the hands of God, humiliations come through those closest to us and through strangers, through the contradictions and failures of life, even through the ways in which God calls us to serve him. Through each of these occasions, God is working to bring down a child of Adam and Eve in order to raise up a child of God. We can be certain that God will be the defender of our dignities and reputations, for love's design is to heal what is broken and to mend what is wounded. But we can be equally sure that he will do everything in love's power to make low those "mountains and hills" that stand against what is best for his own daughters and sons (Luke 3:5). And pride is the highest mountain of all.

The early church teacher Cyril of Alexandria wrote of Jesus: "He became like us that we might become like him. The work of the Spirit seeks to transform us by grace into a perfect copy of his humbling." It would appear, therefore, that the call of Moses was as much for his benefit as it was for the benefit of Israel's children. God was making a man even as he was making a nation. It required only that, despite his fear of humiliation, Moses say "yes."

A PRAYER

Lord Jesus, you humbled yourself to become like one of us, and to be born into the world for our salvation. Teach me the grace of humility; root out of my heart all pride and haughtiness, and so fashion me after your holy likeness in this world, that in the world to come I may reflect your everlasting glory; for your mercy's sake. Amen.

(Bishop Walsham How, d. 1823, adapt.)

REFLECT | *What are some of the humiliating experiences that you have suffered that make you fear humiliation today? In what area(s) have you already found that a humiliation actually worked to your benefit? What is God asking of you right now, that you are resisting because you are afraid of humiliation?*

Day 7 When I am Afraid

READ | Psalm 56

When I am afraid, I put my trust in thee. (v. 3)

During this week we have visited with some our most basic fears—fear of others, fear of conflict, fear of death, fear of want, and fear of humiliation. Today, we turn once more to the psalms for a final word of encouragement.

It is clear from this prayer that the writer is in great danger. His enemies are very real and very strong. He is outnumbered and overpowered. But it is equally clear that there are some very real alternatives to the psalmist's fear. A few simple words tell us what they are:

When I am afraid, I put my trust in thee (v. 3)—A small child is sometimes afraid in the dark. A noise wakes her up and her bleary eyes see shapes moving on the wall like menacing figures. She pulls the covers up over her head in the hopes that the shadows will go away, but this doesn't stop her imagination from "seeing" even worse things. Fear has now taken on a life of its own, and soon turns to panic. In a fraction of a second, she makes her decision. Risking everything (especially being grabbed by the monster that is now under the bed), she throws off the covers, makes a single daring leap to the door, runs down the hallway like the wind, and bounds into her parents' bed. There, in the comfort of their embrace, and with only a soothing "shhh" from their lips, she ever so slowly falls back to a peaceful sleep.

When you are afraid, child, where do you run?

This I know, that God is for me (v. 9)—Confidence is rarely innate to our characters. More likely, it is born of repeated positive experiences that tell us that our trust is being put in the right place. In other words, confidence really is "built." The dancer who must fling herself into the arms of her partner may at first hold back. She tries to relax, but she stiffens each time her feet leave the floor, and her own arms brace for the expected fall. But the fall never comes. Each time, her partner's arms are there to receive her. Not once does he falter, despite how awkwardly and hesitantly she comes. With every successful jump she finds her trust in him growing until, finally, she throws herself without caution, and the dance becomes all grace.

What can you do now, child, with what you already know about me?

What can man do to me? (v. 11)—Plenty, I might answer. With the psalmist I might describe all that trampling and lurking they do, thinking bad things about me and working to frustrate my every move. But really, can man do something to destroy me? Can he separate me from the love of God? Can she take away my birthright as a child of God? Can they stop God's work in my life? Can they keep me from putting my trust in the God who is for me?

Do you know, child, that the answer to all these questions is "no"?

God's might to uphold me,
God's wisdom to guide me,
God's eye to look before me,
God's ear to hear me,
God's word to speak to me,
God's hand to guard me,
God's way to lie before me,
God's shield to protect me,
God's hosts to save me.
—St. Patrick
(Phyllis Tickle, *The Divine Hours:
Prayers for Autumn and Wintertime*, 312)

REFLECT | *Consider the questions that are asked in this
reflection. How would you answer them?*

Week Eleven Who Has The Reins Anyway?

Day 1 According to Your Will

READ | Luke 1:26-38

And Mary said, "Behold, I am the handmaid of the Lord; let it be to me according to your word." (v. 38)

Ten weeks ago, we began this series of reflections by looking at the terrible consequences of Adam and Eve's disobedience to God—the severing of their relationship with their Creator and with one another. It was as if a beautiful vessel formed by God, with the intention that it always be brimming with his life and love, was violently shattered on the rocks into countless fragments and splinters. Only God, out of sheer mercy and grace, could see the possibility of putting it all back together, and he set forth to do just that. You and I are now part of this miraculous re-creative plan. Every blessing we receive and every trial we undergo, every circumstance we encounter and every person in our lives—all these and much more, God uses in order to gather and mend and reshape the broken pieces of his own sacred handiwork. All he asks of us is that, unlike our first parents, we agree this time with the way he intends to do things, that we not try to come up with our own better ideas, but, instead, trust that he knows what he is doing.

For all this re-creation to even be possible, of course, God sent forth a "new Adam" to open the way for us (1 Corinthians 15:45). With the coming of Jesus Christ, God started over, not by throwing everything away but by reclaiming it all for a new and even better purpose. But in order to do so, he counted on one of us to agree with his plan. A young Hebrew girl was his choice: Mary, who became the mother of our Lord and, in a sense, a "new Eve." She was very much favored and "full of grace," not only because of the unimaginable honor (and burden) she would know for bringing Jesus into the world, but also because she was able so freely and wholly to give herself to God's will. Mary's "let it be to me according to your word" was the response that God had been looking for in the Garden. Adam and Eve (with a little help) rejected God's plans in favor of their own. In every way they are the prime examples of what happens in the kingdom of God when someone other than the King is in charge. Mary, on the other hand, is the prime example of what happens when God has his way, when his will prevails, and when we agree to his purposes.

A "disciple" is literally a "student." This means that, by following Jesus, you and I are learning things that we did not know before. One of the most important lessons we must learn, one that is taught at absolutely every "grade level" of the Christian life, is that God is in charge and that his ways, not ours, are always and everywhere the best. And the reason the lesson is taught so often is that we don't learn it the first time, or the second, or the third. Not surprisingly, given what happened in the Garden, this is one of the hardest subjects to master.

"Who is in charge of my life?" "Whose way of doing things is the best?" "Whose hands are really holding the reins?" These are the questions we are looking at this week. Of course, we all know what the *right* answer is, but, unlike Mary, when the question is asked at very specific moments we are often very, very slow to raise our hands and answer with our own voices. Why is that? This week, by reflecting on some of the choices made by a few other "students" who have already passed through this classroom, we may be able to better understand what we are up against.

REFLECT | *In what kinds of circumstances do you find it most difficult to want God's will? Why? What does it mean to you for God to "be in charge" of your life? What does it not mean?*

Day 2   Wrestling With God

READ | Genesis 32

And Jacob was left alone; and a man wrestled with him until the breaking of the day. (v. 24)

The story of Jacob's nocturnal wrestling match with the angel of the Lord illustrates for us the lengths to which God is willing to go in order to convince us that his ways are true and good. It is a good image for our own scuffles with the Almighty.

We have had some insight into Jacob's life already, when we discussed the preferential treatment he received from his mother and that he, in turn, passed on to his son. In neither case, you remember, did their "idolatry"—putting their desires for their children before the righteousness of God—produce good results (Week 4). But there is much more to his story. The writer of Genesis presents Jacob as an ambitious conniver, even in birth, when he came forth from his mother's womb grasping the heel of his twin, Esau. From that very day, Jacob lived up to the meaning of his name, "he who supplants." By his shrewd scheming he successfully stole his brother's birthright, deceived his father into imparting to him the paternal blessing meant for Esau, and made a fortune for himself off his future father-in-law, Laban. What is more, by the time he left Laban's employment he had become the father of eleven sons who, together with his youngest son, Joseph, would be the patriarchs of the twelve tribes of Israel. Jacob had "climbed the ladder," rung by rung, and made of himself a great man.

However, there was still this matter of swindling his brother that had gone unsettled for years. Hearing the news that Esau and his men were approaching his camp, Jacob came up with one more plan for getting what he wanted, this time his brother's pardon. (It turns out, of course, that Esau was happy and held no grudge whatsoever.) These are the circumstances in which we find Jacob at the river Jabbok, nervously waiting for what the coming dawn will bring. There is nothing more he can do. And this is precisely when God chooses to meet him, face-to-face and hand-to-hand. Through those few dark hours, it is as if Jacob's entire life of self-will and self-sufficiency is being played out with God on that muddy shore. (Another act of "re-creation" by the hand of God?)

The remarkable thing is that God would come down to his creature in such a way, and actually engage with him so intimately and tirelessly. It almost seems as if he has been waiting for just the right time and place to have this struggle with Jacob. God is not averse to having us take hold of him and "wrestle." He looks for our doubts and questions and even our accusations against him to be forthright and honest. He may even be waiting for us to "have it out" with him, knowing that this may be the only way for us to know the strong grip of his love and his truth.

Who is the declared winner in this contest? Is it Jacob, who "strove with God and with men, and prevailed" (v. 28), or is it God, who brought an abrupt end to the fight by dislocating Jacob's hip with only a touch of his finger? In fact, don't they both win? God wins by demonstrating to Jacob, through affliction, that he is merely mortal and no match for the almighty arm of God. God has won his chosen son over to a new relationship of trust and dependence. Jacob wins, too . . . and for the exact same reason.

REFLECT | *Think about your own wrestling with God. What are you after—your own way or God's blessing? Over what issue in your life right now do you need to take hold of God and not let go until you receive his blessing?*

Day 3 Faithless Planning

READ | Genesis 15:1–6; 16:1–16
And he believed the Lord; and he reckoned it to him as righteousness. (15:6)

Jacob's grandfather was Abraham, and, as they say, the apple doesn't fall far from the tree. We first met Abraham ("Abram" at that time) when God called him to take his wife Sarai and to leave his country and his family and go to a new land which God would show him (see Genesis 12:1ff). From this unexceptional couple God intended to raise up a great nation through whom he would bless the whole earth.

As usual, there was a significant and all-too evident problem with this plan—Abraham and Sarai had no children, and no prospects whatsoever for ever having children.

The writer of Genesis tells us that God repeated his promise to Abraham a number of times, and each time it was greeted with acceptance and faith. In fact, Abraham has become a lasting example of what it means to believe God and trust in his promises. Writing to the Christians in Rome, the apostle Paul commended Abraham for his faith and exhorted his readers to imitate him: "No distrust made [Abraham] waver concerning the promise of God, but he grew strong in his faith as he gave glory to God, fully convinced that God was able to do what he had promised" (4:20–21). But wait. "*No* distrust"? What about this little incident with Hagar?

As we have observed before, the Bible (thankfully) makes no apologies for presenting its character's weaknesses as well as strengths. In the case of Abraham, the "father" of our faith, it is a temporary lapse of faith that, in some ways, endears him to us. It is not that Abraham doubted God's promise to make him the father of a people more numerous than the stars. It is just that, as time wore on and the promise was delayed, Abraham, with Sarai's encouragement, took upon himself the means for fulfilling that promise. In other words, he took things into his own hands.

Waiting upon God is one of the most difficult, yet important things that you and I can do in the Christian life. It is difficult because we are not patient people, and waiting on *anyone* tries what little patience we do have. In Abraham's case, God had a very specific plan, a very specific way he intended to carry out that plan, and a very specific schedule to be followed. In every way, God was in charge. But, after a long delay (is there such a thing on God's timetable?), and there was still no fulfillment in sight, Abraham and Sarai succumbed to the kind of temptation we can all understand—to do it themselves.

Sometimes, the struggle we have letting God have his way in our lives has less to do with our faith in his love than it has to do with our impatience with how that love is expressed. Our conviction that God's ways are best can be put severely to the test when we are waiting to see specific signs of those ways—a child's healing, a new job, reconciliation with a loved one, the answer to a prayer. These are among the many, many very concrete "waiting times" when our faith in God and our agreement with his plans are put to the test. Like Sarai and Abraham, we fail that test from time to time. In our impatience we either take things into our own hands and try to force an answer, or we simply give up altogether. But neither of those two alternatives brings about the will of God for our lives. The promise to Abraham and Sarai was fulfilled. Even their presumptive actions did not prevent it. What was required of them, and of us, was to believe . . . and to wait.

REFLECT | *What examples can you draw from your own life when waiting for God brought the better answer to your need? What are you waiting for these days? Where have you given up hope for any answer to come?*

Day 4 Do You Know What You Are Asking?

READ | Matthew 20:17–34

You know not what you are asking. Are you able to drink the cup I am to drink? (v. 22)

Mrs. Zebedee's prayers were not much different from our own, and her ambitious hopes for her sons are something we can all understand. She wanted the best for them, and, like most parents, she assumed that the "best" also meant the most prominent and important. Most of us would probably not be as brazenly obvious as she was when she approached Jesus, and we are left to wonder if the youthful James and John at first reddened with embarrassment when they heard her make her request. However, the fact that Jesus answered and addressed his questions to them seems to indicate that they had been part of the scheme all the time. In any event, here is a mother putting into words what most of us only think with our minds: I want my children to be successes. Of course, Mrs. Zebedee's forthrightness is what lends this story its degree of humor—but also its sense of tragedy. The things we can do to our children! Had she any idea then of the things her two sons would do and would suffer in the years to come, she would never have been so foolish.

This week we are reflecting on our need to let God have charge of our lives. Surely one of the most complex and difficult ways we do that is to let him have charge of those whom we love most. "Backing off" and letting God be God in the lives of our closest family and friends can be downright painful at times, especially when we see them in pain. Our own upbringings have instilled within us a whole list of do's and don'ts, of "I will always" and "I will nevers" that we apply to our own parenting. Some are helpful and some are not. But, with the realization that God loves our children, our families, and our friends far more than we do, also comes the realization that all the good intentions we can muster can only go so far. In the end, we have been entrusted only as stewards and never as owners of these souls. The only one entitled to that is God, their Creator and Redeemer.

With regard to our children, the world sometimes uses the idea that we have to "let them grow up." This is true, but I am inclined to think that the people who also need to "grow up"—that is, to become the men and women of faith that our children need—are we parents. I once read a sermon by a Russian Orthodox priest who said, "God gave children in order to raise their parents." More than anything else, our children need to know that God loves them and that his ways in their lives will always be the best ways. Then, above all else, they can want to love God and to know the joy of doing his will. This will always require that our faith grow up along with theirs, and that we grow older and stronger in our love for God and in our ability to trust him with everything that is important to us.

Years ago, a little prayer came to mind that I have prayed for my family ever since. Your own probably goes something like it. "Lord, _____ belongs to you. Have your way in her/his life, and may you come to mean more to her/him than anyone or anything else in the world. Amen." Mrs. Zebedee was right to pray for her children, for that is exactly what she was doing when she came to Jesus. In her own way, misdirected as it was, she wanted her sons to be close to Jesus, to always be in his company and to sit with him when he became king. But she didn't really know what she was asking. What parent does? This is why we need to let God be in charge.

REFLECT | *What is it that you most want for your children, for your family, for your closest friends? What does it mean for you to entrust them into God's hands? What will this require of you?*

Day 5   What Are You Doing, Lord?

READ | John 11:1–44
Martha said to Jesus, "Lord, if you had been here, my brother would not have died." (v. 21)

Martha, as we know already, was not shy about speaking her mind to Jesus. What is more, on the two occasions we know of from the Gospels, she is recorded with criticism in her voice: "Lord, do you really know what you are doing?"

On the first occasion, you remember, she was indignant that her sister Mary was sitting at Jesus' feet while leaving her to all the work in the kitchen. "Lord, do you not care?" she asked accusingly (Luke 10:40). Then, she essentially ordered Jesus to set her sister straight. This second occasion, recorded by John, is by far more serious. But still, Martha does not hesitate to question Jesus. As soon as she hears that he has entered the village she takes matters in hand and runs to meet him. The same criticizing question is in her tone—"Lord, what were you thinking?"—when she says, "If you had been here, this would not have happened." In the first instance, Martha is clearly put out. In the second, she is clearly in pain.

"Lord, do you really know what you are doing?" The question lies behind many of our conversations with God, especially in connection with the most painful and difficult circumstances in our lives. Illnesses, accidents, family problems, financial issues—these and many of life's disappointments and failures compel us again and again to ask, "Why, Lord?" This is an honest enough question, but it usually carries with it the conceited notion that, were we in charge, we never would have let the thing happen in the first place.

Martha's questioning continues even after Jesus begins to show signs of doing something. When he commands that Lazarus' tomb be opened, it is Martha who corrects him saying, "Are you kidding, Lord? Do you know what it is going to smell like?" Still the one to think that her view of things is the best, Martha is quick to call Jesus' view into question. "Lord, do you really know what you are doing?"

Jesus was patient with Martha as she stood before him back at the supper, essentially complaining that her sister was being lazy and that he was being indulgent in allowing it. But, on this occasion, at the death of her beloved brother, Martha needed more than patience—she needed comfort and assurance. Jesus read through her accusative tone and heard the cry of pain in her heart . . . and he answered it.

Is this not the image of grace itself? The Lord of all life submits himself to the controlling ways and questions of this woman, and gradually, gently brings her to look at things the way he sees them. What if Jesus *had* been in Bethany while Lazarus was sick? What if he had come *then* and healed Lazarus of his illness? Or, what if Martha had gotten her way and they *had not* taken away the stone? The raising of Lazarus turned out to be the radiant precursor of Jesus' own Resurrection. I will bet you that after that, Martha believed that Jesus really did know what he was doing!

REFLECT | *What are the circumstances in your life in which you are asking, "Lord, do you really know what you are doing"? How can you change that question into a genuine prayer for help?*

Day 6   Not This Way, Lord

READ | Matthew 16:13–28

But he turned and said to Peter, "Get behind me, Satan! You are a hindrance to me, for you are not on the side of God, but of men." (v. 23)

Wow! Now here is a confrontation that we would not want to be on the wrong side of! No discussion of people in the Bible who "wrestled" with God would be complete without a look at Peter.

Certainly we cannot fault Peter for his wanting Jesus to be kept safe from harm. It seems only natural. It *is* only natural. Peter loved Jesus. He wanted to see Jesus' work succeed. He wanted more and more people to find the same truth, the same help, the same hope that he and his fellow disciples had found listening to Jesus and following him. He believed that Jesus had a great future, and he was ready to do everything he could to insure that nothing should stand in the way.

But then Jesus introduces all this talk about betrayal and suffering and death in Jerusalem. Just a short time before he had confirmed Peter's God-given insight into Jesus' true identity—he was the Son of God, the Savior. Now he is talking about dying, and Peter will have none of it. Can you imagine his shock and pain when Jesus turned to him with that stinging rebuke: "Get behind me, Satan! You are a hindrance to me, for you are not on the side of God, but of men"? Maybe Peter took it in his stride. The Gospel writer discreetly omits any mention of his reaction. What he does record are Jesus' following words, in which he calls all of his followers to the same way of the cross that he himself walked. In many ways, it is at the same time both the least pleasant and the most promising aspect of discipleship that there is. But it is not a way that we would choose of our own accord.

Is it possible that, with the noblest of motives and even the strongest of affections, we can still find ourselves in opposition to the ways of God in our own lives or in the lives of others? Can we ever presume, given how mysterious and infinite are the divine designs, that we could fully grasp the most paradoxical of all—that life comes out of death, and that, therefore, death, in all the shapes it takes, may sometimes be the very best thing? "There is a way that seems right to a man," says the writer of Proverbs, "but its end is the way to death" (14:12). In a sense, this is exactly what Jesus was saying to Peter—that the way that seemed "right" to him, the way of self-preservation and security that he wanted to follow, was actually more a reflection of hell than of heaven. Had Peter's will prevailed over his Lord's, death would be the only way that any of us would know.

Peter the Apostle did us all a great favor that day when he so impulsively countered the words of our Lord. He helped us all to see where we might be doing the same thing ourselves.

"For my thoughts are not your thoughts, neither are your ways my ways, says the Lord. For as the heavens are higher than the earth, so are my ways higher than your ways and my thoughts than your thoughts." (Isaiah 55:8–9)

REFLECT | *Describe an event in which you were sure that you knew best, only to find that God had something even better in mind. Where can you see that your desire to protect others from pain may actually deny them of something even better?*

Day 7   Here Am I! Send Me

READ | Isaiah 6
In the year that King Uzziah died I saw the Lord sitting upon a throne, high and lifted up; and his train filled the temple. (v. 1)

We have spent a few days reflecting on the question of "who is in charge" of our lives. By their own "wrestlings" with God, a number of figures from the Bible have challenged us to consider where our own struggles may lie when it comes to giving over the reins to God. We cannot leave this topic without looking at one more figure who, like Mary, gave over those reins in a quick and humble fashion.

Isaiah, like all the prophets, was charged by God to proclaim a message to his people. Most often, that message was one of correction and warning—correction against the sins and wickedness of the people, and warnings of impending judgment if they did not change their ways. In Isaiah's case, however, that message also contains some of the most hopeful promises and the most beautiful language in all of the Old Testament.

—Behold, a young woman shall conceive, and bear a son, and shall call his name Immanuel. (7:14)

—For to us a child is born, to us a son is given. (9:6)

—The wolf shall dwell with the lamb, and the leopard shall lie down with the kid, and the calf and the lion and the fatling together, and a little child shall lead them. (11:6)

—And the ransomed of the Lord shall return, and come to Zion with singing; everlasting joy shall be upon their heads; they shall obtain joy and gladness, and sorrow and sighing shall flee away. (35:10)

—Comfort, comfort my people, says your God. Speak tenderly to Jerusalem, and cry to her, that her warfare is ended, that her iniquity is pardoned. (40:1)

—All we like sheep have gone astray; we have turned every one to his own way; and the Lord has laid on him the iniquity of us all. (53:6)

—The Spirit of the Lord is upon me, because the Lord has anointed me to bring good tidings to the afflicted; he has sent me to bind up the brokenhearted, to proclaim liberty to the captives, and the opening of the prison to those who are bound. (61:1)

All these quotations are by way of saying that Isaiah's "here am I" paved the way for God to reveal the heart of his plan for the salvation of the world. Isaiah, who for a few moments was mesmerized by a vision of the Lord in all his glory, said "yes" to a task that he did not yet comprehend. He could never have understood at that moment the purposes for which he was being called. He could never have imagined the golden tongue with which he would speak, nor the amount of light he would be shedding in a darkened world. He could never have dreamt then of the joy his message would inspire for centuries, nor the hope to which it would give birth.

What must Isaiah have seen that compelled him to such a swift and willing acceptance? Not "what," but "who," and so the question answers itself. For if we can see Jesus, if we can see him filling the temple of our hearts and hear his call echoing to us through all its chambers, if our love for him could be as pure as Mary's and our vision of him as clear as Isaiah's, then would we ever want any other to reign over our lives?

REFLECT | *What would it mean for you to say "yes" to God today? In what way is he asking you to say, "here am I"? What is he asking you to do?*

Day 1   Blessings and Obstacles

READ | Numbers 13:1–14:10

If the Lord delights in us, he will bring us into this land and give it to us, a land which flows with milk and honey. (14:9)

Over the last few weeks, we have spent a good deal of time discussing some of the various obstacles that hinder us on our path of discipleship—things like jealousy and idolatry, anger and self-pity, vindictiveness and fear. These are the "men of great stature," those unattractive *giants* (vv. 32–33) that we find living in our own hearts. Through these weeks, we have been "opening our hearts" in order to take a good look at these giants so that we might understand better how to overcome them. We know their intentions and their tactics. By their sheer size and number, they are able sometimes to distract us from the path that is set before us and obscure our vision of the "promised land" that we seek. Their only purpose is to wreak havoc in our souls, to alienate us from our fellow travelers, and to weaken our resolve to follow the One who goes before us. Ultimately, they would like nothing more than to keep us from going the whole distance and finishing our course. But they cannot be allowed to succeed. Not a single one of them is so strong that it cannot be subdued. Their end, however, will be determined to a large extent by how we choose to look at them.

The twelve spies sent into Canaan by Moses brought back a mixed report to the people of Israel. The land before them was spacious and fruitful, "flowing with milk and honey."

They even carried evidence of its abundance for all the people to see—imagine, a single cluster of grapes that took two men to carry! This truly was the land of promise. But ten of the spies also said that this was as close as the people should ever get to it. Their vision fixed upon the frightening inhabitants of the land, and their hearts fainted within them. All they saw was the impossibility of what lay before them, and all they could imagine was the defeat that they feared would inevitably come. But Hoshea (called Joshua) and Caleb saw differently. Even as their eyes saw the same giants as their colleagues, their hearts saw more. "The Lord is with us," they declared; "do not fear them" (14:9). Their resolute counsel was for the people to move forward, to trust in the promises of God and to count upon his strength. The "giants" were no reason to believe that God had changed his mind about what he intended. They only provided another opportunity for the people to depend upon God, and for God to bless his people.

Joshua's advice went unheeded, and so, for forty years, an entire generation of Israelites wandered and perished in the wilderness. A new generation arose, and, with Joshua at their head, they came to enter and inhabit the land of promise. It is to the story of Joshua that we turn as we conclude these twelve weeks of reflections. His name means "God has saved," another form of that name above all names—"Jesus." Joshua is the Old Testament figure of our Savior, who is leading us to our own land of blessing.

Even as we still stand at a distance from the fulfillment of all the good things that God has in store for us (here in the "wilderness of Paran"), Joshua is telling us to keep moving forward. Can you hear his wise and fervent counsel? As you face the close of these twelve weeks, can you look forward and get a glimpse, through your Savior's eyes, of the destiny that lies ahead? He has been to that land already—he walked the entire distance just as we do; he fought with and defeated the same giants that we now face; he laid claim to the promise of his Father; and now he has returned to lead us to our promised home. Can you hear him as he says, "Come, follow me?"

REFLECT | *What are the "giants"—the forces that tempt you to turn back—that you are facing these days? Which one of them are you most discouraged about overcoming? What can you do in order to "keep moving forward"?*

Day 2 Be Strong and of Good Courage

READ | Joshua 1:1–11

Have I not commanded you? Be strong and of good courage; be not frightened, neither be dismayed; for the Lord your God is with you wherever you go." (v. 9)

Forty years after the twelve Israelite spies reported back to Moses at Kadesh, Joshua and a new generation of Israelites stood at the banks of the Jordan River anticipating their entry into the "promised land." A new and unknown venture lay before them—the promise of great blessing together with the certainty of great challenges—and the opening chapter of the Book of Joshua records God's charge to the man whom he had chosen to lead the way. We can hear in these words the voice of God to us as we look forward to taking the next steps of our own pilgrimage.

Three times the Lord repeated to Joshua: "Be strong and of good courage" (vv. 6, 7, 9). Three times in eleven verses. Do you suppose there is a reason? Only God knew what lay before Joshua. God alone had the eyes to see everything that Joshua would face in the coming years—every step, every stumble, every turn, and every straight way. He knew every setback he would suffer, and every victory he would enjoy. He also had no doubt whatsoever about the final outcome.

Joshua, however, was only a man, and therefore too small to see very far ahead. So, the things that he could not possibly know by himself, God told him. He promised him that the land would be won. He reminded Joshua about the law, the words that he had given to his servant Moses, and told him to cling to it and follow it, without diverting from it in any way. This would be the guarantee of his prosperity and success. God told Joshua that there was no reason to be afraid, that he would never have to face alone the difficulties that came against him, and that he, the Lord his God, would be with him wherever he went. These are the reasons for which Joshua could be strong and courageous—because God promised that he would *never* fail or forsake him (v. 5). Can you hear God as he speaks these words to you today, as he calls you to set your sights forward to the next step of the journey?

I will be with you wherever you go—God has faithfully brought you to the place you stand now. You did not set forth on the path, neither did you arrive here under your own strength. Along the way, you have already seen many signs of his love for you and of his ability to help you. Is there any reason to think that he would leave you on your own now?

Be not frightened, neither be dismayed—The Lord your God, the One who has made you his own child, is greater than you can ever imagine. There is nothing that his love cannot accomplish for you. Do not forget that the highest mountains that loom before you look like tiny knolls when seen from heaven.

I will not fail you or forsake you—God has given you every piece of equipment necessary for a successful journey. Even if you cannot find it right now, not one thing will ever be missing when you need it. All you need do is follow the directions that he gives and you are guaranteed to arrive safely at the destination he has in store.

With all this, and so much more, is there any reason that God should hesitate to expect us to *be strong and of good courage?*

REFLECT | *Which of these assuring words means most to you today? What can you do to firmly lay hold of these truths? God must have spoken these words to Joshua because he knew that Joshua might be afraid. What are you most afraid of in the coming weeks?*

Day 3   A New Journey

READ | Joshua 3

When you see the ark of the covenant of the Lord your God being carried by the Levitical priests, then you shall set out from your place and follow it, that you may know the way you shall go, for you have not passed this way before. (vv. 3–4)

When I was a child, my family would sometimes make a traveling vacation that took me to various parts of the country. I look back fondly upon these trips, and remember with a smile one thing that was common to them all—I could not sleep the night before we left. The thought of getting up early in the morning and setting out on the road to a new and different place was too exhilarating to allow sleep. The fun would be in the destination, but it was also in the journey.

Joshua and the people of Israel were camped at the Jordan River. For forty years they had known only the world of the wilderness. Daily life had gone unchanged since the days of their mothers and fathers—setting up camp, taking down camp, gathering manna, praying in the tabernacle—and all the time they were passing by the same scenery and the same landmarks that they had passed by the month before. On this day, however, they awakened to something new and different . . . and totally unknown.

We don't think about it much, but the truth is that each day that greets us is a new step on our path of discipleship. In countless ways, today's scenery will look similar to yesterday's, and we might succumb to the temptation to believe that we've been this way before. But the life of the disciple regularly brings us to the banks of a new Jordan River—new challenges, new successes, new disappointments, new pains, new joys. Some of the experiences that await us this day will be familiar, but others will be dramatically different. There is no way to prepare for them all, only to walk with God through each one of them as we meet them.

Not knowing the things that lie ahead can be both unnerving and exhilarating. What we can know, however, is the way to get there. Under Joshua's leadership the commanders of Israel directed the people essentially to "keep an eye out." The ark of the covenant—representing the presence of God in their midst—would soon pass by and lead them through the river. Watch carefully, they ordered, and do not assume that you know the way. *You have never passed this way before.*

We can be certain that God knows the way that lies before us. There will be no surprises for him today. This is one of the reasons that you and I can face our futures confidently. The way that God prepared the people of Israel for this very new and very big step of their journey was by teaching them to follow him in all the little steps that got them to this point. All the tedious days they had already lived, learning to love and to obey the Lord, were getting them ready for a new adventure that they could not yet imagine. They had already learned to follow the ark. Today it was more important than ever that they do so.

God knows what is coming into our lives. He knows the rivers we will face, and he knows that the only way we will be able to successfully cross each one of them will be by following his lead. The lessons of love and obedience that we learned yesterday and the day before and the day before that were all getting us ready for today. And today will prepare us for tomorrow. Then, when it comes time to cross that last river, we will be ready for the adventure of a lifetime!

REFLECT | *What lessons have you already learned by following Jesus that you are able to put into practice today? What lesson do you think he has been teaching you lately? For you, what does it mean specifically to watch for the ark going before you?*

Day 4   What Do These Stones Mean?

READ | Joshua 4

[Joshua] said to the people of Israel, "When your children ask their fathers in time to come, 'What do these stones mean?' then you shall let your children know, 'Israel passed over this Jordan on dry ground.' " (v. 21)

Do you keep a record of God's blessings and answers to prayer? Some Christians do, and they find the practice enjoyable and reassuring. "Counting your blessings" can be an effective means of shining light into the shadows of discouragement, but it only works if you remember what those blessings are and have been.

We have remarked before that we human beings are prone to "forgetfulness" with regard to the things of God. In the face of present temptations, for example, we often forget the price we paid the last time we gave in. Or in the face of present pain, we forget how God comforted and healed us before. Or in the face of prosperity, we may forget the Source of all our blessings. Consider the numbers of times that the children of Israel were instructed to "remember" what God had done for them. It sounds as if the Lord knew that someday they would forget:

—You shall remember that you were a servant in the land of Egypt. (Deut. 5:15)

—You shall not be afraid of them, but you shall remember what the Lord your God did to Pharaoh and to all Egypt. (Deut. 7:18)

—You shall remember all the way which the Lord your

—God has led you these forty years in the wilderness.
(Deut. 8:2)

—You shall remember the Lord your God. (Deut. 8:18)

—Take heed lest you forget the Lord, who brought you
out of the land of Egypt, out of the house of bondage.
(Deut. 6:12)

Memorials of all kinds are set up in remembrance
of people and events in our history that should never be
forgotten. The memorial itself becomes our connection to
those events and to those people, and, especially when they
have affected us in some personal way, it can elicit from us
a whole array of remembrances, including all the emotions
that come with them. I once visited the small church and
cemetery of my Irish ancestors. Seeing my own name
inscribed on dozens of gravestones, some of which were
hundreds of years old, actually made me feel surrounded
by this long-forgotten family, and, quite unexpectedly, I
was overwhelmed by a deep sense of belonging. Such is the
power of a stone of remembrance.

The stones that the Lord commanded to be set up in the
Jordan were meant to tell the coming generations that they
belonged as well—belonged to a family whose ancestors had
once passed this way; belonged to a people who had once
been miraculously preserved from destruction; belonged
to a God who had once saved them. All those events, and
many, many more, were contained in those twelve stones.
But, in the case of memorials to the work of God, those
events are still going on. The good things that God has done
in the past are but the assurances for what he can do today,
and will most certainly do tomorrow. In a sense, by the

handiwork of God, you and I are now among those "living stones" that our children and our children's children will look to and ask, "What do these stones mean?" And when they ask, may there be someone to answer and say, "These are the reminders to us, that our God is good."

REFLECT | *Make a list of the good things that God has done for you in the last twelve weeks. What does this list tell you about the future?*

Day 5   Do Not Turn Back

READ | Joshua 23

You know in your hearts and souls, all of you, that not one thing has failed of all the good things which the LORD your God promised concerning you; all have come to pass for you, not one of them has failed. (v. 14)

Jumping to the end of the book of Joshua, we find the children of Israel living securely in their new home. Not all the country has been settled, and not every soul is at rest, but Joshua's work is done. He is now the patriarch of the nation, having faithfully wedded this people to their land in the service of God. Joshua has lived up to his name: through his obedience and perseverance, God saved his people for himself.

Joshua now stands before the people "old and well advanced in years," bequeathing to them a blessed future that has been securely built upon God's deeds of the past. Nevertheless, the blessings of the future that Joshua sees are also dependent upon their own deeds, especially their own obedience and faithfulness to God. Even with their reward in hand, declares Joshua, they will soon face the temptation to "turn back" from the ways of God and join with the ways of those who were once their enemies. Joshua warns that if they do so, they will be ruined.

The call to perseverance is almost harder to hear in times of peace than it is in times of adversity. The pain of suffering usually makes us acutely aware of life's choices and the sharp differences there are among them. When we are at our lowest and weakest, we are likely to be super-sensitive to the temptation to give up and turn back. According to Matthew's account, it was not until *after* Jesus fasted in the wilderness for forty days that the tempter came and said to him, "If you are the Son of God, command these stones to become loaves of bread" (4:2–3). So long as the people of Israel were wandering in the wilderness, utterly dependent upon the water and manna that they found each day and needing the pillar of fire and cloud to lead them from place to place, the temptation to turn back to Egypt was blatantly obvious. But now that they knew prosperity, now that their stomachs were always full, their lands always fertile, and their weapons always in the closet, they were especially susceptible to the more subtle temptations to turn away from God.

Joshua's counsel to Israel is of value to us as well. We recognize temptation when it comes to us in those structured times of self-discipline and self-denial. We may still give in to it, but there is no question about what we are doing. At such times, it is as if we have placed a fence around us. It leaves us a very small space in which to move, but we have no trouble knowing either when we have stepped out of its confining limits, or when something has stepped in and is crowding us. But, once that fence is gone, once there are no more obvious "lines to cross," and our moving about becomes freer and easier, then we have a harder time knowing when we have moved in the wrong direction.

The words of Joshua remind us that when this happens (not *if* this happens), we can still turn to the Lord our God and remember the covenant he has made with us. Our futures hold both the structured times and the unstructured. There is no reason that we should not remain faithful to God in both, because God has remained faithful to us.

REFLECT | *What are you most afraid of about "releasing" yourself from various disciplines or restraints? What would it mean for you to be tempted in times of prosperity? What would be your weakest point?*

Day 6   Choose This Day

READ | Joshua 24
Choose this day whom you will serve, whether the gods your fathers served in the region beyond the River, or the gods of the Amorites in whose land you dwell; but as for me and my house, we will serve the LORD. (v. 15)

The twenty-fourth chapter of Joshua is like a quick review of the entire history of Israel—a "CliffsNotes" study guide to the old covenant. We, too, have met with some of these figures over the past twelve weeks: Abraham, Jacob and Esau, Moses and the children of Israel. Their lives are among those through whom God established his promise on the earth and advanced his plan of salvation. Joshua rehearses this miraculous and glorious past in order to compel the people to hold fast in the future.

Choose this day whom you will serve. Isn't this the choice that you and I face every day? You must choose, says Joshua, because, whether you consciously intend to or not, you will most surely be serving some god. It will either be the God of all heaven and earth, or it will be one of the gods you met yesterday, or one of the gods you will meet tomorrow. Make no mistake about it, he says. You must choose, because, if you don't serve one of them, then you will be serving the other. So, which one will it be?

Most of us are familiar with times of new resolutions and fervent commitments. We make them at special times like the New Year, or our birthday, or the season of Lent. They are designed to set us upon a specific course of action, defined by a fresh sense of priorities and a renewed vision for what our lives can be like. In other words, they are opportunities to "start over." In a sense, Joshua was presenting the people of Israel with just such an opportunity. But, in his words, we also find that the opportunity is presented every day.

Chose *this* day. We look at Joshua and we admire a man who persevered in his commitment to God under adversity as well as prosperity. But perseverance is measured not by great and noble feats, nor by flash fires of determination. The quality of perseverance is measured by one good choice after another, after another, after another. It is a fruit that takes years to ripen, but those years are still only lived one day at a time.

The life of the people of Israel continued long after Joshua died. We know that the choices that they made through the years were a thorough mixture of good and bad, wise and foolish, faithful and blasphemous. Still, one thing never changed—God was always ready for them to choose him. That would be a daily opportunity, and it still is.

REFLECT | *What will it mean for you to "choose God" each day? Who are some of the other "gods" whom you will be tempted to serve?*

Day 7   A New Creation

READ | Revelation 21–22

And he who sat upon the throne said, "Behold, I make all things new." (21:5)

We began this series of reflections in the opening chapters of the Book of Genesis. It is only fitting that we end it with the closing chapters of the Revelation to John. This is a long way from Joshua, I know, but what took place for the people of Israel by Joshua's hand was only a foreshadowing of what would take place for us by the hand of Jesus. The promised land into which he longs to lead us is unimaginably beautiful, primarily because it is his own home and he will be there. It will be a paradise in which all that was lost in Eden will be found, all that was broken will be mended, all that died will be made alive.

I have heard young mothers say that the excruciating pain of childbirth all but vanished with the first warm feel of their newborn child upon their breast. If the touch of one little child can relieve such hurt, if those gentle fingers can somehow lessen the pain of sin's curse (Genesis 3:16), how much more consolation can we expect from the hands of God's own Child? The vision of heaven that John receives is meant to tell us that the pains we endure have both a purpose and an end.

We have talked a good deal about "goals" over these past twelve weeks. Some of the great teachers of the early church used to talk about goals, too, but they warned against mistaking them for the true end of our lives. The goals that we reach (or fail to reach) in this life are only "sub-goals," as one young person I know put it. John was presenting the true end and purpose of our lives. Like Joshua, he was an old man by the time he saw the "promised land," and well experienced with suffering and pain. Imagine how he must have felt when he received this glimpse of heaven. He tells his readers that this is what makes it all worthwhile. This is the destination for every disciple, and when they reach it, there will be no thought left of the rough road that got them there. In the face of Love himself, how can there be any remembrance of pain?

Saint Augustine said that the suffering we endure on earth is only a sign of our longing for heaven. We are "nostalgic" for home, and our hearts ache so long as we are away. When we open our hearts as we have done through these weeks, we can easily read in them the signs of this nostalgia. This is why we should not allow ourselves to become discouraged when the ache grows so strong. It is only an indication of how deeply we long to be delivered.

For the real birth that is taking place is our own. You and I are the ones being "re-made," being born again into the kingdom of heaven. And the real pain to be borne has been borne already by our Savior who, like Adam, opened his own side in order to bring another life—our life—into his world.

So do not lose heart. Instead, open your heart . . . to the One who makes all things new.

Let Your Mind Alone!

Books by James Thurber

Thurber & Company
Credos and Curios
Lanterns and Lances
The Years with Ross
Alarms and Diversions
The Wonderful O
Further Fables for Our Time
Thurber's Dogs
Thurber Country
The Thurber Album
The 13 Clocks
The Beast in Me and Other Animals
The White Deer
The Thurber Carnival
The Great Quillow
Men, Women and Dogs
Many Moons
My World—And Welcome to It
Fables for Our Time
The Last Flower
Let Your Mind Alone!
The Middle-Aged Man on the Flying Trapeze
My Life and Hard Times
The Seal in the Bedroom
The Owl in the Attic
Is Sex Necessary? (with E. B. White)

PLAY

The Male Animal (with Elliott Nugent)

REVUE

A Thurber Carnival

Bateman Comes Home

LET YOUR MIND ALONE!

ALONE!

AND OTHER

MORE OR LESS INSPIRATIONAL PIECES

By

JAMES THURBER

With Drawings by the Author

PERENNIAL LIBRARY
Harper & Row, Publishers
New York, Hagerstown,
San Francisco, London

First PERENNIAL LIBRARY edition published 1976

STANDARD BOOK NUMBER: 06–080375–4

76 77 78 79 80 10 9 8 7 6 5 4 3 2 1

FOR HELEN

¶ The essays and stories in this book were originally printed in *The New Yorker*, with the exception of "After the Steppe Cat, What?", which appeared in *The Forum*, and "Women Go On Forever," which appeared in *For Men Only*.

CONTENTS

Part One

Let your mind alone!

1. Pythagoras and the Ladder

I T WAS IN NONE OTHER THAN THE BLACK, MEMORABLE YEAR 1929 that the indefatigable Professor Walter B. Pitkin rose up with the announcement that "for the first time in the career of mankind happiness is coming within the reach of millions of people." Happy living, he confidently asserted, could be attained by at least six or seven people out of every ten, but he figured that not more than one person in a thousand was actually attaining it. However, all the external conditions required for happy living were present, he said, just waiting to be used. The only obstacle was a psychological one. Figuring on a basis of 130,000,000 population in this country and reducing the Professor's estimates to round numbers, we find that in 1929 only 130,000 people were happy, but that between 78,000,000 and 91,000,000 could have been happy, leaving only 52,000,000, at the outside, doomed to discontent. The trouble with all the unhappy ones (except the 52,000,000) was that they didn't Know Themselves, they didn't understand the Science of Happiness, they had no Technique of Thinking. Professor Pitkin wrote a book on the subject; he is, in fact, always writing a book on the subject. So are a number of other people. I have devoted myself to a careful study of as many of these books as a man of my unsteady eyesight and wandering attention could be expected to encompass. And I decided to write a series of articles of my own on the subject, examining what the Success Experts have to say and offering some ideas of my own, the basic one of which is, I think, that man will be better

3

Conducting a Lady to a Table in a Restaurant

off if he quits monkeying with his mind and just lets it alone. In this, the first of the series, I shall abandon Professor Pitkin to his percentages and his high hopes and consider the author of a best-seller published last summer (an alarming number of these books reach the best-seller list). Let us plunge right into Dr. James L. Mursell's "Streamline Your Mind" and see what he has to contribute to the New Happiness, as Professor Pitkin has called it.

In Chapter VI, which is entitled "Using What You've Got," Dr. Mursell deals with the problem of how to learn and how to make use of what you have learned. He believes, to begin with, that you should learn things by doing them, not by just reading up on them. In this connection he presents the case of a young man who wanted to find out "how to conduct a lady to a table in a restaurant." Although I have been gored by a great many dilemmas in my time, that particular problem doesn't happen to have been one of them. I must have just stumbled onto the way to conduct a lady to a table in a restaurant. I don't remember, as a young man, ever having given the matter much thought, but I know that I frequently worried about whether I would have enough money to pay for the dinner and still tip the waiter. Dr. Mursell does not touch on the difficult problem of how to maintain your poise as you depart from a restaurant table on which you have left no tip. I constantly find these mental authorities avoiding the larger issues in favor of something which seems comparatively trivial. The plight of the Doctor's young man, for instance, is as nothing compared to my own plight one time in a restaurant in Columbus when I looked up to find my cousin Wilmer Thurber standing beside me flecked with buttermilk and making a sound which was something between the bay of a beagle and the cry of a large bird.

I had been having lunch in the outer of two small rooms

which comprised a quiet basement restaurant known as the Hole in the Wall, opposite the State House grounds, a place much frequented by elderly clerks and lady librarians, in spite of its raffish name. Wilmer, it came out, was in the other room; neither of us knew the other was there. The Hole in the Wall was perhaps the calmest restaurant I have ever known; the studious people who came there for lunch usually lunched alone; you rarely heard anybody talk. The aged proprietor of the place, because of some defect, spoke always in whispers, and this added to an effect of almost monasterial quiet. It was upon this quiet that there fell suddenly, that day, the most unearthly sound I have ever heard. My back was to the inner room and I was too disconcerted to look around. But from the astonished eyes of those who sat in front of me facing the doorway to that room I became aware that the Whatever-It-Was had entered our room and was approaching my table. It wasn't until a cold hand was laid on mine that I looked up and beheld Wilmer, who had, it came out, inhaled a draught of buttermilk as one might inhale cigarette smoke, and was choking. Having so fortunately found me, he looked at me with wide, stricken eyes and, still making that extraordinary sound, a low, canine *how-ooo* that rose to a high, birdlike *yeee-eep*, he pointed to the small of his back as who should say "Hit me!" There I was, faced with a restaurant problem which, as I have said, makes that of Dr. Mursell's young man seem very unimportant indeed. What I did finally, after an awful, frozen moment, was to get up and dash from the place, without even paying for my lunch. I sent the whispering old man a check, but I never went back to his restaurant. Many of our mental authorities, most of whom are psychologists of one school or another, will say that my dreadful experience must have implanted in me a fear of restaurants (Restauphobia). It did nothing of the sort; it simply implanted in me a wariness of

Wilmer. I never went into a restaurant after that without first making sure that this inveterate buttermilk-drinker was not there.

But let us get back to Dr. Mursell and his young man's peculiar quandary. I suppose this young man must have got to worrying about who went first, the lady or himself. These things, as we know, always work out; if the young man doesn't work them out, the lady will. (If she wants him to go first, she will say, "You go first.") What I am interested in here is not the correct procedure but Dr. Mursell's advice to the young man in question. He writes, "Do not merely learn it in words, Try it over with your sister." In that second sentence he reveals, it seems to me, what these inspirationalists so frequently reveal, a lack of understanding of people; in this case, brothers and sisters. Ninety-nine brothers out of a hundred who were worrying about how to conduct a lady to a table in a restaurant would starve before they would go to their sisters and ask them how the thing is done. They would as lief go to their mothers and have a good, frank talk about sex. But let us, for the sake of the argument, try Dr. Mursell's system.

Sister, who is twenty-one, and who goes around with a number of young men whom her brother frankly regards as pussy-cats, is sitting by the fire one evening reading André Gide, or *Photoplay*, or something. Brother, who is eighteen, enters. "Where's Mom?" he asks. "How should I know?" she snaps. "Thought you might know that, Stupid. Y'ought to know something," he snaps back. Sister continues to read, but she is obviously annoyed by the presence of her brother; he is chewing gum, making a strange, cracking noise every fifth chew, and this gets on her nerves. "Why don't you spit out that damn gum?" she asks, finally. "Aw, nuts," says her brother, in a falsetto singsong. "Nuts to you, Baby, nuts." There is a long, tense silence; he rustles and re-rustles the evening paper. "Where's Itsy Bitsy Dicky tonight?" he asks, suddenly. "Ditch you for a live gal?" By Itsy Bitsy Dicky, he refers to one Richard Warren, a beau of his sister's, whom he considers a hollyhock. "Why don't you go to hell?" asks his sister, coldly. Brother reads the sports page and begins to whistle "Horses," a song which has annoyed his sister since she was ten and he was seven, and which he is whistling for that reason. "*Stop* that!" she screams, at last. He stops for about five seconds and then bursts out, loudly, "*Cra*-zy over *hor*-ses, *hor*-ses, *hor*-ses, she's a little wi-i-i-ld!" Here we have, I think, a typical meeting between brother and sister. Now, out of it, somehow, we have to arrive at a *tableau vivant* in which the brother asks the sister to show him how to conduct a lady to a table in a restaurant. Let us attempt to work that out. "Oh, say, Sis," the brother begins, after a long pause. "Shut up, you lout!" she says. "No, listen, I want to ask you a favor." He begins walking around the room, blushing. "I've asked Greta Dearing out to dinner tomorrow night and I'm not sure how to get her to the table. I mean whether—I mean I don't know how we both get to the table. Come on out in the hall with me and we'll pretend this room is the restaurant. You show me how to get you over to that table in the corner." The note of falsity is so apparent in this that I need not carry out the embarrassing fiction any longer. Obviously the young man is going to have to read up on the subject or, what is much simpler, just take his girl to the restaurant. This acting-out of things falls down of its own stuffiness.

There is a curious tendency on the part of the How-to-Live men to make things hard. It recurs time and again in the thought-technique books. In this same Chapter VI there is a classic example of it. Dr. Mursell recounts the remarkable experience of a professor and his family who were faced with the necessity of reroofing their country house. They decided, for some obscure reason, to do the work themselves, and they intended to order the materials from Sears, Roebuck. The first thing, of course, was to find out how much roofing material they needed. "Here," writes Dr. Mursell, "they struck a snag." They didn't, he points out, have a ladder, and since the roof was too steep to climb, they were at their wits' end as to how they were going to go about measuring it. You and I have this problem solved already: we would get a ladder. But not, it wonderfully turns out, Dr. Mursell's professor and his family. "For several days," writes Dr. Mursell, "they were completely stumped." Nobody thought of getting a ladder. It is impossible to say how they would have solved their problem had not a guest come finally to visit them. This guest noticed that the angle formed by the two sides of the roof (which were equal in length) was a right angle. Let Dr. Mursell go on, in his ecstatic way, from there. "An isosceles right-angled triangle with the base of known length! Had nobody ever been told that the sum of the squares on the two sides of such a triangle was equal to the square of the hypotenuse? And couldn't anyone do a little arithmetic? How very simple! One could easily figure the measurements for the sides of the roof, and as the length of the house could be found without any climbing, the area could be discovered. The theorem of Pythagoras could be used in place of the ladder."

I think this places Dr. James L. Mursell for you; at any rate it does for me: he is the man who would use the theorem of Pythagoras in place of a ladder. I keep wondering what would have happened if that guest hadn't turned up, or if he had remembered the theorem of Pythagoras the way many people do: the sum of the squares of the two sides of a right-angled triangle is equal to *twice* the sum of the hypotenuse, or some other such variant. Many a person, doing a little arithmetic in this case, would order enough material from

Sears, Roebuck to roof seven houses. It seems to me that borrowing a ladder from next door, or buying one from a hardware store, is a much simpler way to go about measuring a roof than waiting for somebody to show up who knows the theorem of Pythagoras. Most people who show up at my house can't remember anything they learned in school except possibly the rule for compound Latin verbs that take the dative. My roof would never be fixed; it would rain in; probably I'd have to sell the house, at a great loss, to somebody who has a ladder. With a ladder of my own, and the old-fashioned technique of thinking, I could get the job done in no time. This seems to me the simplest way to live.

2. Destructive Forces in Life

THE MENTAL EFFICIENCY BOOKS GO INTO ELABORATE DETAIL about how to attain Masterful Adjustment, as one of them calls it, but it seems to me that the problems they set up, and knock down, are in the main unimaginative and pedestrian: the little fusses at the breakfast table, the routine troubles at the office, the familiar anxieties over money and health—the welter of workaday annoyances which all of us meet with and usually conquer without extravagant wear and tear. Let us examine, as a typical instance, a brief case history presented by the learned Mr. David Seabury, author of "What Makes Us Seem So Queer," "Unmasking Our Minds," "Keep Your Wits," "Growing Into Life," and "How to Worry Successfully." I select it at random. "Frank Fulsome," writes Mr. Seabury, "flung down the book with disgust and growled an insult at his wife. That little lady put her hands to her face and fled from the room. She was sure Frank must hate her to speak so cruelly. Had she known it, he was not really speaking to her at all. The occasion merely gave vent to a pent-up desire to 'punch his fool boss in the jaw.'" This is, I believe, a characteristic Seabury situation. Many of the women in his treatises remind you of nobody so much as Ben Bolt's Alice, who "wept with delight when you gave her a smile, and trembled with fear at your frown." The little ladies most of us know would, instead of putting their hands to their faces and fleeing from the room, come right back at Frank Fulsome. Frank would perhaps be lucky if he didn't get a punch in the jaw himself. In any case, the situation would be cleared up in approximately three minutes. This "had she known" business is not as common among wives today as Mr. Seabury seems to think it is. The Latent Content (as the psychologists call it) of a husband's mind is usually as clear to the wife as the Manifest Content, frequently much clearer.

I could cite a dozen major handicaps to Masterful Adjustment which the thought technicians never touch upon, a dozen

A Mentally Disciplined Husband with Mentally Undisciplined Wife

situations not so easy of analysis and solution as most of theirs. I will, however, content myself with one. Let us consider the case of a man of my acquaintance who had accomplished Discipline of Mind, overcome the Will to Fail, mastered the Technique of Living—had, in a word, practically attained Masterful Adjustment—when he was called on the phone one afternoon about five o'clock by a man named Bert Scursey. The other man, whom I shall call Harry Conner, did not answer the phone, however; his wife answered it. As Scursey told me the story later, he had no intention when he dialled the Conners' apartment at the Hotel Graydon of doing more than talk with Harry. But, for some strange reason, when Louise Conner answered, Bert Scursey found himself pretending to be, and imitating the voice of, a colored woman. This Scursey is by way of being an excellent mimic, and a colored woman is one of the best things he does.

"Hello," said Mrs. Conner. In a plaintive voice, Scursey said, "Is dis heah Miz Commah?" "Yes, this is Mrs. Conner," said Louise. "Who is speaking?" "Dis heah's Edith Rummum," said Scursey. "Ah used wuck fo yo frens was nex doah yo place a Sou Norwuck." Naturally, Mrs. Conner did not follow this, and demanded rather sharply to know who was calling and what she wanted. Scursey, his voice soft with feigned tears, finally got it over to his friend's wife that he was one Edith Rummum, a colored maid who had once worked for some friends of the Conners' in South Norwalk, where they had lived some years before. "What is it you want, Edith?" asked Mrs. Conner, who was completely taken in by the imposter (she could not catch the name of the South Norwalk friends, but let that go). Scursey—or Edith, rather —explained in a pitiable, hesitant way that she was without work or money and that she didn't know what she was going to do; Rummum, she said, was in the jailhouse because of a cutting scrape on a roller-coaster. Now, Louise Conner happened to be a most kind-hearted person, as Scursey well knew, so she said that she could perhaps find some laundry work for Edith to do. "Yessum," said Edith. "Ah laundas." At this point, Harry Conner's voice, raised in the room behind his wife, came clearly to Scursey, saying, "Now, for God's sake, Louise, don't go giving our clothes out to somebody you never saw or heard of in your life." This interjection of Conner's was in firm keeping with a theory of logical behavior which he had got out of the Mind and Personality books. There was no Will to Weakness here, no Desire to

Have His Shirts Ruined, no False Sympathy for the Colored Woman Who Has Not Organized Her Life.

But Mrs. Conner who often did not listen to Mr. Conner, in spite of his superior mental discipline, prevailed.* "Where are you now, Edith?" she asked. This disconcerted Scursey for a moment, but he finally said, "Ah's jes rounda corna, Miz Commah." "Well, you come over to the Hotel Graydon," said Mrs. Conner. "We're in Apartment 7-A on the seventh floor." "Yessm," said Edith. Mrs. Conner hung up and so did Scursey. He was now, he realized, in something of a predicament. Since he did not possess a streamlined mind, as Dr. Mursell has called it, and had definitely a Will to Confuse, he did not perceive that his little joke had gone far enough. He wanted to go on with it, which is a characteristic of woolgatherers, pranksters, wags, wish-fulfillers, and escapists generally. He enjoyed fantasy as much as reality, probably even more, which is a sure symptom of Regression, Digression, and Analogical Redintegration. What he finally did, therefore, was to call back the Conners and get Mrs. Conner on the phone again. "Jeez, Miz Commah," he said, with a hint of panic in his voice, "Ah cain' fine yo apottoman!" "Where are you, Edith?" she asked. "Lawd, Ah doan know," said Edith. "Ah's on *some* floah in de Hotel Graydon." "Well, listen, Edith, you took the elevator, didn't you?" "Dass whut Ah took," said Edith, uncertainly. "Well, you go back to the elevator and tell the boy you want off at the seventh floor. I'll meet you at the elevator." "Yessm," said Edith, with even more uncertainty. At this point, Conner's loud voice, speaking to his wife, was again heard by Scursey. "Where in the hell is she calling from?" demanded Conner, who had developed Logical Reasoning. "She must have wandered into somebody else's apart-

* This sometimes happens even when the husband is mentally disciplined and the wife is not.

ment if she is calling you from this building, for God's sake!" Whereupon, having no desire to explain where Edith was calling from, Scursey hung up.

After an instant of thought, or rather Disintegrated Phantasmagoria, Scursey rang the Conners again. He wanted to prevent Louise from going out to the elevator and checking up with the operator. This time, as Scursey had hoped, Harry Conner answered, having told his wife that he would handle this situation. "Hello!" shouted Conner, irritably. "Who is this?" Scursey now abandoned the rôle of Edith and assumed a sharp, fussy, masculine tone. "Mr. Conner," he said, crisply, "this is the office. I am afraid we shall have to ask you to remove this colored person from the building. She is blundering into other people's apartments, using their phones. We cannot have that sort of thing, you know, at the Graydon." The man's words and his tone infuriated Conner. "There are a lot of sort of things I'd like to see you not have at the Graydon!" he shouted. "Well, please come down to the lobby and do something about this situation," said the man, nastily. "You're damned right I'll come down!" howled Conner. He banged down the receiver.

Bert Scursey sat in a chair and gloated over the involved state of affairs which he had created. He decided to go over to the Graydon, which was just up the street from his own apartment, and see what was happening. It promised to have all the confusion which his disorderly mind so deplorably enjoyed. And it did have. He found Conner in a tremendous rage in the lobby, accusing an astonished assistant manager of having insulted him. Several persons in the lobby watched the curious scene. "But, Mr. Conner," said the assistant manager, a Mr. Bent, "I have no idea what you are talking about." "If you listen, you'll find out!" bawled Harry Conner. "In the first place, this colored woman's coming to the hotel was no idea of mine. I've never seen her in my life and I don't want to see her! I want to go to my *grave* without seeing her!" He had forgotten what the Mind and Personality books had taught him: never raise your voice in anger, always stick to the point. Naturally, Mr. Bent could only believe that his guest had gone out of his mind. He decided to humor him. "Where is this—ah—colored woman, Mr. Conner?" he asked, warily. He was somewhat pale and was fiddling with a bit of paper. A dabbler in psychology books himself, he knew that colored women are often Sex Degradation symbols, and he wondered if Conner had not fallen out of love with his wife without realizing it. (This theory, I believe, Mr. Bent has clung to ever since, although the Conners are one of the happiest couples in the country). "I don't know where she is!" cried Conner. "She's up on some other floor phoning my wife! *You* seemed to know all about it! I had nothing to do with it! I opposed it from the start! But I want no insults from you no matter *who* opposed it!" "Certainly not, certainly not," said Mr. Bent, backing slightly away. He began to wonder what he was going to do with this maniac.

At this juncture Scursey, who had been enjoying the scene at a safe distance, approached Conner and took him by the arm. "What's the matter, old boy?" he asked. "H'lo, Bert," said Conner, sullenly. And then, his eyes narrowing, he began to examine the look on Scursey's face. Scursey is not good at dead-panning; he is only good on the phone. There was a guilty grin on his face. "You ———," said Conner, bitterly, remembering Scursey's pranks of mimicry, and he turned on his heel, walked to the elevator, and, when Scursey tried to get in too, shoved him back into the lobby. That was the end of the friendship between the Conners and Bert Scursey. It was more than that. It was the end of Harry Conner's stay at the Graydon. It was, in fact, the end of his stay in New

York City. He and Louise live in Oregon now, where Conner accepted a less important position than he had held in New York because the episode of Edith had turned him against Scursey, Mr. Bent, the Graydon, and the whole metropolitan area.

Anybody can handle the Frank Fulsomes of the world, but is there anything to be done about the Bert Scurseys? Can we so streamline our minds that the antics of the Scurseys roll off them like water off a duck's back? I don't think so. I believe the authors of the inspirational books don't think so, either, but are afraid to attack the subject. I imagine they have been hoping nobody would bring it up. Hardly anybody goes through life without encountering his Bert Scursey and having his life—and his mind—accordingly modified. I have known a dozen Bert Scurseys. I have often wondered what happened to some of their victims. There was, for example, the man who rang up a waggish friend of mine by mistake, having got a wrong number. "Is this the Shu-Rite Shoestore?" the caller asked, querulously. "Shu-Rite Shoestore, good morning!" said my friend, brightly. "Well," said the other, "I just called up to say that the shoes I bought there a week ago are shoddy. They're made, by God, of cardboard. I'm going to bring them in and show you. I want satisfaction!" "And you shall have it!" said my friend. "Our shoes are, as you say, shoddy. There have been many complaints, many complaints. Our shoes, I am afraid, simply go to pieces on the foot. We shall, of course, refund your money." I know another man who was always being roused out of bed by people calling a certain railroad which had a similar phone number. "When can I get a train to Buffalo?" a sour-voiced woman demanded one morning about seven o'clock. "Not till two A.M. tomorrow, Madam," said this man. "But that's ridiculous!" cried the woman, "I know," said the man, "and we realize that. Hence we include, in the regular fare, a taxi which will call for you in plenty of time to make the train. Where do you live?" The lady, slightly mollified, told him an address in the Sixties. "We'll have a cab there at one-thirty, Madam," he said. "The driver will handle your baggage." "Now I can count on that?" she said. "Certainly, Madam," he told her. "One-thirty, sharp."

Just what changes were brought about in that woman's character by that call, I don't know. But the thing might have altered the color and direction of her life, the pattern of her mind, the whole fabric of her nature. Thus we see that a person might build up a streamlined mind, a mind awakened to a new life, a new discipline, only to have the whole works shot to pieces by so minor and unpredictable a thing as a wrong telephone number. On the other hand, the undisciplined mind would never have the fortitude to consider a trip to Buffalo at two in the morning, nor would it have the determination to seek redress from a shoestore which had sold it a faulty pair of shoes. Hence the undisciplined mind runs far less chance of having its purposes thwarted, its plans distorted, its whole scheme and system wrenched out of line. The undisciplined mind, in short, is far better adapted to the confused world in which we live today than the streamlined mind. This is, I am afraid, no place for the streamlined mind.

3. The Case for the Daydreamer

ALL THE BOOKS IN MY EXTENSIVE LIBRARY ON TRAINING THE mind agree that realism, as against fantasy, reverie, daydreaming, and woolgathering, is a highly important thing. "Be a realist," says Dr. James L. Mursell, whose "Streamline Your Mind" I have already discussed. "Take a definite step to turn a dream into a reality," says Mrs. Dorothea Brande, the "Wake-Up-and-Live!" woman. They allow you a certain amount of reverie and daydreaming (no woolgathering), but only when it is purposeful, only when it is going to lead to realistic action and concrete achievement. In this insistence on reality I do not see as much profit as these Shapers of Success do. I have had a great deal of satisfaction and benefit out of daydreaming which never got me anywhere in their definition of getting somewhere. I am reminded, as an example, of an incident which occurred this last summer.

I had been travelling about the country attending dog shows. I was writing a series of pieces on these shows. Not being in the habit of carrying press cards, letters of introduction, or even, in some cases, the key to my car or the tickets to a show which I am on my way to attend, I had nothing by which to identify myself. I simply paid my way in, but at a certain dog show I determined to see if the officials in charge would give me a pass. I approached a large, heavy-set man who looked somewhat like Victor McLaglen. His name was Bustard. Mr. Bustard. "You'll have to see Mr. Bustard," a ticket-taker had told me. This Mr. Bustard was apparently

Child Making Flat Statements about a Gentleman's Personal Appearance

very busy trying to find bench space for old Miss Emily Van Winkle's Pomeranians, which she had entered at the last minute, and attending to a number of other matters. He glanced at me, saw that he outweighed me some sixty pounds, and decided to make short shrift of whatever it was I wanted. I explained I was writing an article about the show and would like a pass to get in. "Why, that's impossible!" he cried. "That's ridiculous! If I gave you a pass, I'd have to give a pass to everyone who came up and asked me for a pass!" I was pretty much overwhelmed. I couldn't, as is usual in these cases, think of anything to say except "I see." Mr. Bustard delivered a brief, snarling lecture on the subject of people who expect to get into dog shows free, unless they are showing dogs, and ended with "Are you showing dogs?" I tried to think of something sharp and well-turned. "No, I'm not showing any dogs," I said, coldly. Mr. Bustard abruptly turned his back on me and walked away.

As soon as Mr. Bustard disappeared, I began to think of things I should have said. I thought of a couple of sharp cracks on his name, the least pointed of which was Buzzard. Finely edged comebacks leaped to mind. Instead of going into the dog show—or following Mr. Bustard—I wandered up and down the streets of the town, improving on my retorts. I fancied a much more successful encounter with Mr. Bustard. In this fancied encounter, I, in fact, enraged Mr. Bustard. He lunged at me, whereupon, side-stepping agilely, I led with my left and floored him with a beautiful right to the jaw. "Try that one!" I cried aloud. "Mercy!" murmured an old lady who was passing me at the moment. I began to walk more rapidly; my heart took a definite lift. Some people, in my dream, were bending over Bustard, who was out cold. "Better take him home and let the other bustards pick his bones," I said. When I got back to the dog show, I was in high fettle.

After several months I still feel, when I think of Mr. Bustard, that I got the better of him. In a triumphant daydream, it seems to me, there is felicity and not defeat. You can't just take a humiliation and dismiss it from your mind, for it will crop up in your dreams, but neither can you safely carry a dream into reality in the case of an insensitive man like Mr. Bustard who outweighs you by sixty pounds. The thing to do is to visualize a triumph over the humiliator so vividly and insistently that it becomes, in effect, an actuality. I went on with my daydreams about Mr. Bustard. All that day at the dog show I played tricks on him in my imagination, I outgeneralled him, I made him look silly, I had him on the run. I would imagine myself sitting in a living room. It was late at night. Outside it was raining heavily. The doorbell rang. I went to the door and opened it, and a man was standing there. "I wonder if you would let me use your phone?" he asked. "My car has broken down." It was, of all people, Mr. Bustard. You can imagine my jibes, my sarcasm, my repartee, my shutting the door in his face at the end. After a whole afternoon of this kind of thing, I saw Mr. Bustard on my way out of the show. I actually felt a little sorry about the tossing around I had given him. I gave him an enigmatic, triumphant smile which must have worried him a great deal. He must have wondered what I had been up to, what superior of his I had seen, what I had done to get back at him—who, after all, I was.

Now, let us figure Dr. Mursell in my place. Let us suppose that Dr. Mursell went up to Mr. Bustard and asked him for a pass to the dog show on the ground that he could streamline the dog's intuition. I fancy that Mr. Bustard also outweighs Dr. Mursell by sixty pounds and is in better fighting trim; we men who write treatises on the mind are not likely to be in as good shape as men who run dog shows. Dr. Mursell, then, is rebuffed, as I was. If he tries to get back at Mr. Bustard right there and then, he will find himself saying "I see" or "Well, I didn't know" or, at best, "I just asked you." Even the streamlined mind runs into this Blockage, as the psychologists call it. Dr. Mursell, like myself, will go away and think up better things to say, but, being a realist dedicated to carrying a dream into actuality, he will perforce have to come back and tackle Mr. Bustard again. If Mr. Bustard's patience gives out, or if he is truly stung by some crack of the Doctor's he is likely to begin shoving, or snap his fingers, or say "'Raus!," or even tweak the Doctor's nose. Dr. Mursell, in that case, would get into no end of trouble. Realists are always getting into trouble. They miss the sweet, easy victories of the day-dreamer.

I do not pretend that the daydream cannot be carried too far. If at this late date, for instance, I should get myself up to look as much like Mr. Bustard as possible and then, gazing into the bathroom mirror, snarl "Bustard, you dog!," that would be carrying the daydream too far. One should never run the risk of identifying oneself with the object of one's scorn. I have no idea what complexes and neuroses might lie that way. The mental experts could tell you—or, if they couldn't, they would anyway.

Now let us turn briefly to the indomitable Mrs. Brande, eight of whose precious words of advice have, the ads for her book tell us, changed the lives of 860,000 people, or maybe it is 86,000,000—Simon & Schuster published her book. (These words are "act as if it were impossible to fail," in case your life hasn't been changed.) Discussing realistic action as against the daydream, she takes up the case of a person, any person, who dreams about going to Italy but is getting nowhere. The procedure she suggests for such a person is threefold: (1) read a current newspaper in Italian, buy some histories, phrase books, and a small grammar; (2) put aside a small coin each day; (3) do something in your spare time to make money—"if it is nothing more than to sit with children while their parents are at parties." (I have a quick picture of the parents reeling from party to party, but that is beside the point.)

I can see the newspaper and the books intensifying the dream, but I can't somehow see them getting anybody to Italy. As for putting a small coin aside each day, everybody who has tried it knows that it does not work out. At the end of three weeks you usually have $2.35 in the pig bank or the cooky jar, a dollar and a half of which you have to use for something besides Italy, such as a C.O.D. package. At that rate, all that you would have in the bank or the jar at the end of six years would be about $87.45. Within the next six years Italy will probably be at war, and even if you were well enough to travel after all that time, you couldn't get into the country. The disappointment of a dream nursed for six years, with a reality in view that did not eventuate, would be enough to embitter a person for life. As for this business of sitting with children while their parents are at parties, anybody who has done it knows that no trip to anywhere, even Utopia, would be worth it. Very few people can sit with children, especially children other than their own, more than an hour and a half without having their dispositions and even their characters badly mauled about. In fifteen minutes the average child whose parents are at a party can make enough flat statements of fact about one's personal appearance and ask enough pointed questions about one's private life to send one away feeling that there is little, if any, use in going on with anything at all, let alone a trip to Italy.

The long and hard mechanics of reality which these inspirationalists suggest are, it seems to me, far less satisfactory than the soft routine of a dream. The dreamer builds up for himself no such towering and uncertain structure of hope; he has no depleted cooky jar to shake his faith in himself. It is significant that the line "Oh, to be in England now that April's there," which is a definite dream line, is better known than any line the poet wrote about actually being in England. (I guess *that* will give the inspirationalists something to think about.) You can sit up with children if you want to, you can put a dime a day in an empty coffee tin, you can read the Fascist viewpoint in an Italian newspaper, but when it comes to a choice between the dream and the reality of present-day Italy, I personally shall sit in a corner by the fire and read "The Ring and the Book." And in the end it will probably be me who sends you a postcard from Italy, which you can put between the pages of the small grammar or the phrase book.

4. A Dozen Disciplines

MRS. DOROTHEA BRANDE, WHOSE THEORY OF HOW TO GET TO Italy I discussed in the preceding pages, has a chapter in her "Wake Up and Live!" which suggests twelve specific disciplines. The purpose of these disciplines, she says, is to make our minds keener and more flexible. I'll take them up in order and show why it is no use for Mrs. Brande to try to sharpen and limber up my mind, if these disciplines are all she has to offer. I quote them as they were quoted in a Simon & Schuster advertisement for the book, because the advertisement puts them more succinctly than Mrs. Brande does herself.

"1. Spend one hour a day without speaking except in answer to direct questions."

No hour of the day goes by that I am not in some minor difficulty which could easily become major if I did not shout for help. Just a few hours ago, for example, I found myself in a dilemma that has become rather familiar about my house: I had got tied up in a typewriter ribbon. The whole thing had come unwound from the spool and was wound around me. What started as an unfortunate slip of the hand slowly grew into an enormous involvement. To have gone a whole hour waiting for someone to show up and ask me a question could not conceivably have improved my mind. Two minutes of silence now and then is all right, but that is as far as I will go.

"2. Think one hour a day about one subject exclusively."

Such as what, for example? At forty-two, I have spent a

great many hours thinking about all sorts of subjects, and there is not one of them that I want to go back to for a whole solid hour. I can pretty well cover as much of any subject as I want to in fifteen minutes. Sometimes in six. Furthermore, it would be impossible for me, or for Mrs. Brande, or for Simon & Schuster to think for an hour exclusively on one

American Male Tied up in Typewriter Ribbon

subject. What is known as "psychological association" would be bound to come into the thing. For instance, let us say that I decide to think for a solid hour about General Grant's horse (as good a subject as any at a time when practically all subjects are in an unsettled state). The fact that it is General Grant's horse would remind me of General Grant's beard and that would remind me of Charles Evans Hughes and that would remind me of the NRA. And so it would go. If I resolutely went back to General Grant's horse again, I would, by association, begin thinking about General Lee's horse, which was a much more famous horse, a horse named Traveller. I doubt if Mrs. Brande even knows the name of General Grant's horse, much less enough about it to keep her mind occupied for sixty minutes. I mean sixty minutes of real constructive thinking that would get her somewhere. Sixty minutes of thinking of any kind is bound to lead to confusion and unhappiness.

"3. Write a letter without using the first person singular." What for? To whom? About what? All I could possibly think of to write would be a letter to a little boy telling him how to build a rabbit hutch, and I don't know how to build a rabbit hutch very well. I never knew a little boy who couldn't tell me more about building a rabbit hutch than I could tell him. Nobody in my family was ever good at building rabbit hutches, although a lot of us raised rabbits. I have sometimes wondered how we managed it. I remember the time that my father offered to help me and my two brothers build a rabbit hutch out of planks and close-meshed chicken wire. Somehow or other he got inside of the cage after the wire had been put up around the sides and over the top, and he began to monkey with the stout door. I don't know exactly what happened, but he shut the door and it latched securely and he was locked in with the rabbits. The place was a shambles before he got out, because nobody was home at the time and he couldn't get his hand through the wire to unlatch the door. He had his derby on in the hutch all during his captivity and that added to his discomfiture. I remember, too, that we boys (we were not yet in our teens) didn't at first know what the word "hutch" meant, but we had got hold of a pamphlet on the subject, which my brother Herman read with great care. One sentence in the pamphlet read, "The rabbits' hutches should be cleaned thoroughly once a week." It was this admonition which caused my brother one day to get each of the astonished rabbits down in turn and wash its haunches thoroughly with soap and water.

No, I do not think that anybody can write a letter without using the first person singular. Even if it could be done, I see no reason to do it.

"4. Talk for fifteen minutes without using the first person."

No can do. No going to *try* to do, either. You can't teach an old egoist new persons.

"5. Write a letter in a placid, successful tone, sticking to facts about yourself."

Now we're getting somewhere, except that nothing is more stuffy and conceited-sounding than a "placid, successful tone." The way to write about yourself is to let yourself go. Build it up, exaggerate, make yourself out a person of importance. Fantasy is the food for the mind, not facts. Are we going to wake up and live or are we going to sit around writing factual letters in a placid, successful tone?

"6. Pause before you enter any crowded room and consider your relations with the people in it."

Now, Mrs. Brande, if I did that there would be only about one out of every thirty-two crowded rooms I approached that I would ever enter. I always shut my mind and plunge into a crowded room as if it were a cold bath. That gives me and everybody in the room a clean break, a fresh starting point. There is no good in rehashing a lot of old relations with people. The longer I paused outside a crowded room and thought about my relations with the people in it, the more inclined I would be to go back to the checkroom and get my hat and coat and go home. That's the best place for a person, anyway—home.

"7. Keep a new acquaintance talking, exclusively about himself."

And then tiptoe quietly away. He'll never notice the dif-ference.

"8. Talk exclusively about yourself for fifteen minutes."

And see what happens.

"9. Eliminate the phrases 'I mean' and 'As a matter of fact' from your conversation."

Okie-dokie.

"10. Plan to live two hours a day according to a rigid time schedule."

Well, I usually wake up at nine in the morning and lie there till eleven, if that would do. Of course, I could *plan* to do a lot of different things over a period of two hours, but if I actually started out to accomplish them I would instantly begin to worry about whether I was going to come out on the dot in the end and I wouldn't do any of them right. It would be like waiting for the pistol shot during the last quarter of a close football game. This rule seems to me to be devised simply to make men irritable and jumpy.

"11. Set yourself twelve instructions on pieces of paper, shuffle them, and follow the one you draw. Here are a few samples: 'Go twelve hours without food.' 'Stay up all night and work.' 'Say nothing all day except in answer to questions.'"

In that going twelve hours without food, do you mean I can have drinks? Because if I can have drinks, I can do it easily. As for staying up all night and working, I know all about that: that simply turns night into day and day into night. I once got myself into such a state staying up all night that I was always having orange juice and boiled eggs at twilight and was just ready for lunch after everybody had gone to bed. I had to go away to a sanitarium to get turned around. As for saying nothing all day except in answer to questions, what am I to do if a genial colleague comes into my office and says, "I think your mother is one of the nicest people I ever met" or "I was thinking about giving you that twenty dollars you lent me"? Do I just stare at him and walk out of the room? I lose enough friends, and money, the way it is.

"12. Say 'Yes' to every reasonable request made of you in the course of one day."

All right, start making some. I can't think of a single one offhand. The word "reasonable" has taken a terrible tossing around in my life—both personal and business. If you mean watering the geraniums, I'll do that. If you mean walking around Central Park with you for the fresh air and exercise, you are crazy.

Has anybody got any more sets of specific disciplines? If anybody has, they've got to be pretty easy ones if I am going to wake up and live. It's mighty comfortable dozing here and waiting for the end.

5. How to Adjust Yourself to Your Work

I FIND THAT THE INSPIRATIONAL BOOKS ARE FREQUENTLY DISposed to touch, with pontifical cheerfulness or owlish mysticism, on the problem of how to get along in the business world, how to adjust yourself to your employer and to your fellow-worker. It seems to me that in this field the trainers of the mind, both lady and gentleman, are at their unhappiest. Let us examine, in this our fourth lesson, what Mrs. Dorothea Brande, who is reputedly changing the lives of almost as many people as the Oxford Group, has to say on the subject. She presents the case of a man (she calls him "you") who is on the executive end of an enterprise and feels he should be on the planning end. "In that case," she writes, "your problem is to bring your talents to the attention of your superior officers with as little crowding and bustling as possible. Learn to write clear, short, definite memoranda and present them to your immediate superior until you are perfectly certain that he will never act upon them. In no other circumstances are you justified in going over his head." Very well, let us start from Mrs. Brande's so-called point of justification in going over your superior's head, and see what happens.

Let us suppose that you have presented your favorite memoranda to your immediate superior, Mr. Sutphen, twice and nothing has happened. You are still not perfectly certain that

B. J. ("Two-Gun") Winfall, of New York City

he will never act upon them. To be sure, he has implied, or perhaps even said in so many words, that he never will, but you think that maybe you have always caught him at the wrong moment. So you get up your memoranda a third time. Mr. Sutphen, glancing at your paper and noting that it is that same old plan for tearing out the west wall, or speeding up the out-of-town truck deliveries, or substituting colored lights for bells, is pretty well convinced that all you do in your working hours is write out memoranda. He figures that you are probably suffering from a mild form of monomania and determines to dispense with your services if you submit any memoranda again. After waiting a week and hearing nothing from Mr. Sutphen, you decide, in accordance with Mrs. Brande's suggestion, to go over his head and take the matter up with Mr. Leffley. In doing so, you will not be stringing along with me. I advise you not to go over Mr. Sutphen's head to Mr. Leffley; I advise you to quit writing memoranda and get to work.

The Mr. Leffleys of this country have enough to do the way it is, or think they have, and they do not like to have you come to them with matters which should be taken up with the Mr. Sutphens. They are paying the Mr. Sutphens to keep you and your memoranda from suddenly bobbing up in front of them. In the first place, if you accost the Mr. Leffleys personally, you become somebody else in the organization whose name and occupation they are supposed to know. Already they know who too many people are. In the second place, the Mr. Leffleys do not like to encounter unexpected memoranda. It gives them a suspicion that there is a looseness somewhere; it destroys their confidence that things are going all right; it shakes their faith in the Mr. Sutphens—and in the Mr. Bairds, the Mr. Crowfuts, and the old Miss Bendleys who are supposed to see that every memorandum has been filed away, or is being acted on. I know of one young man who was always sending to his particular Mr. Leffley, over Mr. Sutphen's head, memoranda done up in limp-leather covers and tied with ribbon, this to show that he was not only clear, short, and definite, but neat. Mr. Leffley did not even glance between the leather covers; he simply told Miss Bendley to turn the thing over to Mr. Sutphen, who had already seen it. The young man was let go and is now a process-server. Keep, I say, your clear, short, and definite memoranda to yourself. If Mr. Sutphen has said no, he means no. If he has taken no action, no action is going to be taken. People who are all the time submitting memoranda are put down as jealous, disgruntled, and vaguely dangerous. Employers do not want them around. Sooner or later Mr. Sutphen, or Mr. Leffley himself, sees to it that a printed slip, clear, short, and definite, is put in their pay envelopes.

My own experience, and the experience of many of my friends, in dealing with superiors has covered a wide range of crucial situations of which these success writers appear to be oblivious and for which they therefore have no recommended course of action (which is probably just as well). I am reminded of the case of Mr. Russell Soames, a friend of mine, who worked for a man whom we shall call Mr. B. J. Winfall. This Winfall, some five or six years ago, in the days when Capone was at large and wholesale shootings were common in Chicago, called Soames into his office and said, "Soames, I'm going out to Chicago on that Weltmer deal and I want you to go along with me." "All right, Mr. Winfall," said Soames. They went to Chicago and had been there only four or five hours when they were calling each other Russell and B. J. and fighting for the check at the bar. On the third day, B. J. called Russell into his bedroom (B. J. had not left his bedroom in thirty-six hours) and said, "Russell, before we go back to New York, I want to see a dive, a hideout, a joint. I want to see these gangsters in their haunts. I want to see them in action, by God, if they ever get into action. I think most of it is newspaper talk. Your average gangster is a yellow cur." B. J. poured himself another drink from a bottle on his bedside table and repeated, "A yellow cur." Drink, as you see, made B. J. pugnacious (he had already gone through his amorous phase). Russell Soames tried to argue his chief out of this perilous plan, but failed. When Russell would not contact the right parties to arrange for B. J.'s little expedition, B. J. contacted them himself, and finally got hold of a men who knew a man who could get them into a regular hangout of gorillas and finger men.

Along about midnight of the fourth day in Chicago, B. J. Winfall was ready to set out for the dive. He wore a cap, which covered his bald spot, and he had somehow got hold of a cheap, ill-fitting suit, an ensemble which he was pleased to believe gave him the effect of a hardboiled fellow; as a matter of fact, his nose glasses, his pink jowls, and his paunch betrayed him instantly for what he was, a sedentary businessman. Soames strove to dissuade his boss, even in the taxi on their way to the tough spot, but Winfall pooh-poohed him. "Pooh pooh, Russell," he snarled out of the corner of his mouth, unfamiliarly. "These kind of men are rats." He had brought a flask with him and drank copiously from it. "Rats," he said, "of the first order. The first order, Russell, my boy." Soames kept repeating that he felt B. J. was underating the dangerousness of the Chicago gangster and begged him to be on his good behavior when they got to the joint, if only for the sake of B. J.'s wife and children and his (Russell's) old mother. He exacted a reluctant promise that B. J. would behave himself, but he was by no means easy in his mind when their taxi finally stopped in front of a low, dark building in a far, dark street. "Leave it to me, Russell, my boy," said B. J. as they got out of the cab. "Leave it to me." Their driver refused to wait, and Russell, who paid him off, was just in time to restrain his employer from beating on the door of the place with both fists. Russell himself knocked, timidly. A thin Italian with deadly eyes opened the door a few inches, Russell mentioned a name, falteringly, and the man admitted them.

As Russell described it to me later, it was a dingy, smoky place with a rough bar across the back attended by a liver-faced barman with a dirty rag thrown over one shoulder, and only one eye. Leaning on the bar and sitting at tables were a lot of small tough-faced men. They all looked up sullenly when Russell and B. J. walked in. Russell felt that there was a movement of hands in pockets. Smiling amiably, blinking nervously, Russell took his companion's arm, but the latter broke away, strode to the bar, and shouted for whiskey. The bartender fixed his one eye on B. J. with the glowering, steady gaze Jack Dempsey used to give his opponents in the ring. He took his time slamming glasses and a bottle down on the bar. B. J. filled a glass, tossed it off, turned heavily, and faced the roomful of men. "I'm Two-Gun Winfall from New York City!" he shouted. "Anybody *want* anything?"

By the most cringing, obsequious explanations and apologies, Russell Soames managed to get himself and his boss out of the place alive. The secret of accomplishing such a feat as he accomplished that night is not to be found in any of the inspirational books. Not a single one of their impressive bits of advice would get you anywhere. Take Mrs. Brande's now famous italicized exhortation, *"Act as if it were impossible to fail."* Wasn't B. J. Winfall doing exactly that? And was that any way to act in this particular situation? It was not. It was Russell Soames' craven apologies, his abject humility, his (as he told me later) tearful admission that he and B. J. were just drunken bums with broken hearts, that got them out of there alive. The success writers would never suggest, or even tolerate, any such behavior. If Russell Soames had followed their bright, hard rules of general conduct, he would be in his grave today and B. J. Winfall's wife would be a widow.

If Mrs. Brande is not, as in the case of the memoranda-writer, suggesting a relationship with a superior which I believe we have demonstrated to be dangerous and unworkable (and missing altogether the important problem of how to handle one's employer in his more difficult moments), she is dwelling mystically on the simple and realistic subject of how to deal with one's fellow-workers. Thus, in embroidering the theme that imagination can help you with your fellow-workers, she writes, "When you have seen this, you can work out a code for yourself which will remove many of the irritations and dissatisfactions of your daily work. Have you ever been amused and enlightened by seeing a familiar room from the top of the stepladder; or, in mirrors set at angles to each other, seen yourself as objectively for a second or two as anybody else in the room? It is that effect you should strive for in imagination." Here again I cannot hold with the dear lady. The nature of imagination, as she describes it, would merely terrify the average man. The idea of bringing such a distorted viewpoint of himself into his relation with his fellow-workers would twist his personality laboriously out of shape and, in the end, appall his fellow-workers. Men who catch an unfamiliar view of a room from the top of a stepladder are neither amused nor enlightened; they have a quick, gasping moment of vertigo which turns rapidly into plain terror. No man likes to see a familiar thing at an unfamiliar angle, or in an unfamiliar light, and this goes, above all things, for his own face. The glimpses that men get of themselves in mirrors set at angles to each other upset them for days. Frequently they shave in the dark for weeks thereafter. To ask a man to steadily contemplate this thing he has seen fleetingly in a mirror and to figure it as dealing with his fellow-workers day by day is to ask him to abandon his own character and to step into another, which he both disowns and dislikes. Split personality could easily result, leading to at least fifteen of the thirty-three "varieties of obliquity" which Mr. David Seabury lists in his "How to Worry Successfully," among them Cursory Enumeration, Distortion of Focus, Nervous Hesitation (superinduced by Ambivalence), Pseudo-Practicality, Divergency, Retardation, Emotionalized Compilation, Negative Dramatization, Rigidism, Secondary Adaptation, False Externalization, Non-Validation, Closure, and Circular Brooding.

I don't know why I am reminded at this point of my Aunt Kate Obetz, but I am. She was a woman without any imaginative la-di-da, without any working code save that of direct action, who ran a large dairy farm near Sugar Grove, Ohio, after her husband's death, and ran it successfully. One day something went wrong with the cream separator, and one of her hands came to her and said nobody on the farm could fix it. Should they send to town for a man? "No!" shouted my Aunt Kate. "I'll fix it myself!" Shouldering her way past a number of dairy workers, farm hands and members of her family, she grasped the cream separator and began monkeying with it. In a short time she had reduced it to even more pieces than it had been in when she took hold of it. She couldn't fix it. She was just making things worse. At length, she turned on the onlookers and bawled, "Why doesn't somebody take this goddam thing away from me?" Here was a woman as far out of the tradition of inspirationalist conduct as she could well be. She admitted failure; she had no code for removing irritations and dissatisfactions; she viewed herself as in a single mirror, directly; she lost her temper; she swore in the presence of subordinates; she confessed complete surrender in the face of a difficult problem; she didn't think of herself as a room seen from the top of a stepladder. And yet her workmen and her family continued to love and respect her. Somebody finally took the cream separator away from her; somehow it was fixed. Her failure did not show up in my aunt's character; she was always the same as ever.

For true guidance and sound advice in the business world we find, I think, that the success books are not the place to look, which is pretty much what I thought we would find all along.

6. Anodynes for Anxieties

I SHOULD LIKE TO BEGIN THIS LESSON WITH A QUOTATION FROM Mr. David Seabury's "How to Worry Successfully." When things get really tough for me, I always turn to this selection and read it through twice, the second time backward, and while it doesn't make me feel fine, exactly, it makes me feel better. Here it is:

"If you are indulging in gloomy fears which follow each other round and round until the brain reels, there are two possible procedures:

"First, quit circling. It doesn't matter where you cease whirling, as long as you stop.

"Second, if you cannot find a constant, think of something as different from the fact at which you stopped as you possibly can. Imagine what would happen if you mixed that contrast into your situation. If nothing results to clarify your worry, try another set of opposites and continue the process until you do get a helpful answer. If you persist, you will soon solve any ordinary problem."

I first read this remarkable piece of advice two months ago and I vaguely realized then that in it, somewhere, was a strangely familiar formula, not, to be sure, a formula that would ever help me solve anything, but a formula for something or other. And one day I hit on it. It is the formula by which the Marx brothers construct their dialogue. Let us take their justly famous scene in which Groucho says to Chico, "It is my belief that the missing picture is hidden in the house next door." Here Groucho has ceased whirling, or circling, and has stopped at a fact, that fact being his belief that the picture is hidden in the house next door. Now Chico, in accordance with Mr. Seabury's instructions, thinks of something as different from that fact as he possibly can. He says, "There isn't any house next door." Thereupon Groucho "mixes that contrast into his situation." He says, "Then we'll build one!"

The Filing-card System

Mr. Seabury says, "If you persist you will soon solve any ordinary problem." He underestimates the power of his formula. If you persist, you will soon solve anything at all, no matter how impossible. That way, of course, lies madness, but I would be the last person to say that madness is not a solution.

It will come as no surprise to you, I am sure, that throughout the Mentality Books with which we have been concerned there runs a thin, wavy line of this particular kind of Marxist philosophy. Mr. Seabury's works are heavily threaded with it, but before we continue with him, let us turn for a moment to dear Dorothea Brande, whose "Wake Up and Live!" has changed the lives of God knows how many people by this time. Writes Mrs. Brande, "One of the most famous men in America constantly sends himself postcards, and occasionally notes. He explained the card sending as being his way of relieving his memory of unnecessary details. In his pocket he carries a few postals addressed to his office. I was with him one threatening day when he looked out the restaurant window, drew a card from his pocket, and wrote on it. Then he threw it across the table to me with a grin. It was addressed to himself at his office, and said. 'Put your raincoat with your hat.' At the office he had other cards addressed to himself at home."

We have here a muzziness of thought so enormous that it is difficult to analyze. First of all, however, the ordinary mind is struck by the obvious fact that the famous American in question has, to relieve his memory of unnecessary details, burdened that memory with the details of having to have postcards at his office, in his pockets, and at his home all the time. If it isn't harder to remember always to take self-addressed postcards with you wherever you go than to remember to put your raincoat with your hat when the weather looks threatening, then you and I will eat the postcards or even the raincoat. Threatening weather itself is a natural sharp reminder of one's raincoat, but what is there to remind one that one is running out of postcards? And supposing the famous man does run out of postcards, what does he do—hunt up a Western Union and send himself a telegram? You can see how monstrously wrapped up in the coils of his own little memory system this notable American must soon find himself. There is something about this system of buying postcards, addressing them to oneself, writing messages on them, and then mailing them that is not unlike one of those elaborate Rube Goldberg contraptions taking up a whole room and involving bicycles, shotguns, parrots, and little colored boys, all set up for the purpose of eliminating the bother of, let us say, setting an alarm clock. Somehow, I can just see Mrs. Brande's famous man at his desk. On it there are two phones, one in the Bryant exchange, the other in the Vanderbilt exchange. When he wants to remind himself of something frightfully urgent, he picks up the Bryant phone and calls the Vanderbilt number, and when that phone rings, he picks it up and says hello and then carries on a conversation with himself. "Remember tomorrow is wifey's birthday!" he shouts over one phone. "O.K.!" he bawls back into the other. This, it seems to me, is a fair enough extension of the activities of our famous gentleman. There is no doubt, either, but that the two-phone system would make the date stick more sharply in his mind than if he just wrote it down on a memo pad. But to intimate that all this shows a rational disciplining of the mind, a development of the power of the human intellect, an approach to the Masterful Adjustment of which our Success Writers are so enamored, is to intimate that when Groucho gets the house built next door, the missing picture will be found in it.

When it comes to anxieties and worries, Mr. Seabury's elaborate systems for their relief or solution make the device of Mrs. Brande's famous American look childishly simple. Mr. Seabury knows, and apparently approves of, a man "who assists himself by fancied interviews with wise advisers. If he is in money difficulties, he has mental conversations with a banker; when business problems press, he seeks the aid of a great industrialist and talks his problems over with this ghostly friend until he comes to a definite conclusion." Here, unless I am greatly mistaken, we have wish fulfillment, fantasy, reverie, and woolgathering at their most perilous. This kind of goings-on with a ghostly banker or industrialist is an escape mechanism calculated to take a man so far from reality he might never get back. I tried it out myself one night just before Christmas when I had got down to $60 in the bank and hadn't bought half my presents yet. I went to bed early that night and had Mr. J. P. Morgan call on me. I didn't have to go to his office; he heard I was in some difficulty and called on me, dropping everything else. He came right into my bedroom and sat on the edge of the bed. "Well, well, well," he said, "what's this I hear about you being down?" "I'm not so good, J. P.," I said, smiling wanly. "We'll have the roses back in those cheeks in no time," he said. "I'm not really sick," I told him. "I just need money." "Well, well, well," he exclaimed, heartily, "is *that* all we need?" "Yes, sir," I said. He took out a checkbook. "How'd a hundred thousand dollars do?" he asked, jovially. "That would be all right," I said. "Could you give it to me in cash, though—in tens and twenties?" "Why, certainly, my boy, certainly," said Mr. Morgan, and he gave me the money in tens and twenties. "Thank you very much, J. P.," I said. "Not at all, Jim, not at all!" cried my ghostly friend. "What's going on in there?" shouted my wife, who was in the next room. It seems that I had got to talking out loud, first in my own voice and then louder, and with more authority, in Mr. Morgan's. "Nothing, darling," I answered. "Well, cut it out," she said. The depression that settled over me when I realized that I was just where I had been when I started to talk with Mr. Morgan was frightful. I haven't got completely over it yet.

This mental-conversation business is nothing, however, compared to what Mr. Seabury calls "picture-puzzle making in worry." To employ this aid in successful thinking, you have to have fifty or sixty filing cards, or blank cards of some kind or other. To show you how it works, let us follow the case history of one Frank Fordson as Mr. Seabury relates it. It seems that this Fordson, out of work, is walking the streets. "He enters store after store with discouraged, pessimistic proprietors. There are poor show windows and dusty sidewalks. They make Frank morbid. His mind feels heavy. He wishes he could happen on a bright idea." He does, as you shall see. Frank consults a psychologist. This psychologist tells him to take fifty filing cards and write on each of them a fact connected with his being out of work. So he writes on one "out of work" and on another "dusty sidewalks" and on another "poor show windows," etc. You and I would not be able to write down more than fifteen things like that before getting off onto something else, like "I hate Joe Grubig" or "Now is the time for all good men," but Frank can do fifty in his stride, all about how tough things are. This would so depress the ordinary mind that it would go home to bed, but not Frank. Frank puts all of the fifty cards on the floor of the psychologist's office and begins to couple them up at random, finally bringing into accidental juxtaposition the one saying "out of work" and one saying "dull sign." Well, out of this haphazard arrangement of the cards, Frank, Mr. Seabury says, got an idea. He went to a hardware store the next day and offered to shine the store's dull sign if the proprietor would give him a can of polish and let him keep what was left. Then he went around shining other signs, for money, and made $3 that day. Ten days later he got a job as a window-dresser and, before the year was out, a "position in advertising."

"Take one of your own anxieties," writes Mr. Seabury. "Analyze it so as to recall all the factors. Write three score of these on separate cards. Move the cards about on the floor into as many different relations as possible. Study each combination." Mr. Seabury may not know it, but the possible different relations of sixty cards would run into the millions.

If a man actually studied each of these combinations, it would at least keep him off the streets and out of trouble—and also out of the advertising business, which would be something. after all. Toy soldiers, however, are more fun.

Now, if this kind of playing with filing cards doesn't strike your fancy, there is the "Worry Play." Let me quote Mr. Seabury again. "You should write out a description of your worry," he says, "divide it into three acts and nine scenes, as if it were a play, and imagine it on the stage, or in the movies, with various endings. Look at it as impersonally as you would look at a comedy and you might be surprised at the detachment you would gain." I have tried very hard to do this. I try out all these suggestions. They have taken up most of my time and energy for the past six months and got me into such a state that my doctor says I can do only three more of these articles at the outside before I go to a sanitarium. A few years ago I had an old anxiety and I was reminded of it by this "Worry Play" idea. Although this old anxiety has been dead and gone for a long time, it kept popping up in my mind because, of all the worries I ever had, it seemed to lend itself best to the drama. I tried not to think about it, but there it was, and I finally realized I would have to write it out and imagine it on the stage before I could dismiss it from my consciousness and get back to work. Well, it ran almost as long as "Mourning Becomes Electra" and took me a little over three weeks to dramatize. Then, when I thought I was rid of it, I dreamed one night I had sold the movie rights, and so I had to adapt it to the movies (a Mr. Sam Maschino, a movie agent, kept bobbing up in my dreams, hectoring me). This took another two weeks. I could not, however, attain this detachment that Mr. Seabury talks about. Since the old anxiety was my own anxiety, I was the main character in it. Sometimes, for as many as fifteen pages of the play script and the movie continuity, I was the only person on the set. I visualized myself in the main rôle, naturally—having rejected Leslie Howard, John Gielgud, and Lionel Barrymore for one reason or another. I was lousy in the part, too, and that worried me. Hence I advise you not to write out your worries in the form of a play. It is simpler to write them out on sixty pieces of paper and juggle them around. Or talk about them to J. P. Morgan. Or send postcards to yourself about them. There are a number of solutions for anxieties which I believe are better than any of these, however: go out and skate, or take in a basketball game, or call on a girl. Or burn up a lot of books.

7. The Conscious vs. The Unconscious

IT IS HIGH TIME THAT WE WERE GETTING AROUND TO A CONSIDERAtion of the magnum opus of Louis E. Bisch, M.D., Ph.D., formerly Professor of Neuropsychiatry at the New York Polyclinic Medical School and Hospital, and Associate in Educational Psychology at Columbia University, and the author of "Be Glad You're Neurotic." Some of the reassuring chapter titles of his popular treatise are "I'm a Neurotic Myself and Delighted," "You Hate Yourself. No Wonder!," "No, You're Not Going Insane Nor Will Any of Your Fears Come True," "Are Your Glands on Friendly Terms?," and "Of Course Your Sex Life Is Far from Satisfactory." Some of you will be satisfied with just these titles and will not go on to the book itself, on the ground that you have a pretty good idea of it already. I should like, however, to have you turn with me to Chapter VII, one of my favorite chapters in all psychomentology, "Your Errors and Compulsions Are Calls for Help."

The point of this chapter, briefly, is that the unconscious mind often opposes what the conscious mind wants to do or say, and frequently trips it up with all kinds of evasions, deceits, gags, and kicks in the pants. Our popular psychiatrists try to make these mysteries clear to the layman by the use of simple, homely language, and I am trying to do the same.

Dr. Bisch relates a lot of conflicts and struggles that take place between the Hercules of the Conscious and the Augean Stables of the Unconscious (that is my own colorful, if somewhat labored, metaphor and I don't want to see any of the other boys swiping it). "I myself," writes Dr. Bisch, "forgot the number of a hospital where I was to deliver a lecture when

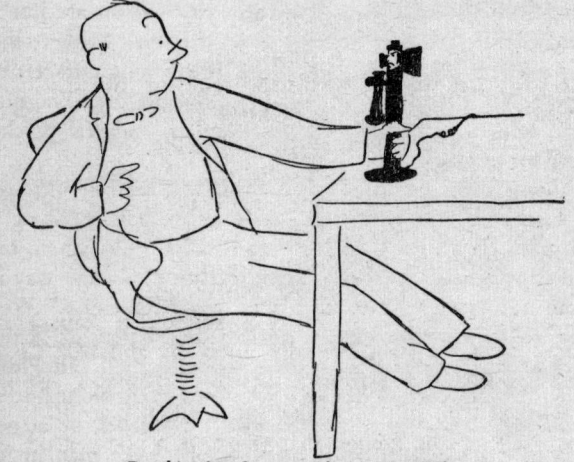

Psychiatrist about to Phone His Wife

I was about to apologize for my delay. I had talked to that particular hospital perhaps a hundred times before. This was the first time, however, that I was consciously trying to do what unconsciously I did not want to do." If you want unconsciously as well as consciously to call a hospital one hundred times out of one hundred and one, I say your conscious and unconscious are on pretty friendly terms. I say you are doing fine. This little experience of Dr. Bisch's is merely to give you a general idea of the nature of the chapter and to ease you into the discussion gently. There are many more interesting examples of conflict and error, of compulsion and obsession, to come. "A colleague," goes on Dr. Bisch, "told me that when he decided to telephone his wife to say he could not be home for dinner he dialled three wrong numbers before he got his own. 'It's because she always flares up when I'm detained at the office,' he explained." This shows that psychiatrists are just as scared of their wives as anybody else. Of course, I believe that this particular psychiatrist dialled the three wrong numbers on purpose. In the case of all husbands, both neurotic and normal, this is known as sparring for time and has no real psychological significance.

I almost never, I find in going slowly and carefully through Dr. Bisch's chapter, taking case histories in their order, agree with him. He writes, "The appearance of persons whom one dislikes or is jealous of, who have offended in some way or whom one fears, tend to be blotted from the mind." Well, some twelve years ago I knew, disliked, was jealous of, feared, and had been offended by a man whom I shall call Philip Vause. His appearance has not only not been blotted from my mind, it hasn't even tended to be. I can call it up as perfectly as if I were holding a photograph of the man in my hand. In nightmares I still dream of Philip Vause. When, in these dreams, I get on subways, he is the guard; when I fly through the air, the eagle that races with me has his face; when I climb the Eiffel Tower, there he is at the top, his black hair roached back, the mole on the left cheek, the thin-lipped smile, and all. Dr. Bisch goes on to say that "the more disagreeable an incident, the deeper is it finally repressed." To which he adds, "The recollection of the pain attending child-birth never lingers long." He has me there.

Dr. Bisch proceeds from that into this: "A man who mislays

his hat either dislikes it, wants a new one, experienced unpleasantness when last he wore it, or he does not want to go out. And what you lose you may be sure you do not value, even if it be your wedding ring. Psychologists claim that we lose things because we want to be rid of them or the association they carry, but that we are unwilling to admit the fact to ourselves and actually throw the thing away." This shows you pretty clearly, I think, the point psychologists have reached. I call it mysticism, but I am a polite fellow; you can call it anything you want to. Under any name, it isn't getting us anywhere. Every husband whose tearful wife has lost her wedding ring will now begin to brood, believing (if he strings along with the psychologists instead of with me) that the little darling threw it away, because she is really in love with Philip Vause, and that her tears over her loss are as phony as the plight of a panhandler's family. Let us leave all the sad young couples on the point of separating and go on to Dr. Bisch's analysis of a certain man.

"A certain man," writes Dr. Bisch, "forgot to wind the alarm on several occasions, in consequence of which he was late for work. He also forgot his keys on two occasions and had to wake up his wife in the early hours of the morning. Twice he forgot the furnace at night with the result that there was no heat the next day. In this case the unconscious was trying to tell him that he did not like living in the country although consciously he maintained that he did, for the good of the children." There are, from the standpoint of my own school of psychology, so many fallacies in this piece of analysis that I hardly know where to begin. But let us begin at the beginning, with the failure to wind the alarm clock. Now, a man who does not want to stay home winds the clock so that it will wake him and he can get the hell out and go to the office. There is surely nothing sounder than this. Hence the failure to wind the alarm clock shows that his unconscious was trying to tell him that he did not want to go to the office any more but wanted to stay at his house in the country all the time. The key-forgetting business I simply do not believe. A man who has had to rout out his wife once in the early hours of the morning is not going to forget his key a second time. This is known as Thurber's Empirical Law No. 1. If Dr. Bisch had lived in the country as long and as happily as I have, he would know this simple and unmystical fact: any man can forget to fix the clock and the furnace; especially the furnace, because the clock is usually right where it can be seen, whereas the furnace isn't. Some husbands "forget" to bank the furnace because they have kept hearing funny noises in the cellar all evening and are simply scared to go down there. Hundreds of simple little conscious motives enter into life, Dr. Bisch, hundreds of them.

"A woman," goes on Dr. Bisch, "who wished to consult an attorney about a divorce wrote to him: 'I have been married 22 years.' But the second 2 had evidently been added afterward, indicating that probably she was embarrassed to admit not being able to make a go of it after living with the man so long." How's that again, Doctor? I may be dumb, but I don't exactly catch all that. Couldn't the woman have really been married only 2 years, and couldn't she have added the second 2 indicating that probably she was embarrassed to admit that she was giving up trying to make a go of it after living with the man so *short* a time? Maybe we better just drop this one.

"A woman," continues Dr. Bisch (this is another woman), "who was talking to me about an intended trip to the lakes of northern Italy said: 'I don't wish to visit Lavonia Bay.' She, herself, was surprised, as no such place exists. Inasmuch as the trip was to be a honeymoon, it was 'love, honor, and obey' that really was bothering her." I take off my hat to the Doctor's astonishing powers of divination here, because I never would have figured it out. Now that he has given me the key, I get it, of course. "Love, honor, and obey," love-honor-obey, Lavonia Bay. I wonder if he knows the one about the woman who asked the librarian for a copy of "In a Garden." What she really wanted was "Enoch Arden." I like Lavonia Bay better, though, because it is psycho-neurotic, whereas there was nothing the matter with the other poor woman; she just thought that the name of the book was "In a Garden." Dr. Bisch might very likely see something more in this, but the way I've always heard it was that she just thought the name was "In a Garden."

"When a usually efficient secretary," writes Dr. Bisch, "makes errors in typing or shorthand, the excuse of fatigue or indisposition should be taken with a grain of salt. Resentment may have developed toward the employer or the work, or something may unconsciously be bothering her. Some years ago my own secretary often hit the *t* key by mistake. I discovered a young man by the name of Thomas was courting her." That doesn't explain the mistakes of a secretary I had five or six years ago. I had never had a secretary before, and had, indeed, never dictated a letter up to that time. We got some strange results. One of these, in a letter to a man I hoped I would never hear from again, was this sentence: "I feel that the cuneo has, at any rate, garbled the deig." This was not owing to fatigue or indisposition, or to resentment, although there *was* a certain resentment—or even to a young man named Cuneo or Deig. It was simply owing to the fact that my secretary, an Eastern girl, could only understand part of what I, a Middle-Westerner, was saying. In those days, I talked even more than I do now as if I had steel wool in my mouth, and the young lady just did not "get" me. Being afraid to keep asking me what I was trying to say, she simply put down what it sounded like. I signed this particular letter, by the way, just as she wrote it, and I never heard again from the man I sent it to, which is what I had hoped would happen. Psychiatrists would contend that I talked unintelligibly because of that very hope, but this is because they don't know that in Ohio, to give just one example, the word "officials" is pronounced "fishuls," no matter what anybody hopes.

We now go on to the case of a gentleman who deviated from the normal, or uninteresting. "In dressing for a formal dinner," says Dr. Bisch, "a man put on a bright red bow tie. His enthusiasm was self-evident." That is all our psychiatrist says about this one, and I think he is letting it go much too easily; I sense a definite drop here. If I were to say to you that in dressing for a formal dinner last night I put on a bright red bow tie and you were to say merely, "Your enthusiasm was self-evident," I would give you a nasty look and go on to somebody else who would get a laugh out of it, or at least ask what the hell was the idea. For the purpose of analysis in this particular case, I think you would have to know who the man was, anyway. If it was Ernest Boyd, that's one thing; if it was Jack Dempsey, that's another thing; if it was Harpo Marx or Dave Chasen, that's still another thing, or two other things. I think you really have to know who the man was. If the idea was to get a laugh, I don't think it was so very good. As for Dr. Bisch's notion that the man was enthusiastic, I don't see that at all. I just don't see it. Enthusiastic about what?

Our psychiatrist, in this meaty chapter, takes up a great many more cases, many more than I can disagree with in the space at my disposal, but I can't very well leave out the one about the man and the potatoes, because it is one of my favorites. It seems that there kept running through this unfortunate gentleman's mind the words "mashed potatoes, boiled potatoes, mashed potatoes, boiled potatoes"—*that* old line.

This went on for days, and the poor fellow, who had a lot of other things he wanted to keep repeating, could only keep repeating that. "Here," says Dr. Bisch, "the difficulty lay in the fact that the man had previously received a reprimand from his employer regarding his easy-going ways with the men who were under him in his department. 'Don't be too soft!' the employer had shouted. 'Be hard!' That very evening his wife served French fried potatoes that were burnt. 'I should be hard with her, too,' he mused. The next day the 'mashed potatoes, boiled potatoes' had been born." Now my own analysis is that the fellow really wanted to kill (mash) his wife and then go out and get fried or boiled. My theory brings in the fried potatoes and Dr. Bisch's doesn't, or not so well, anyway. I might say, in conclusion, that I don't like fellows who muse about getting hard with their wives and then take it out in repeating some silly line over and over. If I were a psychiatrist, I would not bother with them. There are so many really important ailments to attend to.

8. Sex ex Machina

WITH THE DISAPPEARANCE OF THE GAS MANTLE AND THE advent of the short circuit, man's tranquillity began to be threatened by everything he put his hand on. Many people believe that it was a sad day indeed when Benjamin Franklin tied that key to a kite string and flew the kite in a thunderstorm; other people believe that if it hadn't been Franklin, it would have been someone else. As, of course, it was in the case of the harnessing of steam and the invention of the gas engine. At any rate, it has come about that so-called civilized man finds himself today surrounded by the myriad mechanical devices of a technological world. Writers of books on how to control your nerves, how to conquer fear, how to cultivate calm, how to be happy in spite of everything, are of several minds as regards the relation of man and the machine. Some of them are prone to believe that the mind and body, if properly disciplined, can get the upper hand of this mechanized existence. Others merely ignore the situation and go on to the profitable writing of more facile chapters of inspiration. Still others attribute the whole menace of the machine to sex, and so confuse the average reader that he cannot always be certain whether he has been knocked down by an automobile or is merely in love.

Dr. Bisch, the Be-Glad-You're-Neurotic man, has a remarkable chapter which deals, in part, with man, sex, and the machine. He examines the case of three hypothetical men who start across a street on a red light and get in the way of an oncoming automobile. A dodges successfully; B stands still, "accepting the situation with calm and resignation," thus becoming one of my favorite heroes in modern belles-lettres; and C hesitates, wavers, jumps backward and forward, and finally runs head on into the car. To lead you through Dr. Bisch's complete analysis of what was wrong with B and C would occupy your whole day. He mentions what the McDougallians would say ("Instinct!"), what the Freudians would retort ("Complexes!"), and what the behaviorists would shout ("Conditioned reflexes!"). He also brings in what the physiologists would say—deficient thyroid, hypoadrenal functioning, and so on. The average sedentary man of our time who is at all suggestible must emerge from this chapter believing that his chances of surviving a combination of instinct, complexes, reflexes, glands, sex, and present-day traffic conditions are about equal to those of a one-legged blind man trying to get out of a labyrinth.

Let us single out what Dr. Bisch thinks the Freudians would say about poor Mr. C, who ran right into the car. He writes, " 'Sex hunger,' the Freudians would declare. 'Always keyed up and irritable because of it. Undoubtedly suffers from insomnia and when he does sleep his dream life must be productive, distorted, and possibly frightening. Automobile unquestionably has sex significance for him . . . to C the car is both enticing and menacing at one and the same time. . . . A thorough analysis is indicated. . . . It might take months. But then, the man needs an analysis as much as food. He is heading for a complete nervous collapse.' " It is my studied opinion, not to put too fine a point on it, that Mr. C is heading for a good mangling, and that if he gets away with only a nervous collapse, it will be a miracle.

I have not always, I am sorry to say, been able to go the whole way with the Freudians, or even a very considerable distance. Even though, as Dr. Bisch says, "One must admit that the Freudians have had the best of it thus far. At least they have received the most publicity." It is in matters like their analysis of men and machines, of Mr. C and the automobile, that the Freudians and I part company. Of course, the analysis above is simply Dr. Bisch's idea of what the Freudians would say, but I think he has got it down pretty well. Dr. Bisch himself leans toward the Freudian analysis of Mr. C, for he says in this same chapter, "An automobile bearing down upon you may be a sex symbol at that, you know, especially if you dream it." It is my contention, of course, that even if you dream it, it is probably not a sex symbol, but merely an automobile bearing down upon you. And if it bears down upon you in real life, I am sure it is an automobile. I have seen the same behavior that characterized Mr. C displayed by a squirrel (Mr. S) that lives in the grounds of my house in the country. He is a fairly tame squirrel, happily mated and not sex-hungry, if I am any judge, but nevertheless he frequently runs out toward my automobile when I start down the driveway, and then hesitates, wavers, jumps forward and backward, and occasionally would run right into the car except that he is awfully fast on his feet and that I always hurriedly put on the brakes of the 1935 V-8 Sex Symbol that I drive.

I have seen this same behavior in the case of rabbits (notoriously uninfluenced by any sex symbols save those of other rabbits), dogs, pigeons, a doe, a young hawk (which flew at my car), a blue heron that I encountered on a country road in Vermont, and once, near Paul Smiths in the Adirondacks, a fox. They all acted exactly like Mr. C. The hawk, unhappily, was killed. All the others escaped with nothing worse, I suppose, than a complete nervous collapse. Although I cannot claim to have been conversant with the private life and the secret compulsions, the psychoneuroses and the glandular activities of all these animals, it is nevertheless my confident and unswervable belief that there was nothing at all the matter with any one of them. Like Mr. C, they suddenly saw a car swiftly bearing down upon them, got excited, and lost their heads. I do not believe, you see, there was anything the matter with Mr. C, either. But I do believe that, after a thorough analysis lasting months, with a lot of harping on the incident of the automobile, something might very well come to be the

Happily-mated Rabbit Terrified by Motor-car

matter with him. He might even actually get to suffering from the delusion that he believes automobiles are sex symbols.

It seems to me worthy of note that Dr. Bisch, in reciting the reactions of three persons in the face of an oncoming car, selected three men. What would have happened had they been Mrs. A, Mrs. B, and Mrs. C? You know as well as I do: all three of them would have hesitated, wavered, jumped forward and backward, and finally run head on into the car if some man hadn't grabbed them. (I used to know a motorist who, every time he approached a woman standing on a curb preparing to cross the street, shouted, "Hold it, stupid!") It is not too much to say that, with a car bearing down upon them, ninety-five women out of a hundred would act like Mr. C—or Mr. S, the squirrel, or Mr. F, the fox. But it is certainly too much to say that ninety-five out of every hundred women look upon an automobile as a sex symbol. For one thing, Dr. Bisch points out that the automobile serves as a sex symbol because of the "mechanical principle involved." But only one woman in a thousand really knows anything about the mechanical principle involved in an automobile. And yet, as I have said, ninety-five out of a hundred would hesitate, waver, and jump, just as Mr. C did. I think we have the Freudians here. If we haven't proved our case with rabbits and a blue heron, we have certainly proved it with women.

To my notion, the effect of the automobile and of other mechanical contrivances on the state of our nerves, minds, and spirits is a problem which the popular psychologists whom I have dealt with know very little about. The sexual explanation of the relationship of man and the machine is not good enough. To arrive at the real explanation, we have to begin very far back, as far back as Franklin and the kite, or at least as far back as a certain man and woman who appear in a book of stories written more than sixty years ago by Max Adeler. One story in this book tells about a housewife who bought a combination ironing board and card table, which some New England genius had thought up in his spare time. The husband, coming home to find the devilish contraption in the parlor, was appalled. "What is that thing?" he demanded. His wife explained that it was a card table, but that if you pressed a button underneath, it would become an ironing board. Whereupon she pushed the button and the table leaped a foot into the air, extended itself, and became an ironing board. The story goes on to tell how the thing finally became so finely sensitized that it would change back and forth if you merely touched it—you didn't have to push the button. The husband stuck it in the attic (after it had leaped up and struck him a couple of times while he was playing euchre), and on windy nights it could be heard flopping and banging around, changing from a card table to an ironing board and back. The story serves as one example of our dread heritage of annoyance, shock, and terror arising out of the nature of mechanical contrivances *per se*. The mechanical principle involved in this damnable invention had, I believe, no relationship to sex whatsoever. There are certain analysts who see sex in anything, even a leaping ironing board, but I think we can ignore these scientists.

No man (to go on) who has wrestled with a self-adjusting card table can ever be quite the man he once was. If he arrives at the state where he hesitates, wavers, and jumps at every mechanical device he encounters, it is not, I submit, because he recognizes the enticements of sex in the device, but only because he recognizes the menace of the machine as such. There might very well be, in every descendant of the man we have been discussing, an inherited desire to jump at, and conquer, mechanical devices before they have a chance to turn into something twice as big and twice as menacing. It is not reasonable to expect that his children and their children will have entirely escaped the stigma of such traumata. I myself will never be the man I once was, nor will my descendants probably ever amount to much, because of a certain experience I had with an automobile.

I had gone out to the barn of my country place, a barn

which was used both as a garage and a kennel, to quiet some
large black poodles. It was 1 A.M. of a pitch-dark night in
winter and the poodles had apparently been terrified by some
kind of a prowler, a tramp, a turtle, or perhaps a fiend of
some sort. Both my poodles and I myself believed, at the time,
in fiends, and still do. Fiends who materialize out of nothing
and nowhere, like winged pigweed or Russian thistle. I had
quite a time quieting the dogs, because their panic spread to
me and mine spread back to them again, in a kind of vicious
circle. Finally, a hush as ominous as their uproar fell upon
them, but they kept looking over their shoulders, in a kind
of apprehensive way. "There's nothing to be afraid of," I told
them as firmly as I could, and just at that moment the klaxon
of my car, which was just behind me, began to shriek. Everybody has heard a klaxon on a car suddenly begin to sound;
I understand it is a short circuit that causes it. But very few
people have heard one scream behind them while they were
quieting six or eight alarmed poodles in the middle of the
night in an old barn. I jump now whenever I hear a klaxon,
even the klaxon on my own car when I push the button
intentionally. The experience has left its mark. Everybody,
from the day of the jumping card table to the day of the
screaming klaxon, has had similar shocks. You can see the
result, entirely unsuperinduced by sex, in the strained faces
and muttering lips of people who pass you on the streets of
great, highly mechanized cities. There goes a man who picked
up one of those trick matchboxes that whir in your hands;
there goes a woman who tried to change a fuse without turning off the current; and yonder toddles an ancient who
cranked an old Reo with the spark advanced. Every person
carries in his consciousness the old scar, or the fresh wound,
of some harrowing misadventure with a contraption of some
sort. I know people who would not deposit a nickel and a dime

in a cigarette-vending machine and push the lever even if a diamond necklace came out. I know dozens who would not climb into an airplane even if it didn't move off the ground. In none of these people have I discerned what I would call a neurosis, an "exaggerated" fear; I have discerned only a natural caution in a world made up of gadgets that whir and whine and whiz and shriek and sometimes explode.

I should like to end with the case history of a friend of mine in Ohio named Harvey Lake. When he was only nineteen, the steering bar of an old electric runabout broke off in his hand, causing the machine to carry him through a fence and into the grounds of the Columbus School for Girls. He developed a fear of automobiles, trains, and every other kind of vehicle that was not pulled by a horse. Now, the psychologists would call this a complex and represent the fear as abnormal, but I see it as a purely reasonable apprehension. If Harvey Lake had, because he was catapulted into the grounds of the Columbus School for Girls, developed a fear of girls, I would call that a complex; but I don't call his normal fear of machines a complex. Harvey Lake never in his life got into a plane (he died in a fall from a porch), but I do not regard that as neurotic, either, but only sensible.

I have, to be sure, encountered men with complexes. There was, for example, Marvin Belt. He had a complex about airplanes that was quite interesting. He was not afraid of machinery, or of high places, or of crashes. He was simply afraid that the pilot of any plane he got into might lose his mind. "I imagine myself high over Montana," he once said to me, "in a huge, perfectly safe tri-motored plane. Several of the passengers are dozing, others are reading, but I am keeping my eyes glued on the door to the cockpit. Suddenly the pilot steps out of it, a wild light in his eyes, and in a falsetto like that of a little girl he says to me, 'Conductor, will you please let me off at One-Hundred-and-Twenty-fifth Street?'" "But," I said to Belt, "even if the pilot does go crazy, there is still the co-pilot." "No, there isn't," said Belt. "The pilot has hit the co-pilot over the head with something and killed him." Yes, the psychoanalysts can have Marvin Belt. But they can't have Harvey Lake, or Mr. C, or Mr. S or Mr. F, or, while I have my strength, me.

9. Sample Intelligence Test

THE FUZZINESS THAT CREEPS INTO THE THOUGHT PROCESSES of those inspirationalists who seek to clarify the human scene reaches an interesting point in Chapter XIV of "How to Develop Your Personality," by Sadie Myers Shellow, Ph.D. Dr. Shellow was formerly psychologist with the Milwaukee Electric Railway & Light Company. These things happen in a world of endless permutations. I myself was once connected with the Central Ohio Optical Company. I was hired because I had a bicycle, although why an optical company would want a bicycle might appear on the face of it as inexplicable as why a railway-and-light company would want a psychologist. My experience of motormen leads me to believe that they are inarticulate to the point of never saying anything at all, and I doubt if there is a motorman in all Wisconsin who would reveal the story of his early childhood to a psychologist. Dr. Shellow, of course, may have proceeded along some other line, but most psychologists start with your childhood. Or with your sex life. I somehow have never thought of motormen as having sex lives, but this doesn't mean that they don't have them. I feel that this speculation is not getting us anywhere.

Let us return to Dr. Shellow's book. It was first published five years ago, but her publishers have just brought out a dollar edition, which puts the confusion in Chapter XIV within reach of everyone. In 1932, the book went into six printings. The present edition was printed from the original plates, which means that the mistakes which appear in it have gone on and

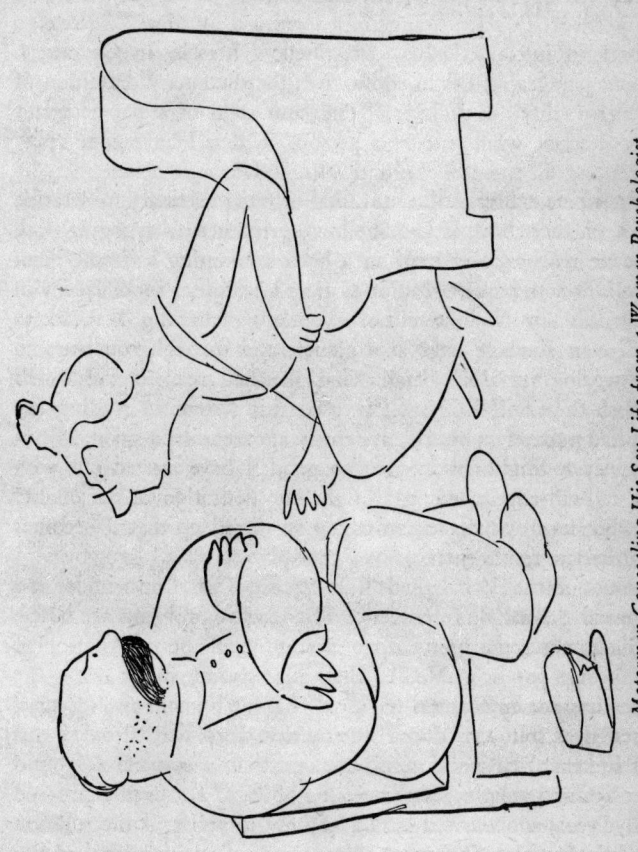

Motorman Concealing His Sex Life from a Woman Psychologist

on through the years. The book begins with a prefatory note by Albert Edward Wiggam, a foreword by Morris S. Viteles, and an introduction by Dr. Shellow herself. In Chapter I, first paragraph, Dr. Shellow gives the dictionary definition of "personality" as follows: "The sum total of traits necessary to describe what is to be a person." Unless I have gone crazy reading all these books, and I think I have, that sentence defines personality as the sum total of traits necessary to describe an unborn child. If Dr. Shellow's error here is typographical, it looms especially large in a book containing a chapter that tells how to acquire reading skill and gives tests for efficiency in reading. Dr. Shellow tells of a young woman who "was able to take in a whole page at a glance, and through concentrated attention relate in detail what she had read as the words flashed by." If Dr. Shellow used this system in reading the proofs of her book, the system is apparently no good. It certainly *sounds* as if it were no good. I have started out with an admittedly minor confusion—the definition of personality —but let us go on to something so mixed up that it becomes almost magnificent.

Chapter XIV is called "Intelligence Tests," and under the heading "Sample Intelligence Test" twelve problems are posed. There are some pretty fuzzy goings-on in the explanation of No. 11, but it is No. 12 that interests me most; what the Milwaukee motormen made of it I can't imagine. No. 12 is stated as follows: "Cross out the *one* word which makes this sentence absurd and substitute one that is correct: A pound of feathers is lighter than a pound of lead." Let us now proceed to Dr. Shellow's explanation of how to arrive at the solution of this toughy. She writes, "In 12 we get at the critical ability of the mind. Our first impulse is to agree that a pound of feathers is lighter than a pound of lead, since feathers are lighter than lead, but if we look back, we will see that a *pound* of feathers could be no lighter than a *pound* of lead since a pound is always the same. What one word, then, makes the whole sentence absurd? We might cross out the second pound and substitute ounce, in which case we would have: A pound of feathers is heavier than an ounce of lead, and that would be correct. Or we might cross out the word heavier and substitute bulkier, in which case we would have eliminated the absurdity."

We have here what I can only call a paradise of errors. I find, in Dr. Shellow's presentation of the problem and her solution of it, Transference, Wishful Thinking, Unconscious Substitution, Psychological Dissociation, Gordian Knot Cutting, Cursory Enumeration, Distortion of Focus, Abandonment of Specific Gravity, Falsification of Premise, Divergence from Consistency, Overemphasis on Italics, Rhetorical Escapism, and Disregard of the Indefinite Article. Her major error—the conjuring up of the word "heavier" out of nowhere—is enough to gum up any problem beyond repair, but there are other interesting pieces of woolly reasoning in No. 12. Dr. Shellow gets off on the wrong foot in her very presentation of the problem. She begins, "Cross out the *one* word which makes this sentence absurd." That means there is *only* one word which can be changed and restricts the person taking the test to that one word, but Dr. Shellow goes on, in her explanation, to change first one and then another. As a matter of fact, there are five words in the sentence any one of which can be changed to give the sentence meaning. Thus we are all balled up at the start. If Dr. Shellow had written, "Cross out one word which makes this sentence absurd," that would have been all right. I think I know how she got into trouble. I imagine that she originally began, "Cross out one of the words," and found herself face to face with that ancient stumbling block in English composition, whether to say "which *makes* this sentence absurd" or "which *make* this sentence absurd." (I don't like to go into italics, but to straighten Dr. Shellow out you got to go into italics.) I have a notion that Dr. Shellow decided that "make" was right, which of course it is, but that she was dissatisfied with "Cross out one of the words which make this sentence absurd" because here "words" dominates "one." Since she wanted to emphasize "one," she italicized it and then, for good measure, put the definite article "the" in front of it. That would have given her "Cross out the *one* of the words which make this sentence absurd." From there she finally arrived at what she arrived at, and the problem began slowly to close in on her.

I wouldn't dwell on this at such length if Dr. Shellow's publishers had not set her up as a paragon of lucidity, precision, and logical thought. (Come to think that over, I believe I would dwell on it at the same length even if they hadn't.) Some poor fellows may have got inferiority complexes out of being unable to see through Dr. Shellow's authoritative explanation of No. 12, and I would like to restore their confidence in their own minds. You can't just go batting off any old sort of answer to an intelligence test in this day when every third person who reads these books has a pretty firm idea that his mind is cracking up.

Let us go on to another interesting fuzziness in the Doctor's explanation. Take her immortal sentence: "We might cross out the second pound and substitute ounce," etc. What anybody who followed those instructions would arrive at is: "A pound of feathers is lighter than *a* ounce of lead." Even leaving the matter of weight out of it (which I am reluctant to do, since weight is the main point), you can't substitute "ounce" for "pound" without substituting "an" for "a," thus changing two words. If "an" and "a" are the same word, then things have come to a pretty pass, indeed. If such slipshoddery were allowed, you could solve the problem with "A pound of feathers is lighter than two pound of lead." My own way out was to change "is" to "ain't," if anybody is interested.

Let us close this excursion into the wonderland of psychology with a paragraph of Dr. Shellow's which immediately follows her explanation of No. 12: "If the reader went through this test quickly before reading the explanation, he may have discovered some things about himself. A more detailed test would be even more revealing. Everyone should at some time or other take a good comprehensive intelligence test and analyze his own defects so that he may know into what errors his reasoning takes him and of what faulty habits of thought he must be aware." I want everybody to file out quietly, now, without any wisecracks.

10. Miscellaneous Mentation

IN GOING BACK OVER THE WELL-THUMBED PAGES OF MY LIBRARY of recent books on mental technique, I have come upon a number of provocative passages which I marked with a pencil but, for one reason or another, was unable to fit into any of my preceding chapters. I have decided to take up this group of miscellaneous matters here, treating the various passages in the order in which I come to them. First, then, there is a paragraph from Dr. Louis E. ("Be Glad You're Neurotic") Bisch, on Overcompensation. He writes, "To overcome a handicap and overcompensate is much the same as consciously and deliberately setting out to overcome a superstition. We will say that you are afraid to pass under a ladder. But suppose you defy the superstition and do it anyway? You may feel uneasy for a few hours or a few days. To your surprise, perhaps, nothing dreadful happens to you. This gives you courage. You try the ladder stunt again. Still you find yourself unharmed. After a while you look for ladders; you delight in walking under them; your ego has been pepped up and you defy all the demons that may be!"

Of course, the most obvious comment to be made here is that if you keep looking for and walking under ladders long enough, something *is* going to happen to you, in the very nature of things. Then, since your defiance of "all the demons that may be" proves you still believe in them, you will be right back where you were, afraid to walk under a ladder again. But what interests me most in Dr. Bisch's study of

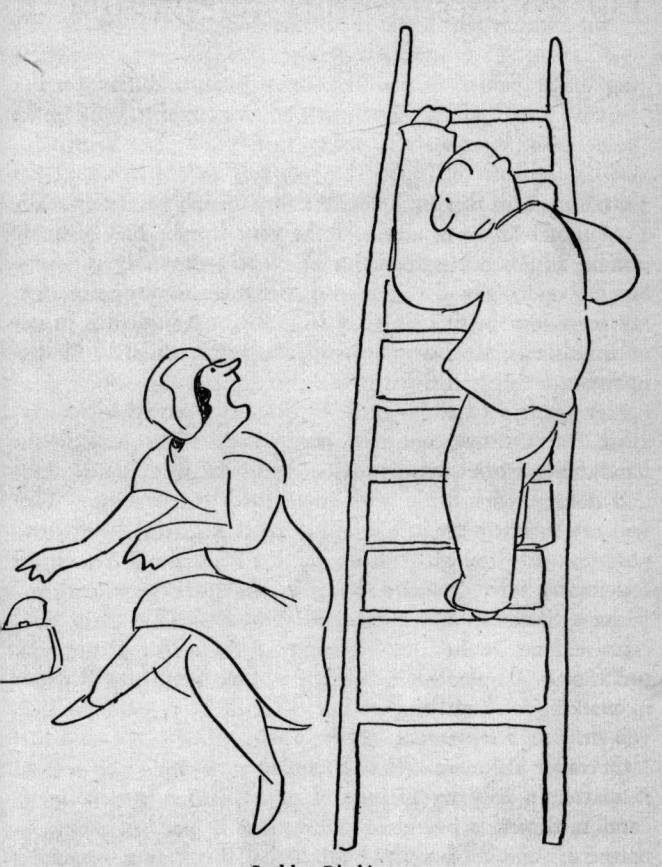

Ladder Phobia

how to "pep up the ego" is its intensification of the very kind of superstition which the person in this case sets out to defy and destroy. To substitute walking under ladders for not walking under ladders is a distinction without a difference. For here we have, in effect, a person who was afraid to walk under ladders, and is now afraid not to. In the first place he avoided ladders because he feared the very fear that that would put into him. This the psychologists call phobophobia (they really do). But *now* he is afraid of the very fear he had of being afraid and hence is a victim of what I can only call phobophobophobia, and is in even deeper than he was before. Let us leave him in this perfectly frightful mess and turn to our old authority, Mr. David Seabury, and a quite different kind of problem.

"A young woman," writes Mr. Seabury, "remarked recently that she had not continued her literary career because she found her work commonplace. 'And,' she went on, 'I don't want to fill the world with more mediocre writing.' 'What sort of finished product do you expect a girl of twenty-two to produce?' I asked. 'You are judging what you can be in the future by what you are doing in the present. Would you have a little elm tree a year old compare itself with a giant tree and get an inferiority feeling? An elm tree of one year is a measly little thing, but given time it shades a whole house.'" Mr. Seabury does not take into consideration that, given time, a lady writer shades a whole house, too, and that whereas a little elm tree is bound to grow up to be a giant elm tree, a lady writer who at twenty-two is commonplace and mediocre is bound to grow to be a giant of commonplaceness and mediocrity. I think that this young woman is the only young woman writer in the history of the United States who thought that she ought not to go on with her writing because it was mediocre. If ever a psychologist had it

in his power to pluck a brand from the burning, Mr. Seabury
had it here. But what did he do? He made the young writer
of commonplace things believe she would grow to be a veritable elm in the literary world. I hope she didn't listen to
him, but I am afraid she probably did. Still, she sounds like
a smart girl, and maybe she saw the weakness in Mr. Seabury's
"You are judging what you can be in the future by what you
are doing in the present." I can think of no sounder judgment
to make.

Let us now look at something from Dr. James L. ("Streamline Your Mind") Mursell. In a chapter on "Mastering and
Using Language," he brings out that most people do not
know how to read. Dr. Mursell would have them get a
precise and dogmatic meaning out of everything they read,
thus leaving nothing to the fantasy and the imagination.
This is particularly unfortunate, it seems to me, when applied
to poetry, as Dr. Mursell applies it. He writes, "A large group
of persons *seemed* to read the celebrated stanza beginning

> The Assyrian came down like the wolf on the fold
> And his cohorts were gleaming in purple and gold,

and ending

> Where the blue wave rolls nightly on deep Galilee.

"But when a suspicious-minded investigator tested them,
quite a number turned out to suppose that the Assyrian's
cohorts were an article of wearing apparel and that the last
line referred to the astronomical discoveries of Galileo. Is
this reading?"

Well, yes. What the second line means is simply that the
cohorts' articles of wearing apparel were gleaming in purple
and gold, so nothing much is distorted except the number of
people who came down like the wolf on the fold. The readers

who got it wrong had, it seems to me, as deep a poetic feeling (which is the main thing) as those who knew that a cohort was originally one of the ten divisions of a Roman legion and had, to begin with, three hundred soldiers, later five hundred to six hundred. Furthermore, those who got it wrong had a fine flaring image of one Assyrian coming down valiantly all alone, instead of with a couple of thousand soldiers to help him, the big coward. As for "Where the blue wave rolls nightly on deep Galilee," the reading into this of some vague association with the far, lonely figure of Galileo lends it a misty poetic enchantment which, to my way of thinking, the line can very well put up with. Dr. Mursell should be glad that some of the readers didn't think "the blue wave" meant the Yale football team. And even if they had, it would be all right with me. There is no person whose spirit hasn't at one time or another been enriched by some cherished transfiguring of meanings. Everybody is familiar with the youngster who thought the first line of the Lord's Prayer was "Our Father, who art in heaven, Halloween be thy Name." There must have been for him, in that reading, a thrill, a delight, and an exaltation that the exact sense of the line could not possibly have created. I once knew of a high-school teacher in a small town in Ohio who for years had read to his classes a line that actually went "She was playing coquette in the garden below" as if it were "She was playing croquet in the garden below." When, one day, a bright young scholar raised his hand and pointed out the mistake, the teacher said, grimly, "I have read that line my way for seventeen years and I intend to go on reading it my way." I am all for this point of view. I remember that, as a boy of eight, I thought "Post No Bills" meant that the walls on which it appeared belonged to one Post No Bill, a man of the same heroic proportions as Buffalo

Bill. Some suspicious-minded investigator cleared this up for me, and a part of the glamour of life was gone.

We will now look at a couple of items from the very latest big-selling inspirational volume, no less a volume than Mr. Dale Carnegie's "How to Win Friends and Influence People." Writes Mr. Carnegie, "The New York Telephone Company conducts a school to train its operators to say 'Number please' in a tone that means 'Good morning, I am happy to be of service to you.' Let's remember that when we answer the telephone tomorrow." Now it seems to me that if this is something we have deliberately to remember, some thing we have to be told about, then obviously the operators aren't getting their message over. And I don't think they are. What I have always detected in the voices of telephone operators is a note of peremptory willingness. Their tone always conveys to me "What number do you want? And don't mumble!" If it is true, however, that the operator's tone really means "Good morning, I am happy to be of service to you," then it is up to the sub scriber to say, unless he is a curmudgeon, "Thank you. How are you this morning?" If Mr. Carnegie doesn't know what the operator would say to that, I can tell him. She would say, "I am sorry, sir, but we are not allowed to give out that information." And the subscriber and the operator would be right back where they are supposed to be, on a crisp, business-like basis, with no genuine "good morning" and no real happiness in it at all.

I also want to examine one of Mr. Carnegie's rules for behavior in a restaurant. He writes, "You don't have to wait until you are Ambassador to France or chairman of the Clam-bake Committee of the Elk's Club before you use this philosophy of appreciation. You can work magic with it every day. If, for example, the waitress brings us mashed potatoes when we ordered French fried, let's say 'I'm sorry to trouble you, but I prefer French fried.' She'll reply. 'No trouble at all,' and will be glad to do it because you have shown respect for her." Now, it is my belief that if we said to the waitress, "I'm sorry to trouble you, but I prefer French fried," she would say, "Well, make up ya mind." The thing to say to her is simply, "I asked for French fried potatoes, not mashed potatoes." To which, of course, she might reply, under her breath, "Well, take the marbles outa ya mouth when ya talkin'." There is no way to make a waitress really glad to do anything. Service is all a matter of business with her, as it is with the phone operators, and Mr. Carnegie might as well face the fact. Anyway, I do not see any "philosophy of appreciation" in saying to a waitress, "I'm sorry to trouble you, but I prefer French fried." Philosophy and appreciation are both capable of higher flights than that. "How are you, Beautiful?" is a higher form of appreciation than what Mr. Carnegie recommends, and it is not very high. But at least it isn't stuffy, and "I'm sorry to trouble you, but I prefer French fried" is; waitresses hate men who hand them that line.

For a final example of mistaken observation of life and analysis of people, I must turn again to the prolific Mr. Seabury. He writes that once, at a dinner, he sat opposite "a tall, lanky man with restless fingers" who was telling the lady on his right about his two dogs and their four puppies. "It was obvious," says Mr. Seabury, "that he had identified himself with the mother dog and was accustomed to spend a good deal of his time in conversation with her about the welfare of her young." Having been a dog man myself for a great many years, I feel that I am on sounder ground there than Mr. Seabury. I know that no dog man ever identifies himself with the mother dog. There is a type of dog man who sometimes wistfully identifies himself with the father dog, or would like to, at any rate, because of the comparative freedom, lack of responsibility, and general carefree attitude that marks the family life of all father dogs. But no dog man, as I have said, ever identifies himself with the mother dog. He may, to be sure, spend a good deal of his time in conversation with her, but this conversation is never about the welfare of her young. Every dog man knows that there is nothing he can say to any mother dog about the welfare of her young that will make the slightest impression on her. This is partly because she does not know enough English to carry on a conversation that would get very far, and partly because, even if she did, she would not let any suggestions or commands, coaxings or wheedlings, influence her in the least.

Every dog man, when his mother dog has had her first pups, has spent a long time fixing up a warm bed in a nice, airy corner for the mother dog to have her pups in, only to discover that she prefers to have them under the barn, in a hollow log, or in the dark and inaccessible reaches of a storeroom amidst a lot of overshoes, ice skates, crokinole boards, and ball bats. Every dog man has, at the risk of his temper and his limbs, grimly and resolutely dug the mother dog and her pups out from among the litter of debris that she prefers, stepping on the ball bats, kneeling on the ice skates, and put her firmly into the bassinet he has prepared for her, only to have her carry the pups back to the nest among the overshoes and the crokinole boards during the night. In the end, every dog man has let the mother dog have her way, having discovered that there is nothing he can do, much less say, that will win her over to his viewpoint in the matter. She refuses to identify herself with him and he becomes too smart to try to identify himself with her. It would wear him to a frazzle in a week.

Part Two

Other More or Less Inspirational Pieces

1. The Breaking Up of the Winships

THE TROUBLE THAT BROKE UP THE GORDON WINSHIPS SEEMED to me, at first, as minor a problem as frost on a window-pane. Another day, a touch of sun, and it would be gone. I was inclined to laugh it off, and, indeed, as a friend of both Gordon and Marcia, I spent a great deal of time with each of them, separately, trying to get them to laugh it off, too—with him at his club, where he sat drinking Scotch and smoking too much, and with her in their apartment, that seemed so large and lonely without Gordon and his restless moving around and his quick laughter. But it was no good; they were both adamant. Their separation has lasted now more than six months. I doubt very much that they will ever go back together again.

It all started one night at Leonardo's, after dinner, over their Bénédictine. It started innocently enough, amiably even, with laughter from both of them, laughter that froze finally as the clock ran on and their words came out sharp and flat and stinging. They had been to see "Camille." Gordon hadn't liked it very much. Marcia had been crazy about it because she is crazy about Greta Garbo. She belongs to that consider-able army of Garbo admirers whose enchantment borders almost on fanaticism and sometimes even touches the edges of frenzy. I think that, before everything happened, Gordon

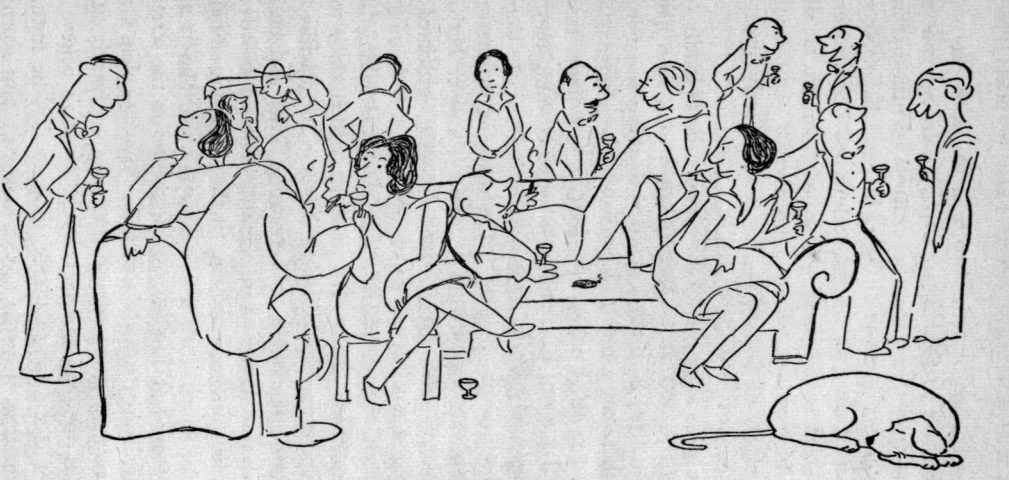

Cocktail Party, 1937

admired Garbo, too, but the depth of his wife's conviction that here was the greatest figure ever seen in our generation on sea or land, on screen or stage, exasperated him that night. Gordon hates (or used to) exaggeration, and he respects (or once did) detachment. It was his feeling that detachment is a necessary thread in the fabric of a woman's charm. He didn't like to see his wife get herself "into a sweat" over anything and, that night at Leonardo's, he unfortunately used that expression and made that accusation.

Marcia responded, as I get it, by saying, a little loudly (they had gone on to Scotch and soda), that a man who had no abandon of feeling and no passion for anything was not altogether a man, and that his so-called love of detachment simply covered up a lack of critical appreciation and understanding of the arts in general. Her sentences were becoming long and wavy, and her words formal. Gordon suddenly began to pooh-pooh her; he kept saying "Pooh!" (an annoying mannerism of his, I have always thought). He wouldn't answer her arguments or even listen to them. That, of course, infuriated her. "Oh, pooh to you, too!" she finally more or less shouted. He snapped at her, "Quiet, for God's sake! You're yelling like a prizefight manager!" Enraged at that, she had recourse to her eyes as weapons and looked steadily at him for a while with the expression of one who is viewing a small and horrible animal, such as a horned toad. They then sat in moody and brooding silence for a long time, without moving a muscle, at the end of which, getting a hold on herself, Marcia asked him, quietly enough, just exactly what actor on the screen or on the stage, living or dead, he considered greater than Garbo. Gordon thought a moment and then said, as quietly as she had put the question, "Donald Duck." I don't believe that he meant it at the time, or even thought that he meant it. However that may have been, she looked at him scornfully and said that that speech just about perfectly represented the shallowness of his intellect and the small range of his imagination. Gordon asked her not to make a spectacle of herself—she had raised her voice slightly—and went on to say that her failure to see the genius of Donald Duck proved conclusively to him that she was a woman without humor. That, he said, he had always suspected; now, he said, he knew it. She had a great desire to hit him, but instead she sat back and looked at him with her special Mona Lisa smile, a smile rather more of contempt than, as in the original, of mystery. Gordon hated that smile, so he said that Donald Duck happened to be exactly ten times as great as Garbo would ever be and that anybody with a brain in his head would admit it instantly. Thus the Winships went on and on, their resentment swelling, their sense of values blurring, until it ended up with her taking a taxi home alone (leaving her vanity bag and one glove behind her in the restaurant) and with him making the rounds of the late places and rolling up to his club around dawn. There, as he got out, he asked his taxi-driver which he liked better, Greta Garbo or Donald Duck, and the driver said he liked Greta Garbo best. Gordon said to him, bitterly, "Pooh to you, too, my good friend!" and went to bed.

The next day, as is usual with married couples, they were both contrite, but behind their contrition lay sleeping the ugly words each had used and the cold glances and the bitter gestures. She phoned him, because she was worried. She didn't want to be, but she was. When he hadn't come home, she was convinced he had gone to his club, but visions of him lying in a gutter or under a table, somehow horribly mangled, haunted her, and so at eight o'clock she called him up. Her heart lightened when he said, "Hullo," gruffly: he was alive, thank God! His heart may have lightened a little, too, but not very much, because he felt terrible. He felt terrible and he felt that it was her fault that he felt terrible. She said that she was sorry and that they had both been very silly, and he growled something about he was glad she realized *she'd* been silly, anyway. That attitude put a slight edge on the rest of her words. She asked him shortly if he was coming home. He said sure he was coming home; it was his home, wasn't it? She told him to go back to bed and not be such an old bear, and hung up.

The next incident occurred at the Clarkes' party a few days later. The Winships had arrived in fairly good spirits to find themselves in a buzzing group of cocktail-drinkers that more or less revolved around the tall and languid figure of the guest of honor, an eminent lady novelist. Gordon late in the evening won her attention and drew her apart for one drink together and, feeling a little high and happy at that time, as is the way with husbands, mentioned lightly enough (he wanted to get it out of his subconscious), the argument that he and his wife had had about the relative merits of Garbo and Duck. The tall lady, lowering her cigarette-holder, said, in the spirit of his own gaiety, that he could count her in on his side. Unfortunately, Marcia Winship, standing some ten feet away, talking to a man with a beard, caught not the spirit but only a few of the words of the conversation, and jumped to the conclusion that her husband was deliberately reopening the old wound, for the purpose of humiliating her in public. I think that in another moment Gordon might have brought her over, and put his arm around her, and admitted his "defeat" —he was feeling pretty fine. But when he caught her eye, she gazed through him, freezingly, and his heart went down. And then his anger rose.

Their fight, naturally enough, blazed out again in the taxi they took to go home from the party. Marcia wildly attacked the woman novelist (Marcia had had quite a few cocktails), defended Garbo, excoriated Gordon, and laid into Donald Duck. Gordon tried for a while to explain exactly what had happened, and then he met her resentment with a resentment that mounted even higher, the resentment of the misunderstood husband. In the midst of it all she slapped him. He looked at her for a second under lowered eyelids and then said, coldly, if a bit fuzzily, "This is the end, but I want you to go to your grave knowing that Donald Duck is *twenty times* the artist Garbo will ever be, the longest day you, or she, ever live, if you *do*—and I can't understand, with so little to live for, why you should!" Then he asked the driver to stop the car, and he got out, in wavering dignity. "Caricature! Cartoon!" she screamed after him. "You and Donald Duck both, you—" The driver drove on.

The last time I saw Gordon—he moved his things to the club the next day, forgetting the trousers to his evening clothes and his razor—he had convinced himself that the point at issue between him and Marcia was one of extreme importance involving both his honor and his integrity. He said that now it could never be wiped out and forgotten. He said that he sincerely believed Donald Duck was as great a creation as any animal in all the works of Lewis Carroll, probably even greater, perhaps much greater. He was drinking and there was a wild light in his eye. I reminded him of his old love of detachment, and he said to the hell with detachment. I laughed at him, but he wouldn't laugh. "If," he said, grimly, "Marcia persists in her silly belief that that Swede is great and that Donald Duck is merely a caricature, I cannot conscientiously live with her again. I believe that he is great, that the man who created him is a genius, probably our only genius. I believe, further, that Greta Garbo is just another actress. As God is my judge, I believe that! What does she expect me to do, go whining back to her and pretend that

I think Garbo is wonderful and that Donald Duck is simply a cartoon? Never!" He gulped down some Scotch straight. "Never!" I could not ridicule him out of his obsession. I left him and went over to see Marcia.

I found Marcia pale, but calm, and as firm in her stand as Gordon was in his. She insisted that he had deliberately tried to humiliate her before that gawky so-called novelist, whose clothes were the dowdiest she had ever seen and whose affectations obviously covered up a complete lack of individuality and intelligence. I tried to convince her that she was wrong about Gordon's attitude at the Clarkes' party, but she said she knew him like a book. Let him get a divorce and marry that creature if he wanted to. They can sit around all day, she said, and all night, too, for all I care, and talk about their precious Donald Duck, the damn comic strip! I told Marcia that she shouldn't allow herself to get so worked up about a trivial and nonsensical matter. She said it was not silly and nonsensical to her. It might have been once, yes, but it wasn't now. It had made her see Gordon clearly for what he was, a cheap, egotistical, resentful cad who would descend to ridiculing his wife in front of a scrawny, horrible stranger who could not write and never would be able to write. Furthermore, her belief in Garbo's greatness was a thing she could not deny and would not deny, simply for the sake of living under the same roof with Gordon Winship. The whole thing was part and parcel of her integrity as a woman and as an—as an, well, as a woman. She could go to work again; he would find out.

There was nothing more that I could say or do. I went home. That night, however, I found that I had not really dismissed the whole ridiculous affair, as I hoped I had, for I dreamed about it. I had tried to ignore the thing, but it had tunnelled deeply into my subconscious. I dreamed that I was out hunting with the Winships and that, as we crossed a snowy field, Marcia spotted a rabbit and, taking quick aim, fired and brought it down. We all ran across the snow toward the rabbit, but I reached it first. It was quite dead, but that was not what struck horror into me as I picked it up. What struck horror into me was that it was a white rabbit and was wearing a vest and carrying a watch. I woke up with a start. I don't know whether that dream means that I am on Gordon's side or on Marcia's. I don't want to analyze it. I am trying to forget the whole miserable business.

2. My Memories of D. H. Lawrence

IF YOU WANDER AROUND IN BOOKSTORES YOU WILL HAVE COME upon several books about D. H. Lawrence: Mr. John Middleton Murry's autobiography, Frieda Lawrence's memoirs, Keith Winter's *roman à clef* called "Impassioned Pygmies," etc. These are all comparatively recent; a complete bibliography going back to the time of Lawrence's death would run into hundreds of items, maybe thousands. The writing man is pretty much out of it if he hasn't written something about how hard it was to understand, to talk to, and to get along generally with D. H. Lawrence; and I do not propose to be out of it. I had my difficult moments on account of the Master, and I intend to tell about them—if Mr. Murry will quit talking for a moment and let me talk.

I first met D. H. Lawrence on a train platform in Italy twelve years ago. He was pacing up and down. There was no mistaking the reddish, scraggly beard, the dark, beetling eyebrows, the intense, restless eyes. He had the manner of a man who was waiting for something; in this case, I think it was the train. I had always wanted to meet the great artist and here was my golden opportunity. I finally screwed my courage up to the accosting point and I walked over and accosted him. "D. H. Lawrence?" I said. He frowned, stopped, pulled a watch out of his vest pocket, and held it up to me so that

I could see the dial. "No speak Eyetalian," he said. "Look for yourself." Then he walked away. It had been about 10:12 or 10:13 A.M. by his watch (I had 10:09 myself, but I may have been slow). Since we both got on the train that pulled into the station a few minutes later, I contrived to get into

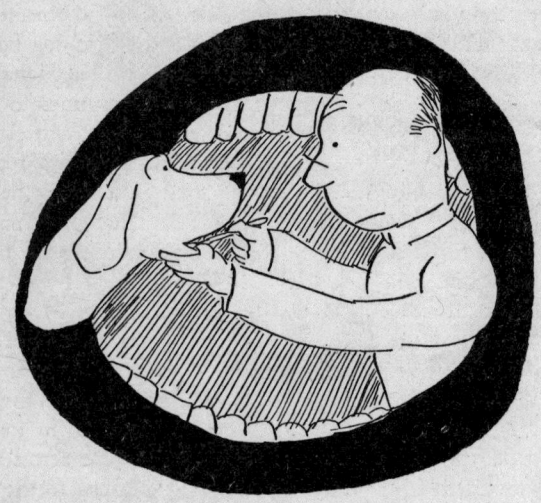

Dr. Karns

the same compartment with him and to sit down next to him. I found him quite easy to talk to. He seemed surprised that I spoke English—on the platform he had taken me for an Italian who wanted to know what time it was. It turned out after a few minutes of rather puzzling conversation that his name was George R. Hopkins and that he had never heard of D. H. Lawrence. Hopkins was a resident of Fitchburg, Massachusetts, where he had a paper factory. He wished to God he was back in the United States. He was a strong Coolidge man, thought every French person was depraved, and hadn't been able to find a decent cup of coffee in all Europe. He had a married daughter, and two sons in Penn State, and had been having trouble with a molar in his lower jaw ever since he arrived at Le Havre, some three weeks before. He wouldn't let anybody monkey with it, he said, except a certain Dr. Karns in Fitchburg. Karns was an Elk and a bird-dog fancier in addition to being the best dentist in the United States.

This encounter did not discourage me. I determined to meet D. H. Lawrence before I came back to America, and eventually I sat down and wrote him a note, asking him for the opportunity of meeting him (I had found out where he was living at the time—in Florence, I believe, though I may be wrong). I explained that I was a great admirer of his—I addressed him simply as Dear Master—and that I had some ideas about sex which I thought might interest him. Lawrence never received the letter, it transpired later, because I had unfortunately put it in the wrong envelope. He got instead a rather sharp note which I had written the same evening to a psychoanalyst in New York who had offered to analyze me at half his usual price. This analyst had come across some sketches I had made and had apparently jumped to the conclusion that it would be interesting to try to get at what was behind them. I had addressed this man in my note simply as "sir" and I had told him that if he wanted to analyze somebody he had better begin with himself, since it was my opinion there was something the matter with him. As for me, I said, there was nothing the matter with me. This, of course, was the letter that Lawrence got, owing to the shifting of envelopes, and I was later to understand why I never heard from Lawrence and also why I kept hearing from the analyst all the time. I hung around Europe for several months waiting for a letter from Lawrence, and finally came home, in a low state of mind.

I eventually met, or rather talked with, D. H. Lawrence about six months after I got back to New York. He telephoned me one evening at my apartment. "Hello," I said into the transmitter. "Hello," a voice said. "Is this Mr. Thurber?" "Yes," I said. "Well, this is D. H. Lawrence," said the voice. I was taken back; for a moment I couldn't say a word, I was so surprised and excited. "Well, well," I said, finally, "I didn't know you were on this side." "This is the right side to be on, isn't it?" he asked, in a rather strained voice (I felt that he was excited, too). "Yes, it is," I said. "Well," said Lawrence, "they turned me over on my right side because my left side hurt me so." Thereupon he began to sing "Frankie and Johnny." He turned out to be a waggish friend of mine who had heard my stories about trying to get in touch with D. H. Lawrence, and was having me on.

I never did get to meet D. H. Lawrence, but this I rarely admit. Whenever I am at a cocktail party of literary people and the subject of Lawrence comes up, I tell my own little anecdote about the Master: how he admired Coolidge, how he had trouble with his teeth, how he liked to sing "Frankie and Johnny." These anecdotes are gaining considerable currency and I have no doubt that they will begin to creep into autobiographies of the man in a short time. Meanwhile I have become what you could almost call allergic to famous writers. I suppose this is the natural outgrowth of my curious and somewhat disturbing relationship with D. H. Lawrence. I cannot truthfully say that any part of that relationship was satisfactory, and therefore I am trying to forget D. H. Lawrence, which makes me about the only writer in the world who is. It is a distinction of a sort.

3. The Case Against Women

A BRIGHT-EYED WOMAN, WHOSE SPARKLE WAS RATHER MORE of eagerness than of intelligence, approached me at a party one afternoon and said, "Why do you hate women, Mr. Thurberg?" I quickly adjusted my fixed grin and denied that I hated women; I said I did not hate women at all. But the question remained with me, and I discovered when I went to bed that night that I had been subconsciously listing a number of reasons I do hate women. It might be interesting—at least it will help pass the time—to set down these reasons, just as they came up out of my subconscious.

In the first place, I hate women because they always know where things are. At first blush, you might think that a perverse and merely churlish reason for hating women, but it is not. Naturally, every man enjoys having a woman around the house who knows where his shirt studs and his briefcase are, and things like that, but he detests having a woman around who knows where *everything* is, even things that are of no importance at all, such as, say, the snapshots her husband took three years ago at Elbow Beach. The husband has never known where these snapshots were since the day they were developed and printed; he hopes, in a vague way, if he thinks about them at all, that after three years they have been thrown out. But his wife knows where they are, and so do his mother, his grandmother, his great-grandmother, his daughter, and the maid. They could put their fingers on them in a moment, with that quiet air of superior knowledge which makes a man feel that he is out of touch with all the things that count in life.

A man's interest in old snapshots, unless they are snapshots of himself in action with a gun, a fishing rod, or a tennis

The Cold, Flat Look

racquet, languishes in about two hours. A woman's interest in old snapshots, particularly of groups of people, never languishes; it is always there, as the years roll on, as strong and vivid as it was right at the start. She remembers the snapshots when people come to call, and just as the husband, having mixed drinks for everybody, sits down to sip his own, she will say, "George, I wish you would go and get those snapshots we took at Elbow Beach and show them to the Murphys." The husband, as I have said, doesn't know where the snapshots are; all he knows is that Harry Murphy doesn't want to see them; Harry Murphy wants to talk, just as he himself wants to talk. But Grace Murphy says that she wants to see the pictures; she is crazy to see the pictures; for one thing, the wife, who has brought the subject up, wants Mrs. Murphy to see the photo of a certain costume that the wife wore at Elbow Beach in 1933. The husband finally puts down his drink and snarls, "Well, where are they, then?" The wife, depending on her mood, gives him either the look she reserves for spoiled children or the one she reserves for drunken workmen, and tells him he knows perfectly well where they are. It turns out, after a lot of give and take, the slightly bitter edge of which is covered by forced laughs, that the snapshots are in the upper right-hand drawer of a certain desk, and the husband goes out of the room to get them. He comes back in three minutes with the news that the snapshots are not in the upper right-hand drawer of the certain desk. Without stirring from her chair, the wife favors her husband with a faint smile (the one that annoys him most of all her smiles) and reiterates that the snapshots *are* in the upper right-hand drawer of the desk. He simply didn't look, that's all. The husband knows that he looked; he knows that he prodded and dug and excavated in that drawer and that the snapshots simply are not there. The wife tells him to go look again and he will find them. The husband goes back and looks again— the guests can hear him growling and cursing and rattling papers. Then he shouts out from the next room. "They are *not* in this *drawer,* just as I told you, Ruth!" The wife quietly excuses herself and leaves the guests and goes into the room where her husband stands, hot, miserable, and defiant—and with a certain nameless fear in his heart. He has pulled the desk drawer out so far that it is about to fall on the floor, and he points at the disarray of the drawer with bitter triumph (still mixed with that nameless fear). "Look for your-self!" he snarls. The wife does not look. She says with quiet coldness, "What is that you have in your hand?" What he has in his hand turns out to be an insurance policy and an old bankbook—and the snapshots. The wife gets off the old line about what it would have done if it had been a snake, and the husband is upset for the rest of the evening; in some cases he cannot keep anything on his stomach for twenty-four hours.

Another reason I hate women (and I am speaking, I believe, for the American male generally) is that in almost every case where there is a sign reading "Please have exact change ready," a woman never has anything smaller than a ten-dollar bill. She gives ten-dollar bills to bus conductors and change men in subways and other such persons who deal in nickels and dimes and quarters. Recently, in Bermuda, I saw a woman hand the conductor on the little railway there a bill of such huge denomination that I was utterly unfamiliar with it. I was sitting too far away to see exactly what it was, but I had the feeling that it was a five-hundred-dollar bill. The conductor merely ignored it and stood there waiting—the fare was just one shilling. Eventually, scrabbling around in her handbag, the woman found a shilling. All the men on the train who witnessed the transaction tightened up inside; that's what a woman with a ten-dollar bill or a twenty or a five-hundred does to a man in such situations—she tightens him up inside. The episode gives him the feeling that some monstrous triviality is threatening the whole structure of civilization. It is difficult to analyze this feeling, but there it is.

Another spectacle that depresses the male and makes him fear women, and therefore hate them, is that of a woman looking another woman up and down, to see what she is wearing. The cold, flat look that comes into a woman's eyes when she does this, the swift coarsening of her countenance, and the immediate evaporation from it of all humane quality make the male shudder. He is likely to go to his stateroom or his den or his private office and lock himself in for hours. I know one man who surprised that look in his wife's eyes and never afterward would let her come near him. If she started toward him, he would dodge behind a table or a sofa, as if he were engaging in some unholy game of tag. That look, I believe, is one reason men disappear, and turn up in Tahiti or the Arctic or the United States Navy.

I (to quit hiding behind the generalization of "the male") hate women because they almost never get anything exactly right. They say, "I have been faithful to thee, Cynara, after my fashion" instead of "in my fashion." They will bet you that Alfred Smith's middle name is Aloysius, instead of Emanuel. They will tell you to take the 2:57 train, on a day that the 2:57 does not run, or, if it does run, does not stop at the station where you are supposed to get off. Many men, separated from a woman by this particular form of imprecision, have never showed up in her life again. Nothing so embitters a man as to end up in Bridgeport when he was supposed to get off at Westport.

I hate women because they have brought into the currency of our language such expressions as "all righty" and "yes indeedy" and hundreds of others. I hate women because they throw baseballs (or plates or vases) with the wrong foot advanced. I marvel that more of them have not broken their backs. I marvel that women, who coordinate so well in languorous motion, look uglier and sillier than a goose-stepper when they attempt any form of violent activity.

I had a lot of other notes jotted down about why I hate women, but I seem to have lost them all, except one. That one is to the effect that I hate women because, while they never lose old snapshots or anything of that sort, they invariably lose one glove. I believe that I have never gone anywhere with any woman in my whole life who did not lose one glove. I have searched for single gloves under tables in crowded restaurants and under the feet of people in darkened movie theatres. I have spent some part of every day or night hunting for a woman's glove. If there were no other reason in the world for hating women, that one would be enough. In fact, you can leave all the others out.

4. No Standing Room Only

THE THEATRE PAGE OF THE "WORLD-TELEGRAM" CARRIED THIS little note one evening: "Saturday afternoon was something of an event at the Broadhurst, for 'Victoria Regina' had just rounded out fifty-two weeks on Broadway and Helen Hayes, the sentimentalist, wanted to do something to celebrate the occasion. So she called Harry Essex, the company manager, backstage and suggested that only fifty-two standees be admitted into the matinee. By curtain rise only that number of vertical playgoers were allowed into the playhouse; those turned away got no explanation from the box office."

Robert Browning says somewhere in his poems that Providence often seems to "let twenty pass and stone the twenty-first." Miss Hayes goes Providence thirty-two better and thus is about two and a half times as lenient. She didn't have the fifty-third man stoned, either, or otherwise roughly handled, but he must have been just about as bewildered and sore as if he had been. To celebrate the anniversary of a popular play by refusing to let certain people in to see it sets a new precedent for celebrations, particularly sentimental celebrations. I somehow have the idea that Harry Essex, the company manager, didn't really understand what Miss Hayes said. I think she probably suggested that the first fifty-two persons who asked for standing room be let in free. That's more along the old, established lines of celebration and sentiment, and sounds more like Miss Hayes, somehow. I don't know whether it sounds like Mr. Essex or not, but I imagine

PRICES
WASH 4~.
PULL 10 - 11~~
MARCEL - 1~~

it doesn't. I never heard of a company manager who would let fifty-two people in free; on the other hand, I never heard of one who would keep people out when they wanted to pay to get in. Of course, it may be that the box-office man got mixed up on his instructions, but that doesn't sound like a box-office man. I don't suppose we will ever get to the bottom of it all, but I can't help wondering what happened when the fifty-third person showed up and wanted to pay to get into the show. Let us try to reconstruct his conversation with the box-office man:

MR. FIFTY-THREE: I want a ticket, please.

BOX-OFFICE MAN: Standing room only.

MR. FIFTY-THREE: All right, give me standing room.

BOX-OFFICE MAN: But—uh—I just remembered—there is standing room but I can't sell you any.

MR. FIFTY-THREE: What did you say?

BOX-OFFICE MAN: I say there is standing room but I can't sell you any.

MR. FIFTY-THREE: I don't get it. It sounds as if you kept saying there is standing room but you can't sell me any.

BOX-OFFICE MAN: That's what I said.

MR. FIFTY-THREE: Well, say it again. Some other way.

BOX-OFFICE MAN: All I have is no standing room. No standing room only.

MR. FIFTY-THREE: Huh?

BOX-OFFICE MAN: Look—if you come back *next* Saturday, or even tonight, I could let you in even if it were more crowded in there than it is now, but I can't tell you why.

MR. FIFTY-THREE: I want to get in now. I'd rather stand when there are fewer standees.

BOX-OFFICE MAN: I can't let you in.

MR. FIFTY-THREE: Why can't you?

BOX-OFFICE MAN: I just can't, that's all.

MR. FIFTY-THREE: What's the matter with me?

BOX-OFFICE MAN: Nothing's the matter with you.

MR. FIFTY-THREE: Well, something must be the matter with somebody.

BOX-OFFICE MAN: No, nothing's the matter, exactly.

MR. FIFTY-THREE: Well, *approximately,* what's the matter?

BOX-OFFICE MAN: I can't sell you a ticket to stand.

MR. FIFTY-THREE: You sold the man right ahead of me standing room, because I saw you.

BOX-OFFICE MAN: If he'd been behind you, *you* could have got in, but *he* couldn't.

MR. FIFTY-THREE: Are you Charles MacArthur?

BOX-OFFICE MAN: No.

MR. FIFTY-THREE: Why? Why? Why?

BOX-OFFICE MAN: Because I'm not.

MR. FIFTY-THREE: No, no, I mean why can't I *get in?*

BOX-OFFICE MAN: I can't tell you. I can't give any explanation.

MR. FIFTY-THREE: Do you *know* why I can't get in?

BOX-OFFICE MAN: I don't want to talk about it.

By this time, Mrs. Fifty-Four and Mrs. Fifty-five, and a lot of other women on up to Mrs. Seventy-two, are pushing, and they finally dislodge Mr. Fifty-three and demand standing room. The box-office man has to get rid of them, which is harder than getting rid of Mr. Fifty-three, lots harder. Just how many bewildered people were turned away in all on this sentimental occasion, I don't know, but I'm glad I wasn't the box-office man.

The American Airlines, now, has the good old-fashioned idea of celebrating a sentimental occasion. They recently decided to give a prize to the millionth person who chanced to show up and ask for passage on one of their planes. Up showed the lucky Mr. Theodore Colcord Baker. He was given a free trip to Europe on the Hindenburg and a thousand dollars in cash. It would take a hundred thousand dollars to get me to ride on the Hindenburg or any other Zeppelin, but that is beside the point. The point is that when Mr. Baker showed up he wasn't told that American Airlines wouldn't let him ride on one of their planes. The sentiment of that would have been lost on Mr. Baker, even if it had been explained to him. It would have been lost on Miss Hayes and Mr. Essex, too, particularly if they were in a hurry to fly somewhere. Of course, if Mr. Fifty-three had been in a hurry to see "Victoria Regina" he probably wouldn't have waited a year, but the sentiment in both cases is the same. I'm not trying to compare a plane ride to a matinée, I'm trying to compare Helen Hayes to American Airlines; even so, I would be the last to say that Miss Hayes should have given anyone a thousand dollars. I just think she should have let Mr. Fifty-three in.

I've brooded about this affair for quite a few days and nights now, and out of it I have hit on a kind of revenge for Mr. Fifty-three, if he still is as mad as I think he is. My plan would be hard to work but it would be a lot of fun. In "Victoria Regina," as you know, Prince Albert dies, rather early in the play. Now my idea is to have Mr. Fifty-three, if he has any spunk at all, don the uniform of a court announcer some Saturday afternoon, put on makeup, slip backstage when nobody is looking, and, in the scene after Albert's death, walk boldly onstage and, with a gesture toward the door, say, loudly, "The Royal Consort, Prince Albert!" They would either have to ring the curtain down or else Mr. Vincent Price, who plays Prince Albert, would have to walk on again, as fit as a fiddle but with nothing to say, except maybe that he was feeling a lot better than he had been. That would put Miss Hayes in a very sentimental spot. But perhaps I have brooded about the whole business too long. I guess I have.

5. Nine Needles

ONE OF THE MORE SPECTACULAR MINOR HAPPENINGS OF THE past few years which I am sorry that I missed took place in the Columbus, Ohio, home of some friends of a friend of mine. It seems that a Mr. Albatross, while looking for something in his medicine cabinet one morning, discovered a bottle of a kind of patent medicine which his wife had been taking for a stomach ailment. Now, Mr. Albatross is one of those apprehensive men who are afraid of patent medicines and of almost everything else. Some weeks before, he had encountered a paragraph in a Consumers' Research bulletin which announced that this particular medicine was bad for you. He had thereupon ordered his wife to throw out what was left of her supply of the stuff and never buy any more. She had promised, and here now was another bottle of the perilous liquid. Mr. Albatross, a man given to quick rages, shouted the conclusion of the story at my friend: "I threw the bottle out the bathroom window and the medicine chest after it!" It seems to me that must have been a spectacle worth going a long way to see.

I am sure that many a husband has wanted to wrench the family medicine cabinet off the wall and throw it out the window, if only because the average medicine cabinet is so filled with mysterious bottles and unidentifiable objects of all kinds that it is a source of constant bewilderment and exasperation to the American male. Surely the British medicine cabinet and the French medicine cabinet and all the other

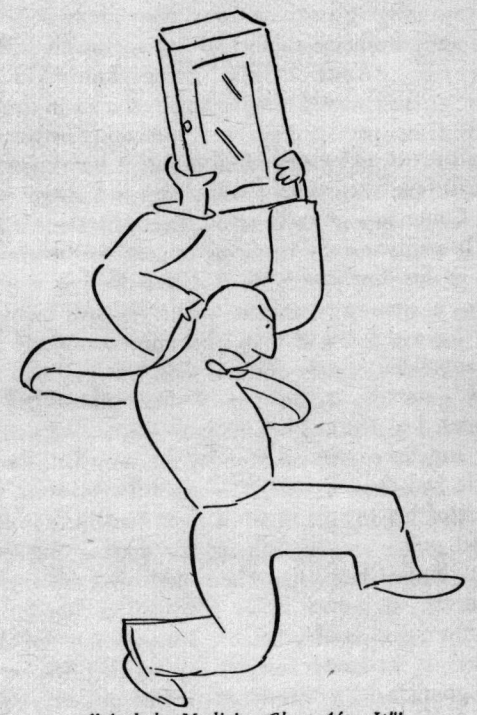

"And the Medicine Chest After It!"

medicine cabinets must be simpler and better ordered than ours. It may be that the American habit of saving everything and never throwing anything away, even empty bottles, causes the domestic medicine cabinet to become as cluttered in its small way as the American attic becomes cluttered in its major way. I have encountered few medicine cabinets in this country which were not pack-jammed with something between a hundred and fifty and two hundred different items, from dental floss to boracic acid, from razor blades to sodium perborate, from adhesive tape to coconut oil. Even the neatest wife will put off clearing out the medicine cabinet on the ground that she has something else to do that is more important at the moment, or more diverting. It was in the apartment of such a wife and her husband that I became enormously involved with a medicine cabinet one morning not long ago.

I had spent the weekend with this couple—they live on East Tenth Street near Fifth Avenue—such a weekend as left me reluctant to rise up on Monday morning with bright and shining face and go to work. They got up and went to work, but I didn't. I didn't get up until about two-thirty in the afternoon. I had my face all lathered for shaving and the washbowl was full of hot water when suddenly I cut myself with the razor. I cut my ear. Very few men cut their ears with razors, but I do, possibly because I was taught the old Spencerian free-wrist movement by my writing teacher in the grammar grades. The ear bleeds rather profusely when cut with a razor and is difficult to get at. More angry than hurt, I jerked open the door of the medicine cabinet to see if I could find a styptic pencil and out fell, from the top shelf, a little black paper packet containing nine needles. It seems that this wife kept a little paper packet containing nine needles on the top shelf of the medicine cabinet. The packet fell into the soapy water of the washbowl, where the paper rapidly disintegrated, leaving nine needles at large in the bowl. I was, naturally enough, not in the best condition, either physical or mental, to recover nine needles from a washbowl. No gentleman who has lather on his face and whose ear is bleeding is in the best condition for anything, even something involving the handling of nine large blunt objects.

It did not seem wise to me to pull the plug out of the washbowl and let the needles go down the drain. I had visions of clogging up the plumbing system of the house, and also a vague fear of causing short circuits somehow or other (I know very little about electricity and I don't want to have it explained to me). Finally, I groped very gently around the bowl and eventually had four of the needles in the palm of one hand and three in the palm of the other—two I couldn't find. If I had thought quickly and clearly, I wouldn't have done that. A lathered man whose ear is bleeding and who has four wet needles in one hand and three in the other may be said to have reached the lowest known point of human efficiency. There is nothing he can do but stand there. I tried transferring the needles in my left hand to the palm of my right hand, but I couldn't get them off my left hand. Wet needles cling to you. In the end, I wiped the needles off onto a bathtowel which was hanging on a rod above the bathtub. It was the only towel that I could find. I had to dry my hands afterward on the bathmat. Then I tried to find the needles in the towel. Hunting for seven needles in a bathtowel is the most tedious occupation I have ever engaged in. I could find only five of them. With the two that had been left in the bowl, that meant there were four needles in all missing— two in the washbowl and two others lurking in the towel or lying in the bathtub under the towel. Frightful thoughts came to me of what might happen to anyone who used that towel or washed his face in the bowl or got into the tub, if I didn't find the missing needles. Well, I didn't find them. I sat down on the edge of the tub to think, and I decided finally that the only thing to do was wrap up the towel in a newspaper and take it away with me. I also decided to leave a note for my friends explaining as clearly as I could that I was afraid there were two needles in the bathtub and two needles in the wash-bowl, and that they better be careful.

I looked everywhere in the apartment, but I could not find a pencil, or a pen, or a typewriter. I could find pieces of paper, but nothing with which to write on them. I don't know what gave me the idea—a movie I had seen, perhaps, or a story I had read—but I suddenly thought of writing a message with a lipstick. The wife might have an extra lipstick lying around and, if so, I concluded it would be in the medicine cabinet. I went back to the medicine cabinet and began poking around in it for a lipstick. I saw what I thought looked like the metal tip of one, and I got two fingers around it and began to pull gently—it was under a lot of things. Every object in the medicine cabinet began to slide. Bottles broke in the washbowl and on the floor; red, brown, and white liquids spurted; nail files, scissors, razor blades, and miscellaneous objects sang and clattered and tinkled. I was covered with perfume, peroxide, and cold cream.

It took me half an hour to get the debris all together in the middle of the bathroom floor. I made no attempt to put anything back in the medicine cabinet. I knew it would take a steadier hand than mine and a less shattered spirit. Before I went away (only partly shaved) and abandoned the shambles, I left a note saying that I was afraid there were needles in the bathtub and the washbowl and that I had taken their towel and that I would call up and tell them everything—I wrote it in iodine with the end of a toothbrush. I have not yet called up, I am sorry to say. I have neither found the courage nor thought up the words to explain what happened. I suppose my friends believe that I deliberately smashed up their bathroom and stole their towel. I don't know for sure, because they have not yet called me up, either.

6. A Couple of Hamburgers

IT HAD BEEN RAINING FOR A LONG TIME, A SLOW, COLD RAIN falling out of iron-colored clouds. They had been driving since morning and they still had a hundred and thirty miles to go. It was about three o'clock in the afternoon. "I'm getting hungry," she said. He took his eyes off the wet, winding road for a fraction of a second and said, "We'll stop at a dog-wagon." She shifted her position irritably. "I wish you wouldn't call them *dog*-wagons," she said. He pressed the klaxon button and went around a slow car. "That's what they are," he said. "Dog-wagons." She waited a few seconds. "*Decent* people call them *diners*," she told him, and added, "Even if you call them diners, I don't like them." He speeded up a hill. "They have better stuff than most restaurants," he said. "Anyway, I want to get home before dark and it takes too long in a restaurant. We can stay our stomachs with a couple hamburgers." She lighted a cigarette and he asked her to light one for him. She lighted one deliberately and handed it to him. "I wish you wouldn't say 'stay our stomachs,'" she said. "You know I hate that. It's like 'sticking to your ribs.' You say that all the time." He grinned. "Good old American expressions, both of them," he said. "Like sow belly. Old pioneer term, sow belly." She sniffed. "My ancestors were pioneers, too. You don't have to be vulgar just because you were a pioneer." "Your ancestors never got as far west as mine did," he said. "The real pioneers travelled on their sow belly and got somewhere." He laughed loudly at that. She looked out at the wet trees and signs and telephone poles going by. They drove on for several miles without a word; he kept chortling every now and then.

"What's that funny sound?" she asked, suddenly. It invariably made him angry when she heard a funny sound. "What funny sound?" he demanded. "You're always hearing

funny sounds." She laughed briefly. "That's what you said when the bearing burned out," she reminded him. "You'd never have noticed it if it hadn't been for me." "I noticed it, all right," he said. "Yes," she said. "When it was too late." She enjoyed bringing up the subject of the burned-out bearing whenever he got to chortling. "It was too late when *you* noticed it, as far as that goes," he said. Then, after a pause, "Well, what does it sound like *this* time? All engines make a noise running, you know." "I know all about that," she answered. "It sounds like—it sounds like a lot of safety pins being jiggled around in a tumbler." He snorted. "That's your imagination. Nothing gets the matter with a car that sounds like a lot of safety pins. I happen to know that." She tossed away her cigarette. "Oh, sure," she said. "You always happen to know everything." They drove on in silence.

"I want to stop somewhere and get something to *eat*!" she said loudly. "All right, all right!" he said. "I been watching for a dog-wagon, haven't I? There hasn't been any. I can't make you a dog-wagon." The wind blew rain in on her and she put up the window on her side all the way. "I won't stop at just any old diner," she said. "I won't stop unless it's a cute one." He looked around at her. "Unless it's a *what* one?" he shouted. "You know what I mean," she said. "I mean a decent, clean one where they don't slosh things at you. I hate to have a lot of milky coffee sloshed at me." "All right," he said. "We'll find a cute one, then. You pick it out. I wouldn't know. I might find one that was cunning but not cute." That struck him as funny and he began to chortle again. "Oh, shut up," she said.

Five miles farther along they came to a place called Sam's Diner. "Here's one," he said, slowing down. She looked it over. "I don't want to stop there," she said. "I don't like the ones that have nicknames." He brought the car to a stop at one side of the road. "Just what's the matter with the ones that have nicknames?" he asked with edgy, mock interest. "They're always Greek ones," she told him. "They're always Greek ones," he repeated after her. He set his teeth firmly together and started up again. After a time, "Good old Sam, the Greek," he said, in a singsong. "Good old Connecticut Sam Beardsley, the Greek." "You didn't see his name," she snapped. "Winthrop, then," he said. "Old Samuel Cabot Winthrop, the Greek dog-wagon man." He was getting hungry.

On the outskirts of the next town she said, as he slowed down, "It looks like a factory kind of town." He knew that she meant she wouldn't stop there. He drove on through the place. She lighted a cigarette as they pulled out into the open again. He slowed down and lighted a cigarette for himself. "Factory kind of town than *I* am!" he snarled. It was ten miles before they came to another town. "Torrington," he growled. "Happen to know there's a dog-wagon here because I stopped in it once with Bob Combs. Damn cute place, too, if you ask me." "I'm not asking you anything," she said, coldly. "You think you're *so* funny. I think I know the one you mean," she said, after a moment. "It's right in the town and it sits at an angle from the road. They're never so good, for some reason." He glared at her and almost ran up against the curb. "What the hell do you mean 'sits at an angle from the road'?" he cried. He was very hungry now. "Well, it isn't silly," she said, calmly. "I've noticed the ones that sit at an angle. They're cheaper, because they fitted them into funny little pieces of ground. The big ones parallel to the road are the best." He drove right through Torrington, his lips compressed. "Angle from the *road*, for God's sake!" he snarled, finally. She was looking out her window.

On the outskirts of the next town there was a diner called The Elite Diner. "This looks—" she began. "I see it, I see it!" he said. "It doesn't happen to look any cuter to me than any goddam—" she cut him off. "Don't be such a sorehead, for Lord's sake," she said. He pulled up and stopped beside the diner, and turned on her. "Listen," he said, grittingly, "I'm going to put down a couple of hamburgers in this place even if there isn't one single inch of chintz or cretonne in the whole—" "Oh, be still," she said. "You're just hungry and mean like a child. Eat your old hamburgers, what do I care?" Inside the place they sat down on stools and the counterman walked over to them, wiping up the counter top with a cloth as he did so. "What'll it be, folks?" he said. "Bad day, ain't it? Except for ducks." "I'll have a couple of—" began the husband, but his wife cut in. "I just want a pack of cigarettes," she said. He turned around slowly on his stool and stared at her as she put a dime and a nickel in the cigarette machine and ejected a package of Lucky Strikes. He turned to the counterman again. "I want a couple of hamburgers," he said. "With mustard and lots of onion. *Lots* of onion!" She hated onions. "I'll wait for you in the car," she said. He didn't answer and she went out.

He finished his hamburgers and his coffee slowly. It was terrible coffee. Then he went out to the car and got in and drove off, slowly humming "Who's Afraid of the Big Bad Wolf?" After a mile or so, "Well," he said, "what was the matter with the Elite Diner, milady?" "Didn't you *see* that cloth the man was wiping the counter with?" she demanded. "Ugh!" She shuddered. "I didn't happen to want to eat any of the counter," he said. He laughed at that comeback. "You didn't even notice it," she said. "You never notice anything. It was filthy." "I noticed they had some damn fine coffee in there," he said. "It was swell." He knew she loved good coffee. He began to hum his tune again; then he whistled it; then he began to sing it. She did not show her annoyance, but she knew that he knew she was annoyed. "Will you be kind enough to tell me what time it is?" she asked. "Big *bad* wolf, big *bad* wolf—five minutes o' five—tum-dee-*doo*-dee-dum-m-m." She settled back in her seat and took a cigarette from her case and tapped it on the case. "I'll wait till we get home," she said. "If you'll be kind enough to speed up a little." He drove on at the same speed. After a time he gave up the "Big Bad Wolf" and there was deep silence for two miles. Then suddenly he began to sing, very loudly,

H-A-double-*R*-*I*-G-A-*N* *spells Harrr*-i-gan—" She gritted her teeth. She hated that worse than any of his songs except "Barney Google." He would go on to "Barney Google" pretty soon, she knew. Suddenly she leaned slighty forward. The straight line of her lips began to curve up ever so slightly. She heard the safety pins in the tumbler again. Only now they were louder, more insistent, ominous. He was singing too loud to hear them. "Is a *name* that *shame* has never been con-*nec*-ted with—*Harrr*-i-gan, that's *me!*" She relaxed against the back of the seat, content to wait.

7. The Case of the Laughing Butler

A LADY WHO SIGNED HERSELF "HOSTESS" WROTE RECENTLY TO Elinor Ames, who clears up matters of etiquette for the distraught readers of the *Daily News,* "How many cocktails should a hostess serve before a meal? Sometimes I feel so embarrassed because the dinner is ready but the guests go right on drinking in the living room and I can't find a tactful way to urge them out to dinner. I have no maid so must announce dinner myself." To which Miss Ames replied, "Never serve more than two cocktails before dinner, for the guest who has several cocktails and an assortment of canapés and hors-d'œuvre will suffer a loss of appetite. Why not try a laughing imitation of a butler? Stand at the door and say, in clear tones, 'Dinner is served.' If your manner is pleasant but pointed—and there are no more cocktails—your guests will follow you into the dining room."

Here we have stated, by Hostess, one of the problems of American home life today, and one which you and I—and, in her hearts of hearts, Miss Ames herself—know cannot be solved by imitating a butler. One might as well try to dispose of some such problem as "What shall one do about sex?" by imitating a butler. To give a brief history of cocktails-before-dinner, every school child knows, of course, that the trouble began when liquor was substituted for tea as a late-

To Enjoy Imitations People Must Have about Five Cocktails

afternoon and early-evening beverage. The old-fashioned tea party was easy to handle; your Aunt Clara or your little neice could handle it, and have the whole house in apple-pie order again by half past six. Nobody ever drank more than one or two cups of tea (three at the outside), and even if he did it had no other effect than to make him slightly stupid. There was never any disposition on the part of tea drinkers to go on and on with the thing; nobody ever crept into the guest room and lay down; nobody shouted. I do not pretend that such things occur at all parties where cocktails are served; what I mean to say is that they never occurred at tea parties. The tea party could be decorous to the point of stuffiness, it had all the drawbacks of the stone-sober, but it was eminently manageable. Then came, as we all know, gin, and with it the problem with which Hostess finds herself confronted.

The weakness of Miss Ames' attempt to cope with the cocktail problem, the proof of her uncertainty and lack of confidence in her own plan, lies in that curious suggestion of hers, "Why not try a laughing imitation of a butler?" If she had had any faith in her ability to help Hostess out, she would not have answered a hard question by asking another question. Well, let me answer that question for Hostess, who must be pretty bewildered. In the first place, if a hostess stands at the door and laughs, nobody is going to get the idea that she is imitating a butler, for the simple reason that butlers do not laugh. You have to give an unsmiling and dignified imitation of a butler or the whole thing falls flat. Furthermore, it is extremely difficult for a woman in a dinner gown to imitate a butler. I doubt if any woman except Beatrice Lillie could get away with it, and she probably has a butler. (Miss Ames' implication that the presence of an actual butler would solve the cocktail problem we need not bother with here further than to say it wouldn't.) Moreover, a roomful of guests who have had only two cocktails are not going to be amused by, or cater to, anybody doing imitations of any kind whatsoever. To enjoy imitations, or even pay attention to imitations, people must have about five cocktails, at which point they will, of course, begin giving imitations themselves—the gentleman with mustaches doing Hitler and Charlie Chaplin. Gentlemen—or ladies—imitating Chaplin are likely to be a nuisance in a crowded room, particularly if they try going around a corner on one foot. Getting people who are doing imitations out to the dining room would be next to impossible.

But let us, for the sake of the argument, consider Miss Ames' specific case, that of a hostess who, having served two cocktails and determining not to serve any more, stands at the door and gives a laughing imitation of a butler. Nothing, beyond a few strained little laughs, is going to happen. The hostess is simply going to stand there, her idiotic laughter dying, while a roomful of people, each holding his empty glass rigidly before him, regard their hostess with cold grins. There is only one thing for Hostess to do at this point, and I shall express it by paraphrasing one of Miss Ames' own sentences, as follows: "If your manner is pleasant but pointed—and there are no more cocktails—you are going to have to make some more cocktails." This has become the accepted thing, and there is nothing to do but accept it. Dinner can always wait for one more round, or if it can't, it is going to, anyway.

There is really only one way for a hostess to speed her guests to the dinner table after two cocktails, but it is a remedy that is worse than the malady. I refer to the serving of purple or blue cocktails or cocktails of any color not ordinarily encountered in liquor glasses. Strangely colored cocktails, made up of liquid odds and ends, can be, and often are, served by women like Hostess. As Marjorie Hillis says in "Live Alone and Like It," "Worse even than the woman who puts marshmallows into a salad is the one who goes in for fancy cocktails." (Miss Hillis knows quite a lot about serving drinks, but she has a one-cocktail delusion about Old-Fashioneds. She writes, "Old-Fashioneds come into the economy class after a fashion, because of the fact that you make them singly, and *usually people don't expect two.*" I believe it can safely be said that nothing in the world depresses a guest so much as only one Old-Fashioned.) The serving of fancy cocktails, then—to get back to the fancy cocktails—is one way out for Hostess. It will be an even better way out if she serves with them canapés made of anchovy paste mixed with marmalade, or something of the sort, and gives each gentleman a dainty little cocktail napkin to worry about. This will get the guests out to dinner all right but it will also get them out of the house right after dinner, probably never to return. There don't have to be any marshmallows in the salad. Thus we see that there is no perfect, or even near-perfect, solution to Hostess's problem in this country.

In France our problem does not come up because the French look on cocktails before dinner as an invention of the devil (*une invention du diable*). No proper French person would ever let himself in for any such quandary as confronts Hostess; first, because it is repugnant to the French to dull the palate with gin and rye, thus spoiling the taste for food, and, second, because it costs too much (*c'est trop cher*). Many Americans have no real taste for food, or, if they have, they are so worried or nervous by late afternoon that they don't care. Thus it has come about that a great number of Americans, instead of giving up cocktails before dinner, are largely giving up dinner after cocktails. A professor out in Ohio has announced that because of this Americans are rapidly becoming a one-meal race, having the time and inclination only for a cup of coffee and a piece of toast in the morning. The professor's conclusion seems to be that when the barbarians come down from the North they will find a people so badly nourished that they will be a pushover.

I happen to be an old-fashioned host who does not believe in the abandonment of dinner after cocktails. This is probably because I rarely have a chance to have more than one cocktail at my own dinner parties, owing to the fact that I usually have to go out for ice, and hence have just worked up an appetite when dinner is announced, or by the time it should be announced. Dinner guests have a way of showing up at my house quite early, bringing anywhere from one to six people with them. Sometimes it is somebody's father who just wanted to stop in and see me before he took his train; sometimes it is four or five friends of one of my guests, with whom he has been having a quick one at Joe's or somewhere, and who thought they would just drop in and say hello; sometimes it is that bald man with the nose glasses and that middle-aged woman in the brown dress who so often show up at people's houses at five-thirty or six o'clock. In these cases the ice, of course, runs out and I have to go out and get some more (the ice-cube system is not, I believe, here to stay, unless it gets a great deal better). Thus I usually find myself over in Bleecker or Sullivan Street at seven o'clock of the evening I am giving a dinner party, trying to explain to some Italian that I have to have ice. Of course, I usually try to phone for the ice first, but that never works, as you know if you have tried it. You can get Tony Angelli or Tony Dibello on the phone, all right, but you can't make him understand that you want ice. You say, "Hello—Angelli's?," and a thick, low voice says, "Hodda wodda poosh?" "Could you deliver some ice right away to such-and-such a number?"

you ask, above the racket of the cocktail drinkers. "You gudda poosh what?" says the voice. You never really get beyond that, whatever it is, so you have to go out for the ice. It is useless to send a servant. No servant has ever been known to find an Italian ice-dealer.

On one occasion I waited for half an hour in the steamy kitchen of a house in Sullivan Street until the Italian ice-man, who had disappeared after a brief and excited talk with me, came back with some white wine. He had thought I wanted white wine. Is was very late when I got back with the ice that time and everybody had a good laugh at me, to be sure, coming in with the ice. When I go out for the ice now, I usually snatch a couple of sandwiches at a delicatessen. It isn't much, but it is something. My own experience is simply one example of why it is impossible to solve the cocktails-before-dinner problem as glibly and briefly as Miss Ames tries to solve it. I don't like to think of Hostess standing there at the door, laughingly imitating a butler, hoping everybody will clap hands and file gaily out to dinner. Life isn't that simple.

8. Bateman Comes Home

(Written After Reading Several Recent Novels about the Deep South and Confusing them a Little—as the Novelists Themselves Do—with "Tobacco Road" and "God's Little Acre")

OLD NATE BIRGE SAT ON THE RUSTED WRECK OF AN ANCIENT sewing machine in front of Hell Fire, which was what his shack was known as among the neighbors and to the police. He was chewing on a splinter of wood and watching the moon come up lazily out of the old cemetery in which nine of his daughters were lying, only two of whom were dead. He began to mutter to himself. "Bateman be comin' back any time now wid a thousan' dollas fo' his ol' pappy," said Birge. "Bateman ain' goin' let his ol' pappy starve nohow." A high, cracked voice spoke inside the house, in a toneless singsong. "Bateman see you in hell afore he do anything 'bout it," said the voice. "Who dat?" cried Birge, standing up. "Who dat sayin' callumy 'bout Bateman? Good gahd amighty!" He sat down quickly again. His feet hurt him, since he had gangrene in one of them and Bless-Yo-Soul, the cow, had stepped on the other one that morning in Hell Hole, the pasture behind Hell Fire. A woman came to the door with a skillet in her hand. Elviry Birge was thin and emaciated and dressed in a tattered old velvet evening gown. "You oughtn' speak thataway 'bout Bateman at thisatime," said Birge. "Bateman's a good boy. He go 'way in 1904 to make his pappy a thousan' dollas." "Thuh hell wuth thut," said

Elviry, even more tonelessly than usual. "Bateman ain' goin'
brang we-all no thousan' dollas. Bateman got heself a place
fo' dat thousan' dollas." She shambled back into the house.
"Elviry's gone crazy," muttered Birge to himself.

A large woman with a heavy face walked into the littered
yard, followed by a young man dressed in a tight blue suit.
The woman carried two suitcases; the young man was smoking a cigarette and running a pocket comb through his hair.
"Who dat?" demanded Birge, peering into the dark. "It's
me, yore Sister Sairy," said the large woman. "An' tuckered
as a truck horse." The young man threw his cigarette on the
ground and spat at its burning end. "Mom shot a policeman
in Chicago," he said, sulkily, "an' we hadda beat it." "Whut
you shoot a policeman fo', Sairy?" demanded Birge, who had
not seen his sister for twenty years. "Gahdam it, you cain' go
'round doin' that!" "That'll be one o' Ramsay's jokes," said
Sairy. "Ramsay's a hand for jokes, he is. Seems like that's
all he *is* a hand for." "Ah, shut yore trap before I slap it shut,"
said Ramsay. He had never been in the deep South before and
he didn't like it. "When do we eat?" he asked. "Ev'body goin'
'round shootin' policemen," muttered Birge, hobbling about
the yard. "Seem lak ev'body shootin' policeman 'cept Bateman. Bateman, he's a good boy." Elviry came to the door
again, still carrying the skillet; as they had had no food since
Coolidge's first term, she used it merely as a weapon. "Whut's
ut?" she asked, frowning into the dark. The moon, grown
tired, had sunk back into the cemetery again. "Come ahn out,
cackle-puss, an' find out," said Ramsay. "Look heah, boy!"
cried Birge. "I want me more rev'rence outa you, gahdam it!"
"Hello, Elviry," said Sairy, sitting on one of her suitcases. "We
come to visit you. Ain't you glad?" Elviry didn't move from
the doorway.

"We-all thought you-all was in *She*cago," said Elviry, in her toneless voice. "We-all was in all Chicago," said Ramsay, "but we-all is here all, now all." He spat. "Dam ef he ain' right, too," said Birge, chuckling. "Lawdy gahd! You bring me a a thousan' dollas, boy?" he asked, suddenly. "I ain't brought nobody no thousand dollers," growled Ramsay. "Whine you make yerself a thousand dollers, you old buzzard?" "Don' lem call me buzzard, Elviry!" shouted Birge. "Cain' you hit him wid somethin'? Hit him wid dat skillet!" Elviry made for Ramsay with her skillet, but he wrested it away from her and struck her over the head with it. The impact made a low, dull sound, like *sponk*. Elviry fell unconscious, and Ramsay sat down on her, listlessly. "Hell va place ya got here," he said.

At this juncture a young blonde girl, thin and emaciated but beautiful in the light of the moon (which had come up again), ran into the yard. "Wheah you bin, gal?" demanded Birge. "Faith is crazy," he said to the others, "an' they ain' nobody knows why, 'cause I give her a good Christian up-bringin' ef evah a man did. Look heah, gal, yo' Aunt Sairy heah fo' a visit, gahdam it, an' nobody home to welcome her. All my daughters 'cept Prudence bin gone fo' two weeks now. Prudence, she bin gone fo' two yeahs." Faith sat down on the stoop. "Clay an' me bin settin' fire to the auditorium," she said. Birge began whittling at a stick. "Clay's her third husban'," he said. "'Pears lak she should pay some 'tention to her fifth husban', or leastwise her fo'th, but she don'. I don' understan' wimmin. Seem lak ev'body settin' fire to somethin' ev'time I turn my back. Wonder any buildin's standin' in the whole gahdam United States. You see anythin' o' Bateman, gal?" "I ain' seen anythin' o' anybody," said Faith. "Now that is a bald-face lie by a daughter I brought up in the feah o' hell fire," said Birge. "Look heah, gal, you cain' set fire to no buildin' 'thout you see somebody. Gahd's love give that truth to this world. Speak to yo' Aunt Sairy, gal. She jest kill hesef a *po*liceman in *She*cago." "Did you kill a policeman, Aunt Sairy?" Faith asked her. Sairy didn't answer her, but she spoke to Ramsay. "You sit on this suitcase an' let me sit on Elviry a while," she said. "Do as yo' Motha tells you boy," said Birge. "Ah, shut up!" said Ramsay, smoking.

Ben Turnip, a half-witted neighbor boy with double pneumonia, came into the yard, wearing only overalls. "Ah seed you-all was a-settin'," he said, bursting into high, toneless laughter. "Heah's Bateman! Heah's Bateman!" cried Birge, hobbling with many a painful gahdam over to the newcomer. "You bring me a thousan' dollas, Bateman?" Elviry came to, pushed Ramsay off her, and got up. "That ain' Bateman, you ol' buzzard," she said, scornfully. "That's only Ben Turnip an' him turned in the haid, too, lak his Motha afore him." "Go 'long, woman," said Birge. "I reckon I know moan son. You bring yo' ol' pappy a thousan' dollars, Bateman?" "Ah seed you-all was a-settin'," said Ben Turnip. Suddenly he became very excited, his voice rising to a high singsong. "He-settin', I-settin', you-settin', we-settin'," he screamed. "Deed-a-bye, deed-a-bye, deed-a-bye, die!" "Bateman done gone crazy," mumbled Birge. He went back and sat down on the sewing machine. "Seem lak ev'body gone crazy. Now, that's a pity," he said, sadly. "Nuts," said Ramsay.

"S'pose you-all did see me a-settin'," said Ben Turnip, belligerently. "Whut uv ut? Cain' Ah set?" "Sho, sho, set yosef, Bateman," said Birge. "I'll whang ovah his haid wid Elviry's skillet fust pusson say anything 'bout you settin'. Set yosef." Ben sat down on the ground and began digging with a stick. "I done brong you a thousan' dollars," said Ben. Birge leaped from his seat. "Glory gahd to Hallerlugie!" he shouted. "You heah de man, Elviry? Bateman done . . ."

If you keep on long enough it turns into a novel.

9. Footnotes on a Course of Study

I HARDLY KNOW WHERE TO BEGIN IN TRYING TO SUMMARIZE FOR you a pamphlet called "The Technique of Good Manners," by one Mary Perin Barker, which has fallen into my hands. I might begin, I suppose, by saying that it was first got up to be used, and was used, as a course of study at Newark College of Engineering, but that would only start you asking questions, and all I know is that Newark College of Engineering is a college. Mrs. Barker's little book was devised to instruct the men students there how to act from the time they got up until the time they went to bed. These students used to meet with the author for two-hour discussion periods; whether they still do or not I don't know; at any rate, the brochure has now been put into general circulation, with an introductory note by Dr. Dexter S. Kimball, Dean of the College of Engineering of Cornell University. Mrs. Barker teaches proper behavior in the classroom, the ballroom, the laboratory, and the office. She tells you how to answer the phone (you should never grab it up and shout "Yeah?"), how to take a girl to a dance, how to greet one's office mates (you say "Hello there," with a smile, and "mean it"), and so on.

Being a woman, Mrs. Barker goes into italics in surprising places now and then. For instance, she writes, early in this course of study, that a man should have "a razor, a *good* hairbrush, a toothbrush, and a pants presser." Well, that's a woman for you, putting the quality of a hairbrush above the quality of a razor. Somehow, I can just see the razor she has in mind, and the hairbrush too, as far as that goes. I don't want any part of either one of them. I don't care whether I'm well groomed or not. I don't want to be groomed, anyway;

For Cleaning Shoes There Is Nothing so Handy as a Handkerchief

never have. I just want to get up and dress and be let alone. This makes me a boor, I know, and Mrs. Barker, being a cultivated lady (she believes that men should shave under their arms and points out that "for years they have done so at the foreign beach resorts"), Mrs. Barker hates a boor, but we all might as well know where we stand to begin with. It just happens that I do practically nothing the way Mrs. Barker says it should be done. For one thing, I usually argue with people when my clothes are rumpled and my hair is in my eyes. Mrs. B. intimates that you get much farther if you are well dressed. She writes, "One friend of mine says that she never starts an argument unless she is well dressed." I know women like that, too, and they're just as well dressed at the end as they were when they started. And yet nothing so upsets the ill-groomed man as to have a woman come out of an argument with him just as well groomed as when she went in, and talking in the same cool tones, with the same faint smile on her lips. I know them.

To go on to other items in Mrs. Barker's code of behavior for men, she says that it is entirely out of place to use handkerchiefs to "clean shoes, to dust furniture, or to wipe automobile grease or laboratory acid from the hands." I don't know about the automobile grease or the laboratory acid, and I don't care about the furniture-dusting, but I do know that for cleaning shoes there is nothing so handy or so efficient as a handkerchief. The handkerchief a man uses on his shoes he can always tuck away quickly in his pocket where his wife can't see it; on the way to the office he can toss it into a trash receptacle. If he uses a towel, on the other hand, his wife is bound to find it, confront him with it, and say, "What have you been doing with this, may I ask—dipping sheep?" That is likely to ruin the man's day.

As to table manners, I concede most of Mrs. Barker's points, but I cannot go the whole way with her about introductions. She contends that in introducing people a clue to their interests is often a kindness. Thus: "Mr. Smith, may I introduce Mr. Jones? Mr. Jones has just returned from South America, where he has been inspecting a mine." I leave out, reluctantly, any discussion of the probability that Mr. Jones' statement about inspecting a mine was just a cock-and-bull story he told his wife when he packed up to go to South America. (I still think it was a cock-and-bull story, though.) Let us suppose that I am the Mr. Smith who has just been introduced to this Mr. Jones. Well, I would be more embarrassed by the introduction than helped. I know absolutely nothing about mines and almost as little about South America. Naturally, after Mrs. Barker's introduction, Mr. Jones would expect me to say something to him about his mine. I can see him standing there, waiting. And I know just how the talk would go for the first few minutes. "Well," I would say, and stop. Then: "How is the mine?" Mr. Jones would raise his eyebrows slightly and say, stiffly, "I beg your pardon?" I would then (sparring for time) wipe my shoes with a handkerchief, look up, find his eyes still on me, and say, "I mean—is the mine all right?" Mr. Jones would be certain to read into this some veiled aspersion on his mine (particulary if it was a woman, and not a mine, that he had down there), and in a short while we would be enemies for life. That would be all right with me, too, because I have enough friends the way it is, but I am thinking of the young Newark engineers who haven't any friends.

I kept trying to remember, in reading Barker on Behavior, that it was originally written for these young Newark engineers and not for me. But even so, I am not sure that it was fitting or fair for her to tell them that "the girl who is a total loss in a ballroom may have a good many attractive girl friends to whom she would gladly introduce you, and furthermore, she may be a real person whom you would like to know outside the ballroom." Now, I don't set myself up as the greatest authority in the world on this subject, but I have known a great many total losses in my day, and I can say in all fairness and calmness that not one of them ever brought up a lot of attractive girl friends whom she was glad to introduce me to. I don't believe that any total loss in the country has a lot of attractive girl friends or, if she has, that she would be eager to introduce you to them. Moreover, I never knew a total loss who proved to be a real person whom I liked very much to know outside the ballroom. I'll admit that I never saw any of these losses outside the first ballroom in which I met them, but a man of the world does not have to go through every experience to know what it is like. Furthermore, I have compared notes with other men of the world. They all say the same thing.

Mrs. Barker takes up a lot of other topics which I should like to go into, but I have neither the time nor the tolerance for all of them. I do, however, feel impelled to discuss her rule No. 1 under "A Few Rules to be Remembered in Your Association with Women." This rule is: "Ladies always go first except going upstairs, or in a possibly dangerous place. The gentleman goes ahead to help her into a boat, up a slippery incline, or up a ladder." That may be a good rule for the stronger and more agile young engineers, but it is hardly a rule which may be applied, as Mrs. Barker applies it here, to all gentlemen, including the sedentary and the nearsighted. In my own case, I can think of no woman friend of mine who would dream of letting me step into a canoe and then try to hand her into it. Most of my women friends would be perfectly willing—and eager—to get into the canoe first, rules or no rules, and then help me in—with the aid of their husbands, a couple of ropes, and a board. My difficulties with watercraft began some fifteen years ago at Green Lake, New York, when in stepping into a canoe I accidentally trod on a sleeping Boston terrier that I didn't know was in the canoe. I had a firm hold on a young woman's hand at the time, since I was about to assist her into the canoe (I was a stickler for rules in my youth). What followed was a deplorable and improbable fiasco, but it followed. The woman I was assisting at the time and the women she has talked to about the happenings of that day—in other words, all my other women friends —would rather stay behind and burn up than follow me up a ladder. And as for a slippery incline, nobody who saw me try to recover a woman's English sheep-dog puppy for her one icy day two years ago in Sixth Avenue at Fourteenth Street—the dog had slipped its leash—would want to follow me up a slippery incline. That goes for the dog, too.

10. Remembrance of Things Past

I READ THE OTHER DAY ABOUT SOME CHICKENS THAT GOT DRUNK on mash; out in Iowa, I believe it was. I was reminded of the last chickens that I got drunk. They belonged to a French woman who owned a farm in Normandy, near Granville, where I stayed from early spring until late autumn, ten years ago. The drunken chickens make as good a point of beginning as any for my recollections of Madame Goriaut, who owned the farm. I feel that I owe her some small memoir.

I recall the little farmhouse clearly. I saw it first in a slanting rain, as I walked past sheep meadows in which poppies were blooming. A garrulous, tall old man with a blowing white beard walked with me to the farm. He dealt in clocks and watches and real estate, and it was in his dim, ticking shop in the village of Cassis that I had heard of Madame Goriaut's and the room on the second floor which she rented out when she could. I think he went along to be sure that he would get his commission for directing me there.

The room was long and high and musty, with a big, soft bed, and windows that looked out on the courtyard of the place. It was like a courtyard, anyway, in form and in feeling. It should have held old wagon wheels and busy men in leather aprons, but the activity I remember was that of several black-and-white kittens stalking each other in a circular bed of red geraniums, which, of course, is not like a courtyard, but nevertheless I remember the space in front of the house as being like a courtyard. A courtyard, let us say, with black-and-white kittens stalking each other in a circular bed of red geraniums.

The kittens were wild and unapproachable. Perhaps the fear of man had been struck into their hearts by Madame Goriaut. She was a formidable woman, almost, in a way, *épouvantable* (*épouvantable* was her favorite word—everything was *épouvantable:* the miserable straw crop, the storms off the Channel, the state of the nation, America's delay in

getting into the war). Madame was large and shapeless and possessed of an unforgettable toothiness. Her smile, under her considerable mustache, was quick and savage and frightening, like a flash of lightning lighting up a ruined woods. Whether she was tremendously amused (as by the fidgetings of a hanging rabbit—they hang rabbits for the table in Normandy) or tremendously angry (as over the breaking of a crock by her sulky little daughter) you could not determine by her expression. She raised her upper lip and showed her teeth and bellowed, in anger as well as in gaiety. You could identify her moods only by her roaring words, which reverberated around the house like the reports of shotguns. There was no mid-point in her spirit: she was either greatly pleased, usually about nothing much, or greatly displeased, by very little more.

Like many French people in the provinces, Madame Goriaut believed that all Americans were rich. She would ask me if I had not paid a thousand francs for my shoes. My spectacle rims were of solid gold, to be sure. I carried—was it not so? —a thousand dollars in my pockets for tobacco and odds and ends. I would turn my pockets inside out to show her this was not true. At these times she frightened me. It was not too fantastic to conceive of Madame Goriaut creeping into one's room at night with a kitchen knife and a basket, come to pluck one's thousand dollars and one's life as she might pluck spinach. I was always slightly alarmed by her. She had but little English—"I love you," "kiss me," "thousand dollars," "no," and "yes." I don't know where she learned these words, but she enjoyed repeating them, in that order, and with heavy delight, like a child who has learned a poem. Sometimes she gave me the shudders saying, apropos of nothing at all, "I love you, kiss me, thousand dollars, no, yes."

Madame Goriaut was a widow. Her husband had been a great professor, she told me. He had died a few years before, leaving her the farm, no money, and two five-act plays in blank verse. She showed the plays to me the first day I was there. They were written in ink in a fine hand. I picked them up and put them down with an imitation of awed pleasure. I wondered what her husband could have been like, the great professor. I found out a little now and then. Once I asked her if she had a photograph of him and she said no, because he had believed that in the transference of one's image to a film or plate there departed a certain measure of one's substance. Did I believe this was true? I said I did indeed. I was afraid to refute any of the convictions of the great professor when Madame put them to me with her leer and her fierce, sudden laugh. Of these convictions the only other I remember is that M. Goriaut believed he would come back after death as a *hirondelle,* or swallow. There were a lot of swallows around the farmhouse and the barns, and Madame Goriaut asked me if I thought that one of them was her husband. I asked her, in turn, if any of the swallows had ever made her a sign. She bellowed with laughter. I couldn't tell much about that laugh. I couldn't tell what she had thought of her husband alive, or what she believed of him dead.

I got the chickens drunk one Sunday morning by throwing to them pieces of bread soaked in Calvados, strong, new Calvados. Madame had invaded my room one Saturday night after dinner to ask me again why America had got into the war so late. She was bitter on that subject. While she talked she noticed that I had a bottle of Bénédictine on my desk. She said that Bénédictine was not the thing; I must have Calvados, the grand *eau de vie* of the region; she would give me a bottle of it. She went downstairs and brought it up to me, a large bottle. *"Voilà!"* she roared, planking it down on the table. I thanked her. Later she charged me seven francs for it on my weekly bill. I couldn't drink the stuff, it was so green and violent, so I fed it to the chickens. They got very drunk and fell down and got up and fell down again. Madame did not know what was the matter, and she raged around the village about a new disease that had come to kill the chickens and to impoverish her. The chickens were all right by Monday morning—that is, physically. Mentally, I suppose, it was their worst day.

Once I went with Madame Goriaut and her daughter, who was about seven but was peaked and whiny and looked twelve, to a village fair in Cassis. The little girl led the family donkey by his halter. It turned out when we got there that they were going to offer the donkey for sale; it seems that they offered

him for sale every year at the fair. Madame hung a little sign
around his neck saying that he was for sale; she had carried
the sign to the fair wrapped in a newspaper. Nobody bought
the donkey, but one man stepped up and asked how old he
was. The little girl replied, "Twelve years!" Madame Goriaut
flew into one of her rages and cuffed the child to the ground
with the back of her hand. "But he has only eight years,
Monsieur!" she bellowed at the man, who was moving away.
She followed him, bellowing, but he evaded her and she returned, still bellowing. She told me later that the donkey was
twenty-four years old. Her daughter, she said, would make
some man a miserable wife one day.

After the fair we went to a three-table *terrasse* on a narrow
sidewalk in front of a tawdy café in the village and she
ordered Calvados. There was, I noticed, a small insect in my
glass when it was set in front of me. I called to the waiter,
but he had gone back into the café and didn't hear me.
Madame asked what was the matter, and I showed her the
insect in the bottom of the glass. She shrugged, said *"Ah, là!,"*
and exchanged glasses with me. She drank the insect placidly.
When I paid for the drinks, I brought out a new five-franc
note. The little girl's eyes widened and she grabbed for it.
"Quel joli billet de cinq francs!" she squealed. Her mother
slapped her down again, shouting that the *joli billet* belonged
to Monsieur, who was a wealthy gentleman unused to *épou-
vantables* children. The little girl cried sullenly. *"Par exemple!"*
cried Madame, with her toothy leer. "But you may make
her a small present when you leave us." We had another
drink against the black day when I should leave them.

The day I left a man came for me and my bags in a two-
wheeled cart. It was getting on toward November and Normandy had grown chill. A cold rain was falling. I piled my
bags in the back of the cart and was about to shake hands

with Madame when the little girl squealed that I had not given her the present I had promised her. I took a five-franc note from my billfold and handed it to her. She grabbed it and ran, screaming in delight, a delight that turned to terror as Madame, bellowing her loudest, set off in pursuit. They disappeared around a corner of the house, and I could hear them screaming and bellowing in the orchard behind the house. I climbed into the cart and told the man to drive on. He said it was always like that with the young ones nowadays, they wanted everything for themselves. I was gone long before Madame came back, as I suppose she did, to say goodbye. I couldn't have faced her. I sometimes wonder about the little girl. She must be seventeen by now, and is probably already making some man a miserable wife.

11. Something About Polk

Hurrying toward Shiloh through the pages of Mr. W. E. Woodward's "Meet General Grant," a book published nine years ago, which I only recently came upon—in the library of a summer hotel—I ran into a provocative marginal note, indignantly written with pencil, on page 73. In the middle of that page occurs this sentence by Mr. Woodward: "James K. Polk, an insignificant Tennessee politician, who was almost unknown to the American people, was nominated by the Democrats . . ." The pencilled note in the margin opposite this said sharply, "Governor of Tennessee. Twice Speaker of the House of Representatives. The Jackson leader in the fight against the U. S. Bank. Almost unknown?"

I left General Grant and Mr. Woodward to shift for themselves, and gave myself up to quiet contemplation of this astonishing note. Here was the bold imprint of a person who, eighty or more years after Polk's death, could actually give three facts about the man. I was moved to wonder and a kind of admiration for this last of the Polk men, rising up so unexpectedly out of that margin, shaking a white, tense fist, defending his hero. For of all our array of Presidents, there was none less memorable than James K. Polk. If ten patriots, picked at random, were asked to list the names of all the Presidents, it is likely that most of them would leave out the name of the eleventh. Even if they remembered his name, surely none of them could put down a fact about him. He was a man of no arresting achievement. The achievements that our mysterious marginal apologist puts down are certainly not the kind of achievements that make a man well known. Who knows the name of the present Governor of Tennessee? How many people know the name of the Speaker of the House? (Did I hear somebody say Joe Cannon?)

There are a number of other Presidents whom the average patriot, in making a list, might leave out, but in his day each of these others was notable for something unusual, no matter how minor. Pierce was thrown from his horse in the Mexican War, wearing the uniform of a brigadier general; he was the youngest man to be elected to the Presidency up to that time. Andrew Johnson's wife taught him to write; he was said to have been cockeyed one day when, as Vice-President, he addressed the Senate; he was the only President who was ever impeached. Buchanan was the only bachelor President. Tyler served eggnogs and mint juleps in the White House. The first Harrison died in office. And so it goes, the enlivening story of all the Presidents except Polk. It is unquestionably true that he was almost unknown to the American people when he was elected. They never got to know him well; after his term was over, he retired to his home and died there three months later.

The trouble with Polk was that he never did anything to catch the people's eye; he never gave them anything to remember him by; nothing happened to him. He never cut down a cherry tree, he didn't tell funny stories, he was not impeached, he was not shot, he didn't drink heavily, he didn't gamble, he wasn't involved in scandal. He was a war President, to be sure, but his activities in the White House during the Mexican War were overshadowed by the activities in the field of an old buzzard named Zachary Taylor, whose soldiers called him "Old Rough and Ready." Polk never had a nickname; it is likely that he was James to his friends, not Jim. His closest friend—his Farley, his Harry Daugherty—was a man you have never heard of. His name was Gideon J. Pillow.

James K. Polk seemed destined to be overshadowed by other men. He was once even overshadowed by a mythical man, and many who have forgotten the name of Polk will remember the name of the mythical man. In 1844 the Whigs circulated the story that Polk had once taken a gang of Negroes to the South to be sold, each one branded "J.K.P." When asked where they got this infamous story, the Whigs said they had read it in an authoritative travel book written by one Baron Von Roorback. There was no such man, but the word "roorback," meaning a last-minute political trick, has gone into the American language. And the real man the mythical man wrote about has been forgotten. I encountered the Roorback story in Carl Sandburg's "Abraham Lincoln: The Prairie Years," in which I also found an anecdote about Mrs. Polk, but none about Mr. Polk. Thus he was even overshadowed by his wife. It seems that at a reception following Polk's inaugural, someone said to Mrs. Polk, "Madam, you have a very genteel assemblage tonight." to which Mrs. Polk replied, "Sir, I have never seen it otherwise." It wasn't very much, to be sure, but it was something; it has lived a hundred years. The President himself that night does not appear to have opened his trap.

One begins to feel sorry for poor Mr. Polk and the oblivion that has fallen upon him. Here is a President of the United States unremembered for any deed, unremembered even for any anecdote. I am for the formation of a Society for the Invention of Amusing Anecdotes about James K. Polk. I am willing to suggest a few myself to get the thing started. In fifty or a hundred years these anecdotes will begin to appear in histories and biographies. The forgotten President deserves a break; after all, he was a splendid gentleman. Let us see what we can do for James K. Polk, whom Abraham Lincoln once called a "bewildered, confounded, miserably perplexed man."

We might begin with that crack of Lincoln's. Old Gideon Pillow, let us say, came to Polk one day and told him that Abe Lincoln had said he was "bewildered, confounded, and miserably perplexed." "You tell Lincoln," said Polk, "that I've never been so bewildered I couldn't tell the back of a shovel from a piece of writing paper." A little cruel, to be sure, but then Lincoln had asked for it; at least we are showing that our man had spirit. He also had a nice whimsey. A Democrat office-seeker once stormed into his office (we will say) and confronted the President. "First they tell me to see Gideon Pillow and then they tell me to see you," said the man. "I don't know *where* to go." "Ah," said the President, "shunted from Pillow to Polk." Not one of the great puns, perhaps, but it shows our man was human and quick on the uptake. Personally, I think everybody is going to like this next anecdote, about Polk and General Zachary Taylor (that's what we need, anecdotes of the Lincoln-Grant variety). It seems that an indignant Whig came to Polk one day and told him that General Taylor was drinking too much. "He has to," said Polk. "If he didn't see twice as many of those cowardly Mexicans as there really are, he wouldn't have the heart to fight them." The Whig visitor was outraged. "Do you mean to say that you recommend drinking?" he demanded. "Not for myself, if that's what you mean," said Polk. "You see, what *I* have to look at is Whigs."

These are all that I can think of myself, and I am afraid that none of them is going to hurl our hero into immortality, but at least they are a start in the right direction. Let somebody else try it. There's no great rush.

12. Aisle Seats in the Mind

I FOLLOW AS CLOSELY AS ANYONE, PROBABLY MORE CLOSELY THAN most people, the pronouncements on life, death, and the future of the movies as given out from time to time by Miss Mary Pickford. Some friends of mine think that it has even become a kind of obsession with me. I wouldn't go so far as to say that, but I do admit that many times when I would ordinarily sit back and drink my brandy and smoke a cigar and become a little drowsy mentally and a little sodden intellectually, something that Mary Pickford has just said engages my inner attention so that instead of dozing off, I am kept as bright-eyed and alert as a hunted deer. Often I wake up at night, too, and lie there thinking about life, and death, and the future of the movies. Miss Pickford's latest arresting observation came in an interview with a *World-Telegram* correspondent out in Beverly Hills. Said Miss Pickford, in part, "Any type of salaciousness is as distasteful to Mr. Lasky as it is to me. There will be no salaciousness at all in our films. Not one little bit! We will consider only those stories which will insure wholesome, healthy, yet vital entertainment. *Be a guardian, not an usher, at the portal of your thought.*"

Miss Pickford has a way which I can only call intriguing, much as I hate the word, of throwing out little rounded maxims, warnings, and morals at the ends of her paragraphs. I had a great-aunt who did the same thing, and in my teens she fascinated and frightened me; perhaps that is why Miss Pickford's exhortations so engross me, and keep me from the dicing tables, the dens of vice, and the more salacious movies, poems, and novels. Miss Pickford's newest precept has occupied a great many of my waking hours since I read it, and quite a few of my sleeping ones. In the first place, it has brought me sharply up against the realization that I am not a guardian at the portal of my thought and that, what is more, being now

A Trio of Thoughts

forty-two years of age, I probably never will be. What I am like at the portal of my thought is one of those six-foot-six ushers who used to stand around the lobby of the Hippodrome during performances of "Jumbo." (They were not really ushers, but doormen, I think, but let us consider them as ushers for the sake of the argument.) What I want to convey is that I am *all* usher, as far as the portal of my thought goes, terribly usher. But I am unlike the "Jumbo" ushers or any other ushers in that I show any and all thoughts to their seats whether they have tickets or not. They can be under-age and without their parents, or they can be completely cockeyed, or they can show up without a stitch on; I let them in and show them to the best seats in my mind (the ones in the royal arena and the gold boxes).

I don't want you to think that all I do is let in *salacious* thoughts. Salacious thoughts can get in along with any others, including those that are under-age and those that are cockeyed, but my mental audience is largely made up of thoughts that are, I am sorry to say, idiotic. For days a thought has been running around in the aisles of my mind, singing and shouting, a thought that, if I were a guardian, I would certainly have barred at the portal or thrown out instantly as soon as it got in. This thought is one without reason or motivation, but it keeps singing, over and over, to a certain part of the tune of "For He's a Jolly Good Fellow," these words:

> A message for Captain Bligh,
> And a greeting to Franchot Tone.

I hope it doesn't slip by the guardian at your own portal of thought, but, whether it does or not, it is sung to that part of the aforementioned tune the words of which go "Which nobody can deny, which nobody can deny." And it is pretty easy, if you are the usher type, to let it into your mind, where it is likely to get all your other thoughts to singing the same thing, just as Donald Duck did to the orchestra in "The Band Concert." Where it came from I don't know. Thoughts like that can spot the usher type of mind a mile away, and they seek it out as tramps seek out the backdoors of generous farm wives.

Just last Sunday another vagrant thought came up to the portal of my mind, or, rather, was shown up to the portal of my mind, and I led it instantly to a seat down front, where much to my relief, it has been shouting even more loudly than the Captain Bligh-Franchot Tone thought and is, in fact, about to cause that thought to leave the theatre. This new thought was introduced at my portal by my colored maid, Margaret, who, in seeking to describe a certain part of the electric refrigerator which she said was giving trouble, called it "doom-shaped." Since Margaret pronounced that wonderful word, everything in my mind and everything in the outside world has taken on the shape of doom. If I were a true guardian of the portal of my thought, I would have refused that expression admittance, because it is too provocative, too edgy, and too dark, for comfort, but then I would have missed the unique and remarkable experience that I had last Sunday, when, just as night was falling, I walked down a doom-shaped street under a doom-shaped sky and up a doom-shaped staircase to my doom-shaped apartment. Like Miss Pickford, I am all for the wholesome, the healthy, and the vital, but sometimes I think one's mind can become, if one is the guardian type, too wholesome, healthy, and vital to be much fun. Any mind, I say boldly here and now, which would not let a doom-shaped thought come in and take a seat is not a mind that I want around.

As in all my discourses about Miss Pickford and her philosophy, I am afraid I have drifted ever so slightly from the main point, which, in this case, I suppose, is the question of keeping salacious thoughts out of the mind, and not doom-shaped ones, or Franchot Tone. Miss Pickford, however, is to blame for my inability to stick to the exact point, because of her way of following up some specific thought, such as the unanimity of her and Mr. Lasky's feelings about salaciousness, with an extremely challenging and all-encompassing injunction, such as that everybody should be a guardian at the portal of his thought, and not an usher.

I have brooded for a long time about the origin of Miss Pickford's injunction. I am not saying that she did not think it up herself. It's hers and she's welcome to it, as far as I am concerned (I'd rather have "doom-shaped" for my own). But I somehow feel that she was quoting someone and that the only reason she didn't add "as the poet has it" or "as the fella said" is that she naturally supposes that everybody would know who wrote the line. I don't happen to know; I don't happen ever to have heard it before. It may be that it is a product of one of the immortal minds, but somehow I doubt that. To me it sounds like Eddie Guest or the late Ella Wheeler Wilcox. It may have been tossed off, of course, in a bad moment, by John Cowper Powys, or Gene Tunney, or Senator Victor Donahey of Ohio, but I am inclined to think not. If you should happen to know, for certain, that it is the work of Shakespeare or Milton, there is no use in your calling me up about it, or sending a telegram. By the time I could hear from you, I would have got it out of my mind, and only "doom-shaped" would be there, sitting in a darkened theatre. I would like that, so please let us alone.

13. Suli Suli

I ALWAYS TRY TO ANSWER ABERCROMBIE & FITCH'S QUESTIONS (in their advertisements) the way they obviously want them answered, but usually, if I am to be honest with them and with myself, I must answer them in a way that would not please Abercrombie & Fitch. While that company and I have always nodded and smiled pleasantly enough when we met, we have never really been on intimate terms, mainly because we have so little in common. For one thing, I am inclined to be nervous and impatient, whereas Abercrombie & Fitch are at all times composed and tranquil. In the case of a man and a woman this disparity in temperament sometimes works out all right, but with Abercrombie & Fitch and me it is different: neither one of us is willing to submerge any part of his personality in the other, or compromise in matters of precedent, habit, or tradition. Yet in spite of all the natural barriers between Abercrombie & Fitch and myself, we are drawn to each other by a curious kind of fascination, or perhaps it is only me who is drawn to them. Not long ago I dropped in at their store to browse around among all the glittering objects, when suddenly I was faced by a tall and courteous but firm clerk who asked me if there was anything he could do for me. I said instantly, "I want to buy a javelin."

Now, it is true that I have always wanted to buy a javelin, because I have always wanted to see how far I could throw one, but two things had, up to the day I am telling about, kept me from going ahead with the thing. First, I had been afraid that I would not be able to throw a javelin as far as Babe Didrikson used to throw one, and I knew that the discovery that a woman could throw anything farther than I could throw it would have a depressing effect on me and might show up in my work and in my relationships with women. Second, I did not know how Abercrombie & Fitch, of whom I have ever been slightly in awe, would take my wanting to buy a javelin. They are, to be sure, a very courteous firm, but they have a way of looking at you sometimes as

if you had left your spoon in your coffee cup. However, all my fears and uncertainties were beside the point, because here I was, finally asking Abercrombie & Fitch for a javelin.

"A *jave*lin?" said Abercrombie & Fitch (I shall call the clerk that), and I knew instantly from his inflection that he did not think I should have a javelin and, furthermore, I knew that I was not going to get one. Somehow or other it was not the thing for a tall, thin man in a blue suit to come in and ask for a javelin. I was, naturally, embarrassed. "I—uh—yes, I had thought some of purchasing a javelin," I said. "It's for a rather—a sort of special use, in a way, I mean, what I want, of course, is *two* javelins; that is, a *pair* of javelins, so that I could cross them, like oars, you know, or guns, above a mantelpiece. I have oars and guns, of course, but I—I—" Beyond this I could not go with a story that was becoming more and more difficult for me and, I daresay, stranger and stranger to Abercrombie & Fitch. A kind of feverish high note was in my voice, a note that always betrays me when I am lying. "I am very sorry," said Abercrombie & Fitch, his eyebrows raised slightly, "but we have no javelins in stock." He paused; then, "I could order one for you." He knew, you see, that I really only wanted one; my story about wanting two had not fooled him for a minute. I think he also suspected that I wanted to find out whether I could throw the thing as far as Babe Didrikson. Abercrombie & Fitch can read me like a book; I don't know just why. I told the clerk to let it go, not to bother, and to cover my confusion I bought a set of lawn bowls, although I have no lawn that I could possibly use for bowls. I believe the clerk knew that, too.

But I am straying from the point I began with, about Abercrombie & Fitch's questions, the ones I can almost never answer the way they would like to have them answered. Take the one recently printed in an advertisement in the *New Yorker*. Under a picture of a man fishing in a stream were these words: "Can't you picture yourself in the middle of the stream with the certain knowledge that a wise old trout is hiding under a ledge and defying you to tempt him with your skillfully cast fly?" My answer, of course, is "No." Especially if I am to be equipped the way the gentleman in the illustration is equipped: with rod, reel, line, net, hip boots, felt hat, and pipe. They might just as well add a banjo and a parachute to my equipment, along with a grandfather's clock, for with anything at all to handle in the middle of a rushing brook I would drown faster than you could say "J. Robins." The wise old trout would have the laugh of his life, especially when I begin to cast. I tried casting in a stream only twice, and the first time I caught a tree and the second time I barely missed landing one of a group of picnickers. Therefore, I cannot agree with Abercrombie & Fitch's ad when it says further: "Words are poor to express the delight of just handling a beautiful rod with a sweet-singing reel and a line that seems alive as it answers the flick of your wrist." It seems alive all right, but it answers different men in different ways; with me, it is surly to the point of impudence. No, I am afraid I am not going to send for one of the fly-fishing catalogues the company advertised or drop in and look at their "complete trout outfits." Abercrombie & Fitch would know, just glancing at me, that I would be at the mercy of the complete trout outfit, and of the trout, too—if they were brave enough to come at me when I went down in a tangle of rod, reel, line, net, boots, pipe, and hat.

I am sorry to have to say this to Abercrombie & Fitch, but fishing of any kind is something I don't like to picture myself doing. Oh, I've tried fishing of various kinds, but I never seemed to get the hang of any of them. I still remember a gay fishing party I went on with a lot of strong men and beautiful girls, when I was still fairly strong myself. It was a fine day and it was a pleasant creek and the fish were biting. Everybody except me was pulling in perch and pickerel, or whatever they were—all fish look exactly alike to me. I kept pulling out of the water an aged and irritable turtle. No matter where I moved along the bank or where I dropped my line, I would hook the turtle. Nobody else got him, but I got him variously, by the leg, the back of his shell, and his belly, but never securely; he wouldn't swallow the hook, he just monkeyed with it. He would always drop back into the water as I was about to haul him in. I didn't really want him, but I wanted to get him out of the way. It furnished a great deal of amusement for everybody, except me and the turtle. Another time I went fishing on Lake Skaneateles with a group of people, including a lovely young woman named Sylvia. On this occasion I actually did hook a fish, even before anybody else had a bite, and I brought it into the rowboat with a great plop. Then, not having had any experience with a caught fish, I didn't know what to do with it. I had had some vague idea that a fish died quietly and with dignity as soon as it was flopped into a boat, but that, of course, was an erroneous idea. It leaped about strenuously. I got pretty far away from it and stared at it. The young lady named Sylvia finally grabbed it expertly and slapped it into insensibility against the sides and bottom of the boat. I think it was perhaps then that I decided to go in for javelin-throwing and began to live with the dream of being able to throw a javelin farther than Babe Didrikson. A man never completely gets over the chagrin and shock of having a woman handle for him the fish he has caught.

As for deep-sea fishing, you and I—and Abercrombie & Fitch—know that an old turtle-catcher is not going to be able to cope with a big-game fish that fights you for ten or twelve hours and drags you from Miami to Jacksonville. Every time I read an article about deep-sea fishing I realize more thoroughly than ever that, as far as I am concerned, all the sailfish and tuna and tarpon are as safe as if they were in bank vaults. In a recent piece in *Esquire,* Mr. Hemingway tells about a man who hooked an eighty-pound fish which, before the man could pull it in, was grabbed up far below the surface by some unknown monster of the deep, who took a bite at it and let it go. When the original quarry was brought up, it was seen that the other fish had "squeezed it and held it so that every bit of the insides of the fish had been crushed out while the huge fish moved off with the eighty-pound fish in its mouth." "What size of a fish would that be?" Mr. Hemingway asks. He needn't look at me. I do not stick in boats very well, particularly if they are being jerked around by a fish that has another fish in its mouth, and I never expect to get near enough to their habitat to make even a wild guess as to their size.

Then there was an article I came on in, of all magazines, the *East African Annual,* for 1934-35, called "Sea Fishing Off the Coast of Kenya," by Mr. Hugh Copley. In Africa, you can get big, strong black natives (Suli Suli they are called, I think) to go out in a boat with you, but I am afraid they would only hamper and confuse me. Mr. Copley lists the names of the big fish you can pursue along the Kenya coast, giving first the English name, then the technical name, and then the native, or Swahili, name. The list begins this way: "1. The sailfish (Istiophorus gladius), Suli Suli. 2. Herschel's spearfish (Makaira herscheli), Suli Suli." The predicaments that an American, and I mean me, might get into deep-sea fishing with a native that called everything Suli Suli are infinite. I don't even like to think about it. Nor would I ever be able to look after my tackle the way Mr. Copley says it should be looked after, because I would never get anything else done except that, day in and day out. He writes, "Lines must be dried every evening. Reels taken apart and greased. When the fishing trip is over soak all the lines for a night in fresh water and they dry thoroughly for a whole day. All hooks, wire traces, must be greased; gaffs cleaned with emery paper and then greased. The rod should be examined for broken whippings; these replaced and the rod given three coats of best coach varnish." I have a pretty vivid picture of what I would look like after all that greasing and regreasing. And then, of course, the whole thing falls down for me when it comes to the three coats that have to be put on the rod. I might go into Abercrombie & Fitch and ask for a javelin, as indeed I did, but I would never think of going up to one of their clerks and saying, "I should like to buy a bottle of coach varnish." I have no idea what would happen, but the episode would be, I am sure, most unfortunate.

14. An Outline of Scientists

Having been laid up by a bumblebee for a couple of weeks, I ran through the few old novels there were in the cottage I had rented in Bermuda and finally was reduced to reading "The Outline of Science, a Plain Story Simply Told," in four volumes. These books were published by Putnam's fifteen years ago and were edited by J. Arthur Thomson, Regius Professor of Natural History at the University of Aberdeen. The volumes contained hundreds of articles written by various scientists and over eight hundred illustrations, forty of which, the editor bragged on the flyleaf, were in color. A plain story simply told with a lot of illustrations, many of them in color, seemed just about the right mental fare for a man who had been laid up by a bee. Human nature being what it is, I suppose the morbid reader is more interested in how I happened to be laid up by a bee than in what I found in my scientific research, so I will dismiss that unfortunate matter in a few words. The bee stung me in the foot and I got an infection (staphylococcus, for short). It was the first time in my life that anything smaller than a turtle had ever got the best of me, and naturally I don't like to dwell on it. I prefer to go on to my studies in "The Outline of Science," if everybody is satisfied.

I happened to pick up Volume IV first and was presently in the midst of a plain and simple explanation of the Einstein theory, a theory about which in my time I have done as much talking as the next man, although I admit now that I never understood it very clearly. I understood it even less clearly after I had tackled a little problem about a man running a hundred-yard dash and an aviator in a plane above him. Everything, from the roundness of the earth to the immortality of the soul, has been demonstrated by the figures of men in action, but here was a new proposition. It seems that if the aviator were travelling as fast as light, the stop watch held by the track

judge would not, from the aviator's viewpoint, move at all. (You've got to make believe that the aviator could see the watch, which is going to be just as hard for you as it was for me.) You might think that this phenomenon of the unmoving watch hand would enable the runner to make a hundred yards in nothing flat, but, if so, you are living in a fool's paradise. To an aviator going as fast as light, the hundred-yard track would shrink to nothing at all. If the aviator were going *twice* as fast as light, the report of the track judge's gun would wake up the track judge, who would still be in bed in his pajamas, not yet having got up to go to the track meet. This last is my own private extension of the general theory, but it seems to me as sound as the rest of it.

I finally gave up the stop watch and the airplane, and went deeper into the chapter till I came to the author's summary of a scientific romance called "Lumen," by the celebrated French astronomer, M. Flammarion (in my youth, the Hearst Sunday feature sections leaned heavily on M. Flammarion's discoveries). The great man's lurid little romance deals, it seems, with a man who died in 1864 and whose soul flew with the speed of thought to one of the stars in the constellation Capella. This star was so far from the earth that it took light rays seventy-two years to get there, hence the man's soul kept catching up with light rays from old historical events and passing them. Thus the man's soul was able to see the battle of Waterloo, fought backward. First the man's soul—oh, let's call him Mr. Lumen—first Mr. Lumen saw a lot of dead soldiers and then he saw them get up and start fighting. "Two hundred thousand corpses, come to life, marched off the field in perfect order," wrote M. Flammarion. Perfect order, I should think, only backward.

I kept going over and over this section of the chapter on the Einstein theory. I even tried reading it backward, twice as fast as light, to see if I could capture Napoleon at Waterloo while he was still home in bed. If you are interested in the profound mathematical theory of the distinguished German scientist, you may care to glance at a diagram I drew for my own guidance, as follows:

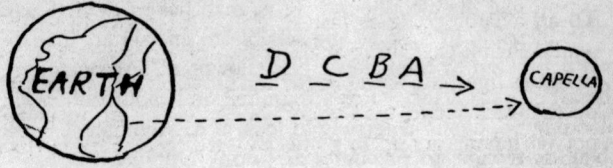

Now, A represents Napoleon entering the field at Waterloo and B represents his defeat there. The dotted line is, of course, Mr. Lumen, going hell-for-leather. C and D you need pay no particular attention to; the first represents the birth of Mr. George L. Snively, an obscure American engineer, in 1819, and the second the founding of the New England Glass Company, in 1826. I put them in to give the thing roundness and verisimilitude and to suggest that Mr. Lumen passed a lot of other events besides Waterloo.

In spite of my diagram and my careful reading and rereading of the chapter on the Einstein theory, I left it in the end with a feeling that my old grip on it, as weak as it may have been, was stronger than my new grip on it, and simpler, since it had not been mixed up with aviators, stop watches, Mr. Lumen, and Napoleon. The discouraging conviction crept over me that science was too much for me, that these brooding scientists, with their bewildering problems, many of which work backward, live on an intellectual level which I, who think of a hundred-yard dash as a hundred-dash, could never attain to. It was with relief that I drifted on to Chapter XXXVI, "The Story of Domesticated Animals." There wouldn't be anything in that going as fast as light or faster, and it was more the kind of thing that a man who has been put to bed by a bee should read for the alleviation of his humiliation. I picked out the section on dogs, and very shortly I came to this: "There are few dogs which do not inspire affection; many crave it. But there are some which seem to repel us, like the bloodhound. True, man has made him what he is. Terrible to look at and terrible to encounter, man has raised him up to hunt down his fellowman." Accompanying the article was a picture of a dignified and mournful-looking bloodhound, about as terrible to look at as Abraham Lincoln, about as terrible to encounter as Jimmy Durante.

Poor, frightened little scientist! I wondered who he was, this man whom Mr. J. Arthur Thomson, Regius Professor of Natural History at the University of Aberdeen, had selected to inform the world about dogs. Some of the chapters were signed, but this one wasn't, and neither was the one on the Einstein theory (you were given to understand that they had all been written by eminent scientists, however). I had the strange feeling that both of these articles had been written by the same man. I had the strange feeling that *all* scientists are the same man. Could it be possible that I had isolated here, as under a microscope, the true nature of the scientist? It pleased me to think so; it still pleases me to think so. I have never liked or trusted scientists very much, and I think now that I know why: they are afraid of bloodhounds. They must, therefore, be afraid of frogs, jack rabbits, and the larger pussycats. This must be the reason that most of them withdraw from the world and devote themselves to the study of the inanimate and the impalpable. Out of my analysis of those few sentences on the bloodhound, one of the gentlest of all breeds of dogs, I have arrived at what I call Thurber's Law, which is that scientists don't really know anything about anything. I doubt everything they have ever discovered. I don't think light has a speed of 7,000,000 miles per second at all (or whatever the legendary speed is). Scientists just think light is going that fast, because they are afraid of it. It's so terrible to look at. I have always suspected that light just plodded along, and now I am positive of it.

I can understand how that big baby dropped the subject of bloodhounds with those few shuddering sentences, but I propose to scare him and his fellow-scientists a little more about the huge and feral creatures. Bloodhounds are sometimes put on the trail of old lost ladies or little children who have wandered away from home. When a bloodhound finds an old lady or a little child, he instantly swallows the old lady or the little child whole, clothes and all. This is probably what happened to Charlie Ross, Judge Crater, Agnes Tufverson, and a man named Colonel Appel, who disappeared at the battle of Shiloh. God only knows how many thousands of people bloodhounds have swallowed, but it is probably twice as many as the Saint Bernards have swallowed. As everybody knows, the Saint Bernards, when they find travellers fainting in the snow, finish them off. Monks have notoriously little to eat and it stands to reason they couldn't feed a lot of big, full-grown Saint Bernards; hence they sick them on the lost travellers, who would never get anywhere, anyway. The brandy in the little kegs the dogs wear around their necks is used by the Saint Bernards in drunken orgies that follow the killings.

I guess that's all I have to say to the scientists right now, except *boo!*

15. Highball Flags

IT IS A MATTER OF COMMON KNOWLEDGE AMONG SMART SEA-going gentlemen (if you keep your eyes open, you will have read about it) that the ubiquitous yachtsman can now purchase a cocktail flag for his pleasure craft. To quote an item I recently read on the subject, the flag has "a red glass on a white field" and it means "We're serving drinks." When it is flown upside down, it means "Who has a drink?" I know very little about the ways of yachtsmen but I have always thought of them as rather reserved, aristocratic gentlemen, not given to garrulity in flags, or to announcing private parties with flags, or to pub-lic—or rather high-seas—cadging of drinks with flags. Appar-ently I was wrong. The ancient practice of sailing a ship, once the prerogative of strong, silent men of retiring disposition, appears about to go the way the canoe went when the ukulele came along. The advent of the cocktail flag, with its strange device, seems likely to lead to a deplorable debasing of the dignity of yachts and yachting—and yachtsmen. Surely any-body will have to be allowed aboard who can climb aboard— that is, when the flag is flown right side up; and certainly all sorts of common and vulgar boats are going to come alongside, roaring and singing (and possibly carrying nothing but gin and ginger ale), when the flag is flown upside down. It is too late now to do anything about this except to suggest some further flag signals; as long as yachts are going in for open drinking and carousing, they may as well do the thing up right. No yachting party which has gone so far as to fly the cocktail flag upside down is going to be satisfied with that. There are a lot of other things the people on board will want to say, after they have run out of drinks and are bawling for more, and an array of signals for these other things might just as well be arranged now. I have a few suggestions to make

"Honey, Honey, Bless Your Heart"

along this line; yachtsmen can take them or they can let them alone. What I propose is a series of highball flags, to be run up after the cocktail flag has been struck.

Flag No. 1: The head of a woman, blue, on a white field. This means "My wife is the finest little girl in all the world."

Flag No. 2: Steel-colored fist on a crimson field. This means "I can lick any other yachtsman within sight of this flag." If flown upside down, this means the same thing plus "with one hand tied behind me."

Flag No. 3: Six gray fists rampant on a dark-blue field. This means "Let's all go over and beat hell out of the Monarch of

Bermuda" (or whatever other large, peaceful ship is lying nearest the yacht and the other yachts it is talking to).

Flag No. 4: White zigzag lightning flash on black field. This means "Let's have one more quick one and then we'll get the hell out of here."

Flag No. 5: Large scarlet question mark on white field. This means "Has anybody got a tenor on board?"

Flag No. 6: Red eye and pendent pear-shaped silver tear on black field. This means "You're bes' frien' ev' had." If hung upside down, it means "You're fines' ship ev' seen."

Flag No. 7: White stocking on scarlet field. This means "We want women!"

Flag No. 8: Black zigzag lightning flash on white field. This means the same as No. 4.

Flag No. 9: Four male heads, white eyes, red, open mouths, on smoky-gray field. This means, if right side up, "Let's sing 'Honey, Honey, Bless Your Heart'"; if upside down, "Let's sing 'I had a Dream, Dear.'" There should be one hundred other similar flags for the one hundred other songs men sing when in their cups, and also, of course, a black flag with a white thumb centered; when hung with the thumb pointing up, this means "O. K., you pitch it"; when hung with the thumb pointing down, it means "No, not 'Sweet Adeline'!"

Flag No. 111: Horizontal white line on sable field. This means "I got to lie down."

Flag No. 112: A large plain yellow flag. This means "I said I got to lie *down*!"

If you have any other ideas, don't send them to me, for my yellow flag is flying, upside down (which means "Gone to bed"); send them to Abercrombie & Fitch. They are selling the cocktail flags, or anyway they have them in stock.

16. Mrs. Phelps

WHEN I WENT TO COLUMBUS, OHIO, ON A VISIT RECENTLY, I called one afternoon on Mrs. Jessie Norton, an old friend of my mother's. Mrs. Norton is in her seventies, but she is in bright possession of all her faculties (except that she does not see very well without her spectacles and is forever mislaying them). She always has a story to tell me over the teacups. She reads my fortune in the tea leaves, too, before I go, and for twenty years has told me that a slim, blonde woman is going to come into my life and that I should beware of the sea. Strange things happen to Mrs. Norton. She is psychic. My mother once told me that Mrs. Norton had been psychic since she was seven years old. Voices speak to her in the night, cryptically, persons long dead appear to her in dreams, and even her waking hours are sometimes filled with a mystic confusion.

Mrs. Norton's story this time dealt with a singular experience she had had only a few months before. It seems that she had gone to bed late on a blowy night, the kind of night on which the wind moans in the wires, and telephone bells ring without benefit of human agency, and there are inexplicable sounds at doors and windows. She had felt, as she got into bed, that something was going to happen. Mrs. Norton has never in her life had the feeling that something was going to happen that something hasn't happened. Once it was the Columbus flood, another time it was the shooting of McKinley, still another time the disappearance forever of her aged cat, Flounce.

On the occasion I am telling about, Mrs. Norton, who lives alone in a vast old graystone apartment building known as Hampton Court, was awakened three hours after midnight by a knocking on her back door. Her back door leads out

into a treeless and rather dreary courtyard, as do all the other back doors in the building. It is really four buildings joined together and running around a whole block, with the courtyard in the center. Mrs. Norton looked out her bedroom window and saw two women standing at her door below—there was a faint light striking down from somewhere. She was for a moment convinced that they were not live women, but this conviction was dispelled when one of them called up to her. Mrs. Norton then recognized the voice of a Mrs. Stokes, a portly, jolly, gray-haired woman, also a resident of Hampton Court, which is inhabited largely by old ladies who are alone in the world. "Something terrible has happened," said Mrs. Stokes. The other woman did not say anything and did not look up. Mrs. Norton had the impression that she was weeping. She told them to wait a moment, pulled a wrapper around herself, and went down and let them in.

It came out that the father of the other woman, a Mrs. Phelps, who had just recently moved into Hampton Court, had dropped dead a few minutes before in her apartment. He had come to visit her that day and now he was dead. Mrs. Phelps, a mild little old woman with white hair, sobbed quietly. It seemed that she had run instantly to Mrs. Stokes, her nearest neighbor in the building, and Mrs. Stokes had suggested that they get Mrs. Norton before going to the old man, because Mrs. Norton was psychic and therefore just the person to turn to in the event of sudden death before dawn. Mrs. Phelps said that she had heard her father fall in his bedroom and, rushing in, had found that he was dead. She was sure that he was dead—there was no need to call a doctor; but would Mrs. Norton telephone for an—an undertaker?

Mrs. Norton, not yet fully awake, suggested that it might be a good idea to make the ladies some tea. Tea was a quieting thing and the brewing of it would give Mrs. Norton a while to think. Mrs. Phelps said that she would take pleasure in a cup of tea. So Mrs. Norton made the tea and the three ladies each drank a cup of it, slowly, talking of other things than the tragedy. Mrs. Phelps seemed to feel much better. Mrs. Norton then wanted to know if there was any particular undertaker that Mrs. Phelps would like to call in and Mrs. Phelps named one, whom I shall call Bellinger. So Mrs. Norton phoned Bellinger's, and a sleepy voice answered and said a man would be right over to Mrs. Phelps' apartment. At this Mrs. Phelps said, "I think I would like to go back to father alone for a moment. Would you ladies be kind enough to come over in a little while?" Mrs. Norton said they would be over as soon as she got dressed, and Mrs. Phelps left. "She seems very sweet," said Mrs. Stokes. "It's the first time I've really talked to her. It's very sad. And at this time of the night, too." Mrs. Norton said that it was a terrible thing, but that, of course, it was to be expected, since Mrs. Phelps' father must have been a very old man, for Mrs. Phelps looked to be sixty-five at least.

When Mrs. Norton was dressed, the two ladies went out into the bleak courtyard and made their way slowly across it and knocked at the back door of Mrs. Phelps' apartment. There was no answer. They knocked more loudly, taking turns, and then together, and there was still no answer. They could see a light inside, but they heard no sound. Bewildered and alarmed (for Mrs. Phelps had not seemed deaf), the two ladies went through Mrs. Stokes' apartment, which was right next door, and around to Mrs. Phelps' front door and rang the bell. It rang loudly and they rang it many times, but no one came to the door. There was a light on in the hall. They could not hear anyone moving inside.

It was at this juncture that Bellinger's man arrived, a small, grumpy man whose overcoat was too large for him. He took over the ringing of the bell and rang it many times, insistently, but without success. Then, grumbling to himself, he turned the doorknob and the door opened and the three walked into the hallway. Mrs. Norton called and then Mrs. Stokes called and then Bellinger's man shouted, but there was no other sound. The ladies looked at Bellinger's man in frank twittery fright. He said he would take a look around. They heard him going from room to room, opening and closing doors, first downstairs and then upstairs, now and then calling out "Madam!" He came back downstairs into the hallway where the ladies were and said there was nobody in the place, dead or alive. He was angry. After all, he had been roused out of his sleep. He said he believed the whole thing was a practical joke, and a damned bad practical joke, if you asked him. The ladies assured him it was not a joke, but he said "Bah" and walked to the door. There he turned and faced them with his hand on the knob and announced that in thirty-three years with Bellinger this was the first and only time he had ever been called out on a case in which there was no corpse, the first and only time. Then he strode out the door, jumped into his car, and drove off. The ladies hurried out of the apartment after him.

They went back to Mrs. Norton's apartment and made some more tea and talked in excited whispers about the curious happenings of the night. Mrs. Stokes said she did not know Mrs. Phelps very well but that she seemed to be a pleasant and kindly neighbor. Mrs. Norton said that she had known her only to nod to but that she had seemed very nice. Mrs. Stokes wondered whether they should call the police, but Mrs. Norton said that the police would be of no earthly use on what was obviously a psychic case. The ladies would go to bed and get some sleep and go over to Mrs. Phelps' apartment when it was daylight. Mrs. Stokes said she didn't feel like going back to her apartment—she would have to pass Mrs. Phelps' apartment on the way—so Mrs. Norton said she could sleep in her extra bed.

The two women, worn out by their experience, fell asleep shortly and did not wake up until almost ten o'clock. They hurriedly got up and dressed and went over to Mrs. Phelps' back door, on which Mrs. Norton knocked. The door opened and Mrs. Phelps stood there, smiling. She was fully dressed and did not look grief-stricken or tired. "Well!" she said. "This *is* nice! Do come in!" They went in. Mrs. Phelps led them into the living room, a neat and well-ordered room, and asked them to take chairs. They sat down, each on the edge of her chair, and waited. Mrs. Phelps talked pleasantly of this and that. Did they ever see anything grow like her giant begonia in the window? She had grown it from a slip that a Mrs. Bricker had given her. Had they heard that the Chalmers child was down with the measles? The other ladies murmured responses now and then and finally rose and said that they must be going. Mrs. Phelps asked them to run in any time; it had been so sweet of them to call. They went out into the courtyard and walked all the way to Mrs. Norton's door without a word, and there they stopped and stared at each other.

That, aggravatingly enough, is where Mrs. Norton's story ended—except for the bit of information that Mrs. Stokes, frightened of Mrs. Phelps, had moved away from Hampton Court a week after the night of alarm. Mrs. Norton does not believe in probing into the psychic. One must take, gratefully, such glimpses of the psychic as are presented to one, and seek no further. She had no theories as to what happened to Mrs. Phelps after Mrs. Phelps "went back to her father." The disappearance fitted snugly into the whole pattern of the night and she let it go at that. Mrs. Norton and Mrs. Phelps have become quite good friends now, and Mrs. Phelps frequently drops in for tea. They have had no further adventures. Mrs. Phelps has not mentioned her father since that night. All that Mrs. Norton really knows about her is that she was born in Bellefontaine, Ohio, and sometimes wishes that she were back there. I took the story for what it was, fuzzy edges and all: an almost perfect example of what goes on in the life that moves slowly about the lonely figure of Mrs. Jessie Norton, reading the precarious future in her tea leaves, listening to the whisperings and knockings of the ominous present at her door. Before I left her she read my fortune in the teacup I had drunk from. It seems that a slight, blonde woman is going to come into my life and that I should beware of the sea.

17. Guns and Game Calls

I WANDERED INTO STOEGER'S FAMOUS GUN HOUSE IN FIFTH Avenue the other morning to see if they could repair my derringer. The way I came to have a derringer is rather odd and quite unlike me, really. I had been up in Winsted, Connecticut, and on the way back I stopped my car in front of a little shop in the town. In the window, on a table, lay the derringer. It was a very old derringer. As you may know, a derringer is a small knob-handled, short-barreled pistol with which ladies and gentlemen used to shoot at one another in the old days. The one I came upon had been found, the man in the shop told me, on Canaan Mountain by a Sunday wanderer a few weeks before. It had lain there in the rains and snows of many years, dropped perhaps by a tired soldier or a fallen duellist. It bore the number 247 in the iron of its barrel, showing that it was one of the very earliest derringers. The man said it was in firing condition and, sure enough, it cocked with a smart click and the hammer fell with a smart click when I pulled the trigger. I bought it for five dollars and brought it to New York, where for more than a week I carried it about with me wherever I went, clicking it at people. Finally I wore the trigger spring out and it wouldn't work any more, so when I was passing Stoeger's the other day, I thought I would go in and ask whether they could repair it.

I know very little about guns, the old derringer being the first gun I have ever owned. Therefore I was a bit awed and uneasy to find myself standing at a counter in Stoeger's facing a muscular, keen-eyed salesman who, I discerned at a glance, knew all about guns. In a hasty look around, as he asked me crisply what he could do for me, I noticed that there did not appear to be, in the whole store, any old guns such as you find on mountains. Everything was modern, shiningly new, elaborately chased and engraved, and apparently expensive (I found out later that a new Luger costs

European Oystercatcher

$100, in case you were thinking of giving anyone a new Luger). Well, there I was, facing this muscular, keen-eyed salesman who knew all about guns, from King micrometered autolocking peep-sights (price $4.50) to the Paragon 236E de luxe special over-and-under shotgun (price $1,150). (I'll tell later how I happen to know the names and prices of those things.)

"It's—ah—it's about a derringer," I said finally, in a low and confidential tone. The man led me promptly, without a word, to a long glass showcase and brought out of it a derringer, a brand-new Remington double-barrelled, two-shot, rim-fire derringer. I looked it over frowningly, felt its weight, sighted along the barrel, and put it back on the counter. I was in a considerable predicament because I didn't want to buy a new derringer and I had led the salesman to believe that I did. I was too timid, of course, to bring up now the subject of my old, rusty, single-barrelled, one-shot, powder-and-ball, flint-fired, mountain-found derringer. The moment for that had gone by. I finally got out of the predicament when he brought up the question of a pistol permit. I haven't got one, of course, and that let me out. I was about to creep away when I noticed a pile of Stoeger's "Catalog and Handbook" on the counter. They cost fifty cents each and I bought one— it seemed the least that I could do.

American Derringer

Every man, I think now, should own a gun catalog and handbook. I spent the whole evening going through mine, from Enfield rifles to Webley automatics, and I know enough names and facts and figures and calibres to impress, if not the average member of what Stoeger's calls "the shooting fraternity," at least the average Desdemona one is likely to encounter in the metropolitan area. I know just off-hand, for instance, that you can buy a Harrington & Richardson vest-pocket revolver that weighs only eight ounces and has a barrel only $1\frac{1}{8}$ inches long, just the thing for a lady to slip into her evening bag when she goes up to see her escort's etchings after the opera. I know a lot of other things, too, but I am saving them all for dinner-table small talk. All, that is, except what I know about English and American game calls. That knowledge I am willing to share with people because it is too complicated for dinner-table small talk and because I am generous enough to let people in on what may solve some of their Christmas-list problems. Not everybody is going to give a set of English and American game calls this season, and whoever does is likely to be thought of among his friends as a sophisticated and ingenious fellow.

Stoeger's then, has stocked sets of fifteen different game calls, twelve English and three American. They are of various shapes and sizes, and look like everything from a patrolman's whistle to something that has been accidentally wrenched off a camshaft (the pheasant and screech-owl call, for example). If you own the whole set of fifteen game calls, you can call all the following creatures: pheasant, screech owl, quail, blackbird, stoat, stag, heath hen (don't waste your breath on this one), moor hen, water hen, grouse, rabbit, fox, partridge, lapwing, hawk, buzzard owl, duck, teal, widgeon, snipe, redshank, sandpiper, goose, turkey, lark, woodcock, and oystercatcher.

Not everyone, of course, is going to be able to call all of these birds and beasts offhand, the way he might shoot dice. To manipulate a game call expertly requires, I could see by the catalog, not only skill and practice but, I suspect, a natural inborn gift, or frenzy. Take the English snipe call, for example. This is an instrument that looks like a combination biscuit-cutter and fountain pen, and it is, I gather, as difficult to play upon as a saxophone. On it you can call not only the snipe but the redshank, sandpiper, and oystercatcher (an oystercatcher is a water bird that catches oysters). Says the catalog: "Redshank: render a series of plaintive, whistling notes by placing the tongue against mouthpiece of whistle and giving five short, sharp blasts, terminating suddenly. Sand-piper: note is similar to redshank only longer and more trill-ing, interspersed by low, mournful notes." None of us, I think, is going to become proficient enough on the snipe call to get a redshank and then a sandpiper in quick succession, and I, for one, am not even going to try to summon an oyster-catcher, much as I would like to see one, because to do that, the catalog says, you must give "a strong, sharp note, made by removing the tongue and quickly replacing it," a little feat that died with Houdini.

On the stag call, which looks like a darning egg, one must produce "a long blow, increasing and then dying down (similar to a cow's 'low')." Stay away, I should advise, from that one. It is extremely difficult to get within earshot of a stag, and the stag-caller is bound to be in constant danger of finding himself entirely surrounded by cows, or, what is worse, bulls. The English rabbit call (the only American calls are the turkey, duck, and American snipe) leaves me somewhat con-fused because it apparently does not attract rabbits at all, but foxes. "With a little practice," says the catalog, "a lifelike imitation of a rabbit can be obtained which acts as an excellent fox decoy." The sound made is a high-pitched squeal, which is not, I suppose, the way one rabbit attracts another rabbit. Most of the foxhunters I know are lusty, florid fellows who hunt foxes in the great tradition of "View hallo!" and "There goes the —— now!" I can't somehow picture any foxhunter I have ever seen standing in a woodsy dell and squealing like a rabbit. And this call, mind you, is an English call! Maybe they are softening up over there.

Passing over the stoat and the widgeon, which I am pleased to regard merely as a bit of mild Stoeger spoofing, I pause, in concluding my survey, to warn you against the lark call. I happen to know the case history of one man who used a lark call. He was a Frenchman who lived near Nice, and the brief and unhappy account of his lark hunt got into the candid pages of the invaluable *Éclaireur de Nice et du Sud-Est* some ten years ago when I was sojourning on the Riviera. It seems that this gentleman climbed a tree and, having cunningly concealed himself in the foliage, began blowing on his lark call—"short, sharp in and out breaths, varying with buzzing sound in mouth at same time," says the catalog (try that on your lark call). Well, this man was so good that he was suddenly riddled with shotgun slugs from the weapon of another hunter, who had been royally taken in by the remarkable imitation. The thing to do with your English and American game-call set is simply to put it away somewhere in your den and think of it as an interesting collection, like so many old derringers. Nobody wants to get shot for a lark, or gored by an unsympathetic and disillusioned bull.

18. The Hiding Generation

ONE AFTERNOON ALMOST TWO YEARS AGO, AT A COCKTAIL PARTY (at least, this is the way I have been telling the story), an eager middle-aged woman said to me, "Do you belong to the Lost Generation, Mr. T?" and I retorted, coldly and quick as a flash, "No, Madam, I belong to the Hiding Generation."

As a matter of fact, no woman ever asked me such a question at a cocktail party or anywhere else. I thought up the little dialogue one night when I couldn't sleep. At the time, my retort seemed pretty sharp and satirical to me, and I hoped that some day somebody *would* ask me if I belonged to the Lost Generation, so that I could say no, I belonged to the Hiding Generation. But nobody ever has. My retort, however, began working in the back of my mind. I decided that since I was apparently never going to get a chance to use it as repartee, I ought to do something else with it, if only to get it out of the back of my mind. About ten months ago I got around to the idea of writing a book called "The Hiding Generation," which would be the story of my own intellectual conflicts, emotional disturbances, spiritual adventures, and journalistic experiences, something in the manner of Malcolm Cowley's "Exile's Return" or Vincent Sheean's "Personal History." The notion seemed to me a remarkably good one, and I was quite excited by it. I bought a new typewriter ribbon and a ream of fresh copy paper; I sharpened a dozen pencils; I got a pipe and tobacco. Then I sat down at the typewriter, lighted my pipe, and wrote on a sheet of paper "The

Hiding Generation, by James Thurber." That was as far as I got, because I discovered that I could not think of anything else to say. I mean anything at all.

Thus passed the first five or six hours of my work on the book. In the late afternoon some people dropped in for cocktails, and I didn't get around to the book again for two more

Some People Dropped in for Cocktails

days. Then I found that I still didn't have anything to say. I wondered if I had already said everything I had to say, but I decided, in looking over what I had said in the past, that I really hadn't ever said anything. This was an extremely depressing thought, and for a while I considered going into some other line of work. But I am not fitted for any other line of work, by inclination, experience, or aptitude. There was consequently nothing left for me but to go back to work on "The Hiding Generation." I decided to "write it in my mind," in the manner of Arnold Bennett (who did practically all of "The Old Wives' Tale" in his head), and this I devoted myself to for about seven months. At length I sat down at the type-writer once more, and there I was again, tapping my fingers on the table, lighting and relighting my pipe, getting up every now and then for a drink of water. I figured finally that maybe I had better make an outline of the book; probably all the writers I had in mind—and there was a pretty big list of them now, including Walter Duranty and Negley Farson—had made an outline of what they were going to say, using Roman numerals for the main divisions and small letters "a" and "b," etc., for the subdivisions. So I set down some Roman numerals and small letters on a sheet of paper. First I wrote "I. Early Youth." I could think of no subdivisions to go under that, so I put down "II. Young Manhood." All I could think of to go under that was "a. Studs Lonigan." Obviously that wouldn't do, so I tore up the sheet of paper and put the whole thing by for another week.

During that week I was tortured by the realization that I couldn't think of anything important that had happened to me up to the time I was thirty-three and began raising Scotch terriers. The conviction that nothing important had happened to me until I was thirty-three, that I had apparently had no intellectual conflicts or emotional disturbances, or anything, reduced me to such a state of dejection that I decided to go to Bridgeport for a few days and stay all alone in a hotel room. The motivation behind this decision is still a little vague in my mind, but I think it grew out of a feeling that I wasn't worthy of going away to Florida or Bermuda or Nassau or any other nice place. I had Bridgeport "coming to me," in a sense, as retribution for my blank youth and my blank young manhood. In the end, of course, I did not go to Bridgeport. I took a new sheet of paper and began another outline.

This time I started out with "I. University Life. a. Intellectual Conflicts." No other workable subdivisions occurred to me. The only Emotional Disturbance that came to my mind was unworthy of being incorporated in the book, for it had to do with the moment, during the Phi Psi May Dance of 1917, when I knocked a fruit salad onto the floor. The incident was as bald as that, and somehow I couldn't correlate it with anything. To start out with such an episode and then just leave it hanging in the air would not give the reader anything to get his teeth into. Therefore I concentrated on "Intellectual Conflicts," but I could not seem to call up any which had torn my mind asunder during my college days. Yet there *must* have been some. I made a lot of little squares and circles with a pencil for half an hour, and finally I remembered one intellectual conflict—if you could call it that. It was really only an argument I had had with a classmate at Ohio State University named Arthur Spencer, about "Tess of the D'Urbervilles." I had taken the view that the hero of the book was not justified in running away to South America and abandoning Tess simply because she had been indiscreet in her youth. Spencer, on the other hand, contended the man was fully justified, and that he (Spencer) would have run away to South America and left Tess, or any other woman, under the circumstances—that is, if he had had the money. As a matter of fact, Spencer settled down in East Liverpool, Ohio, where he is partner in his father's hardware store, and married a very nice girl named Sarah Gammadinger, who had been a Kappa at Ohio State.

I came to the conclusion finally that I would have to leave my university life out of the book, along with my early youth and young manhood. Therefore, my next Roman numeral, which would normally have been IV, automatically became I. I placed after it the words "Paris: A New World. a. Thoughts at Sea." It happened that upon leaving the university, in 1918, I went to Paris as a clerk, Grade B, in the American Embassy. In those days I didn't call it clerk, Grade B, I called it attaché, but it seemed to me that the honest and forceful thing to do was to tell the truth. The book would have more power and persuasion if I told the truth—providing I could remember the truth. There was a lot I couldn't remember, I found out in trying to. For instance, I had put down "Thoughts at Sea" after "a" because I couldn't recall anything significant that had happened to me during the five months I spent in Washington, D. C., before sailing for France. (Furthermore, it didn't seem logical to put a subdivision called "Washington Days" under a general heading called "Paris: A New World.") Something, of course, must have happened to me in Washington, something provocative or instructive, something that added to my stature, but all that comes back to me is a series of paltry little memories. I remember there was a waitress in the Post Café, at the corner of Thirteenth and E Streets, whose last name was Rabbit. I've forgot her first name and even what she looked like, but her last name was Rabbit. A Mrs. Rabbit. Then there was the flu epidemic, during which I gargled glycothymoline three times a day. All the rest has gone from me.

I found I could remember quite a lot about my days at sea on my way to Paris: A New World. In the first place, I had bought a box of San Felice cigars to take with me on the transport, but I was seasick all the way over and the cigars were smoked by a man named Ed Corcoran, who travelled with me. He was not sick a day. I believe he said he had never been sick a day in his life. Even some of the sailors were sick, but not Corcoran. No, sir. He was constantly in and out of our stateroom, singing, joking, smoking my cigars. The other thing I remembered about the voyage was that my trunk and suitcase failed to get on the ship; they were put by mistake on some other ship—the Minnetonka, perhaps, or the Charles O. Sprague, a coastwise fruit steamer. In any case, I didn't recover them until May, 1920, in Paris, and the Hershey bars my mother had packed here and there in both the trunk and the suitcase had melted and were all over everything. All my suits were brown, even the gray one. But I am anticipating myself. All this belongs under "Paris: A New World. b. Paris."

I was just twenty-five when I first saw Paris, and I was still a little sick. Unfortunately, when I try to remember my first impressions of Paris and the things that happened to me, I get them mixed up with my second trip to Paris, which was seven years later, when I was feeling much better and really got around more. On that first trip to Paris I was, naturally enough, without any clothes, except what I had on, and I had to outfit myself at once, which I did at the Galeries Lafayette. I paid $4.75 in American money for a pair of B.V.D.s. I remember that, all right. Nothing else comes back to me very clearly; everything comes back to me all jumbled up. I tried about five times to write down a comprehensive outline of my experiences in Paris: A New World, but the thing remained sketchy and trivial. If there was any development in my character or change in my outlook on life during that phase, I forget just where it came in and why. So I cut out the Paris interlude.

I find, in looking over my accumulation of outlines, that my last attempt to get the volume started began with the heading "I. New York Again: An Old World." This was confusing, because it could have meaning and pertinence only if it followed the chapter outlined as "Paris: A New World," and that had all been eliminated along with my Early Youth, Young Manhood, and University Days. Moreover, while my life back in New York must have done a great deal to change my character, viewpoint, objectives, and political ideals, I forget just exactly how this happened. I am the kind of man who should keep notes about such things. If I do not keep notes, I simply cannot remember a thing. Oh, I remember odds and ends, as you have seen, but they certainly would not tie up into anything like a moving chronicle of a man's life, running to a hundred and fifty thousand words. If they ran to twenty-five hundred words, I would be going good. Now, it's a funny thing: catch me in a drawing-room, over the coffee and liqueurs, particularly the Scotch-and-sodas, and I could hold you, or at least keep talking to you, for five or six hours about my life, but somebody would have to take down what I said and organize it into a book. When I sit down to *write* the story of my life, all I can think of is Mrs. Rabbit, and the Hershey bars, and the B.V.D.'s that came within two bits of costing five bucks. That is, of course, until I get up to the time when I was thirty-three and began raising Scotch terriers. I can put down all of that, completely and movingly, without even making an outline. Naturally, as complete and as moving as it might be, it would scarcely make a biography like, say, Negley Farson's, and it certainly would not sustain so pretentious a title as "The Hiding Generation." I would have to publish it as a pamphlet entitled "The Care and Training of Scotch Terriers." I am very much afraid that that is what my long arduous struggle to write the story of my life is going to come down to, if it is going to come down to anything.

Well, all of us cannot write long autobiographies. But *almost* all of us can.

19. *Wild Bird Hickok and His Friends*

IN ONE OF THE MANY INTERESTING ESSAYS THAT MAKE UP HIS book called "Abinger Harvest," Mr. E. M. Forster, discussing what he sees when he is reluctantly dragged to the movies in London, has set down a sentence that fascinates me. It is: "American women shoot the hippopotamus with eyebrows made of platinum." I have given that remarkable sentence a great deal of study, but I still do not know whether Mr. Forster means that American women have platinum eyebrows or that the hippopotamus has platinum eyebrows or that American women shoot platinum eyebrows into the hippopotamus. At any rate, it faintly stirred in my mind a dim train of elusive memories which were brightened up suddenly and brought into sharp focus for me when, one night, I went to see "The Plainsman," a hard-riding, fast-shooting movie dealing with warfare in the Far West back in the bloody seventies. I knew then what Mr. Forster's curious and tantalizing sentence reminded me of. It was like nothing in the world so much as certain sentences which appeared in a group of French paperback dime (or, rather, twenty-five-centime) novels that I collected a dozen years ago in France. "The Plainsman" brought up these old pulp thrillers in all clarity for me because, like that movie, they dealt mainly with the stupendous activities of Buffalo Bill and Wild Bill Hickok;

but in them were a unique fantasy, a special inventiveness, and an imaginative abandon beside which the movie treatment of the two heroes pales, as the saying goes, into nothing. In moving from one apartment to another some years ago, I somehow lost my priceless collection of *contes héroïques du Far-Ouest*, but happily I find that a great many of the deathless adventures of the French Buffalo Bill and Wild Bill Hickok remain in my memory. I hope that I shall recall them, for anodyne, when with eyes too dim to read, I pluck finally at the counterpane.

In the first place, it should perhaps be said that in the eighteen-nineties the American dime-novel hero who appears to have been most popular with the French youth—and adult —given to such literature was Nick Carter. You will find somewhere in one of John L. Stoddard's published lectures— there used to be a set in almost every Ohio bookcase—an anecdote about how an American tourist, set upon by *apaches* in a dark *rue* in Paris in the nineties, caused them to scatter in terror merely by shouting, *"Je suis Nick Carter!"* But at the turn of the century, or shortly thereafter, Buffalo Bill became the favorite. Whether he still is or not, I don't know—perhaps Al Capone or John Dillinger has taken his place. Twelve years ago, however, he was going great guns—or perhaps I should say great dynamite, for one of the things I most clearly remember about the Buffalo Bill of the French authors was that he always carried with him sticks of dynamite which, when he was in a particularly tough spot—that is, surrounded by more than two thousand Indians—he hurled into their midst, destroying them by the hundred. Many of the most inspired paperbacks that I picked up in my quest were used ones I found in those little stalls along the Seine. It was there, for instance, that I came across one of my favorites, "Les Aventures du Wild Bill dans le Far-Ouest."

Wild Bill Hickok was, in this wonderful and beautiful tale, an even more prodigious manipulator of the six-gun than he seems to have been in real life, which, as you must know, is saying a great deal. He frequently mowed down a hundred or two hundred Indians in a few minutes with his redoubtable pistol. The French author of this masterpiece for some mysterious but delightful reason referred to Hickok

"Vous vous Promenez Très Tard ce Soir, Mon Vieux!"

sometimes as Wild Bill and sometimes as Wild Bird. *"Bonjour, Wild Bill!"* his friend Buffalo Bill often said to him when they met, only to shout a moment later, *"Regardez, Wild Bird! Les Peaux-Rouges!"* The two heroes spent a great deal of their time, as in "The Plainsman," helping each other out of dreadful situations. Once, for example, while hunting Seminoles in Florida, Buffalo Bill fell into a tiger trap that had been set for him by the Indians—he stepped onto what turned out to be sticks covered with grass, and plunged to the bottom of a deep pit. At this point our author wrote, *" 'Mercy me!' s'écria Buffalo Bill."* The great scout was rescued, of course, by none other than Wild Bill, or Bird, who, emerging from the forest to see his old comrade in distress, could only exclaim *"My word!"*

It was, I believe, in another volume that one of the most interesting characters in all French fiction of the Far West appeared, a certain Major Preston, alias Preeton, alias Preslon (the paperbacks rarely spelled anyone's name twice in succession the same way). This hero, we were told when he was introduced, "had distinguished himself in the Civil War by capturing Pittsburgh," a feat which makes Lee's invasion of Pennsylvania seem mere child's play. Major Preeton (I always preferred that alias) had come out West to fight the Indians with cannon, since he believed it absurd that nobody had thought to blow them off the face of the earth with cannon before. How he made out with his artillery against the forest skulkers I have forgotten, but I have an indelible memory of a certain close escape that Buffalo Bill had in this same book. It seems that, through an oversight, he had set out on a scouting trip without his dynamite—he also carried, by the way, cheroots and a flashlight—and hence, when he stumbled upon a huge band of redskins, he had to ride as fast as he could for the nearest fort. He made it just in time. "Buffalo Bill," ran the story, "clattered across the drawbridge and into the fort just ahead of the Indians, who, unable to stop in time, plunged into the moat and were drowned." It may have been in this same tale that Buffalo Bill was once so hard pressed that he had to send for Wild Bird to help him out. Usually, when one was in trouble, the other showed up by a kind of instinct, but this time Wild Bird was nowhere to be found. It was a long time, in fact, before his whereabouts were discovered. You will never guess where he was. He was "taking the baths at Atlantic City under orders of his physician." But he came riding across the country in one day to Buffalo Bill's side, and all was well. Major Preeton, it sticks in my mind, got bored with the service in the Western hotels and went "back to Philadelphia" (Philadelphia appears to have been the capital city of the United States at this time). The Indians in all these tales—and this is probably what gave Major Preeton his great idea—were seldom seen as individuals or in pairs or small groups, but prowled about in well-ordered columns of squads. I recall, however, one drawing (the paperbacks were copiously illustrated) which showed two *Peaux-Rouges* leaping upon and capturing a scout who had wandered too far from his drawbridge one night. The picture represented one of the Indians as smilingly taunting his captive, and the caption read, *"Vous vous promenez très tard ce soir, mon vieux!"* This remained my favorite line until I saw one night in Paris an old W. S. Hart movie called "Le Roi du Far-Ouest," in which Hart, insulted by a drunken ruffian, turned upon him and said, in his grim, laconic way, *"Et puis, après?"*

I first became interested in the French tales of the Far West when, one winter in Nice, a French youngster of fifteen, who, it turned out, devoted all his spending money to them, asked me if I had ever seen a "wishtonwish." This meant nothing to me, and I asked him where he had heard about the wishtonwish. He showed me a Far West paperback he was reading. There was a passage in it which recounted an adventure of Buffalo Bill and Wild Bill during the course of which Buffalo Bill signalled to Wild Bird "in the voice of the wishtonwish." Said the author in a parenthesis which at that time gave me as much trouble as Mr. Forster's sentence about the platinum eyebrows does now, "The wishtonwish was seldom heard west of Philadelphia." It was some time—indeed, it was not until I got back to America—that I traced the wishtonwish to its lair, and in so doing discovered the influence of James Fenimore Cooper on all these French writers of Far

West tales. Cooper, in his novels, frequently mentioned the wishtonwish, which was a Caddoan Indian name for the prairie dog. Cooper erroneously applied it to the whippoorwill. An animal called the "ouapiti" also figured occasionally in the French stories, and this turned out to be the wapiti, or American elk, also mentioned in Cooper's tales. The French writer's parenthetical note on the habitat of the wishtonwish only added to the delightful confusion and inaccuracy which threaded these wondrous stories.

There were, in my lost and lamented collection, a hundred other fine things, which I have forgotten, but there is one that will forever remain with me. It occurred in a book in which, as I remember it, Billy the Kid, alias Billy the Boy, was the central figure. At any rate, two strangers had turned up in a small Western town and their actions had aroused the suspicions of a group of respectable citizens, who forthwith called on the sheriff to complain about the newcomers. The sheriff listened gravely for a while, got up and buckled on his gun belt, and said, *"Alors, je vais demander ses cartes d'identité!"* There are few things, in any literature, that have ever given me a greater thrill than coming across that line.

20. *Doc Marlowe*

I WAS TOO YOUNG TO BE OTHER THAN AWED AND PUZZLED BY Doc Marlowe when I knew him. I was only sixteen when he died. He was sixty-seven. There was that vast difference in our ages and there was a vaster difference in our backgrounds. Doc Marlowe was a medicine-show man. He had been a lot of other things, too: a circus man, the proprietor of a concession at Coney Island, a saloon-keeper; but in his fifties he had traveled around with a tent-show troupe made up of a Mexican named Chickalilli, who threw knives, and a man called Professor Jones, who played the banjo. Doc Marlowe would come out after the entertainment and harangue the crowd and sell bottles of medicine for all kinds of ailments. I found out all this about him gradually, toward the last, and after he died. When I first knew him, he represented the Wild West to me, and there was nobody I admired so much.

I met Doc Marlowe at old Mrs. Willoughby's rooming house. She had been a nurse in our family, and I used to go and visit her over week-ends sometimes, for I was very fond of her. I was about eleven years old then. Doc Marlowe wore scarred leather leggings, a bright-colored bead vest that he said he got from the Indians, and a ten-gallon hat with kitchen matches stuck in the band, all the way around. He was about six feet four inches tall, with big shoulders, and a long, drooping mustache. He let his hair grow long, like General Custer's. He had a wonderful collection of Indian relics and six-shooters, and he used to tell me stories of his

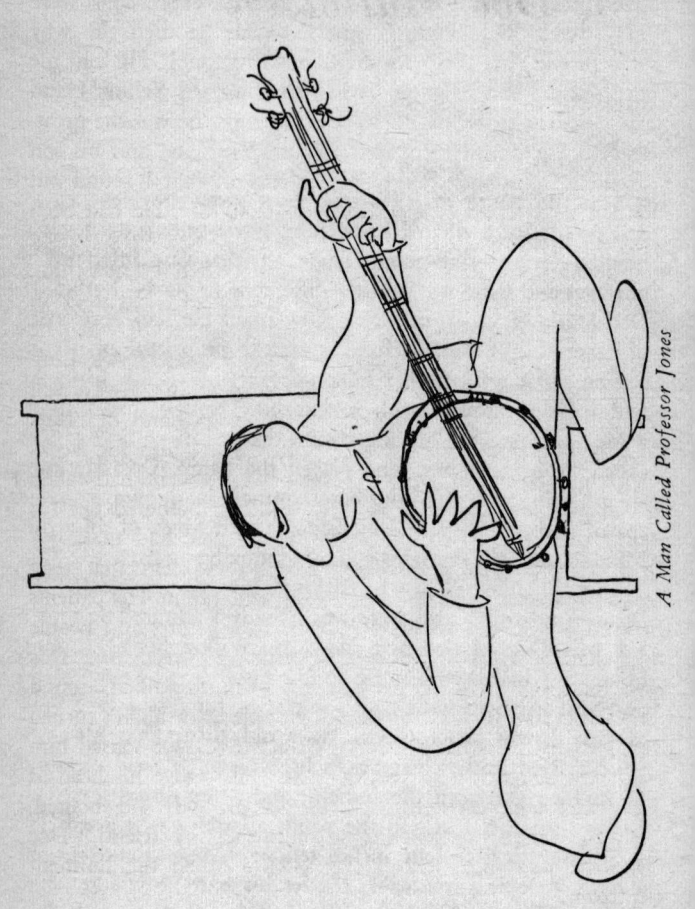

A Man Called Professor Jones

adventures in the Far West. His favorite expressions were "Hay, boy!" and "Hay, boy-gie!," which he used the way some people now use "Hot dog!" or "Doggone!" He told me once that he had killed an Indian chief named Yellow Hand in a tomahawk duel on horseback. I thought he was the greatest man I had ever seen. It wasn't until he died and his son came on from New Jersey for the funeral that I found out he had never been in the Far West in his life. He had been born in Brooklyn.

Doc Marlowe had given up the road when I knew him, but he still dealt in what he called "medicines." His stock in trade was a liniment that he had called Snake Oil when he travelled around. He changed the name to Blackhawk Liniment when he settled in Columbus. Doc didn't always sell enough of it to pay for his bed and board, and old Mrs. Willoughby would sometimes have to "trust" him for weeks at a time. She didn't mind, because his liniment had taken a bad kink out of her right limb that had bothered her for thirty years. I used to see people whom Doc had massaged with Blackhawk Liniment move arms and legs that they hadn't been able to move before he "treated" them. His patients were day laborers, wives of streetcar conductors, and people like that. Sometimes they would shout and weep after Doc had massaged them, and several got up and walked around who hadn't been able to walk before. One man hadn't turned his head to either side for seven years before Doc soused him with Blackhawk. In half an hour he could move his head as easily as I could move mine. "Glory be to God!" he shouted. "It's the secret qualities in the ointment, my friend," Doc Marlowe told him, suavely. He always called the liniment ointment.

News of his miracles got around by word of mouth among the poorer classes of town—he was not able to reach the better people (the "tony folks," he called them)— but there was never a big enough sale to give Doc a steady income. For one thing, people thought there was more magic in Doc's touch than in his liniment, and, for another, the ingredients of Blackhawk cost so much that his profits were not very great. I know, because I used to go to the wholesale chemical company once in a while for him and buy his supplies. Everything that went into the liniment was standard and expensive (and well-known, not secret). A man at the company told me he didn't see how Doc could make much money on it at thirty-five cents a bottle. But even when he was very low in funds Doc never cut out any of the ingredients or substituted cheaper ones. Mrs. Willoughby had suggested it to him once, she told me, when she was helping him "put up a batch," and he had got mad. "He puts a heap of store by that liniment being right up to the mark," she said.

Doc added to his small earnings, I discovered, by money he made gambling. He used to win quite a few dollars on Saturday nights at Freck's saloon, playing poker with the marketmen and the railroaders who dropped in there. It wasn't for several years that I found out Doc cheated. I had never heard about marked cards until he told me about them and showed me his. It was one rainy afternoon, after he had played seven-up with Mrs. Willoughby and old Mr. Peiffer, another roomer of hers. They had played for small stakes (Doc wouldn't play cards unless there was some money up, and Mrs. Willoughby wouldn't play if very much was up). Only twenty or thirty cents had changed hands in the end. Doc had won it all. I remember my astonishment and indignation when it dawned on me that Doc had used the marked cards in playing the old lady and the old man. "You didn't cheat *them*, did you?" I asked him. "Jimmy, my boy," he told me, "the man that calls the turn wins the money." His eyes twinkled and he seemed to enjoy my anger. I was outraged, but I was helpless. I knew I could never tell Mrs. Willoughby about how Doc had cheated her at seven-up. I liked her, but I liked him, too. Once he had given me a whole dollar to buy fireworks with on the Fourth of July.

I remember once, when I was staying at Mrs. Willoughby's, Doc Marlowe was roused out of bed in the middle of the night by a poor woman who was frantic because her little girl was sick. This woman had had the sciatica driven out of her by his liniment, she reminded Doc. He placed her then. She had never been able to pay him a cent for his liniment or his "treatments," and he had given her a great many. He got up and dressed, and went over to her house. The child had colic, I suppose. Doc couldn't have had any idea what was the matter, but he sopped on liniment; he sopped on a whole bottle. When he came back home, two hours later, he said he had "relieved the distress." The little girl had gone to sleep and was all right the next day, whether on account of Doc Marlowe or in spite of him I don't know. "I want to thank you, Doctor," said the mother, tremulously, when she called on him that afternoon. He gave her another bottle of liniment, and he didn't charge her for it or for his "professional call." He used to massage, and give liniment to, a lot of sufferers who were too poor to pay. Mrs. Willoughby told him once that he was too generous and too easily taken in. Doc laughed —and winked at me, with the twinkle in his eye that he had had when he told me how he had cheated the old lady at cards.

Once I went for a walk with him out Town Street on a Saturday afternoon. It was a warm day, and after a while I said I wanted a soda. Well, he said, he didn't care if he took something himself. We went into a drugstore, and I ordered a chocolate soda and he had a lemon phosphate. When we had finished, he said, "Jimmy, my son, I'll match you to see who pays for the drinks." He handed me a quarter and he told me to toss the quarter and he would call the turn. He called heads and won. I paid for the drinks. It left me with a dime.

I was fifteen when Doc got out his pamphlets, as he called them. He had eased the misery of the wife of a small-time printer and the grateful man had given him a special price on two thousand advertising pamphlets. There was very little in them about Blackhawk Liniment. They were mostly about Doc himself and his "Life in the Far West." He had gone out to Franklin Park one day with a photographer—another of his numerous friends—and there the photographer took dozens of pictures of Doc, a lariat in one hand, a six-shooter in the other. I had gone along. When the pamphlets came out, there were the pictures of Doc, peering around trees, crouching behind bushes, whirling the lariat, aiming the gun. "Dr. H. M. Marlowe Hunting Indians" was one of the captions. "Dr. H. M. Marlowe after Hoss-Thieves" was another one. He was very proud of the pamphlets and always had a sheaf with him. He would pass them out to people on the street.

Two years before he died Doc got hold of an ancient, wheezy Cadillac somewhere. He aimed to start traveling around again, he said, but he never did, because the old automobile was so worn out it wouldn't hold up for more than a mile or so. It was about this time that a man named Hardman and his wife came to stay at Mrs. Willoughby's. They were farm people from around Lancaster who had sold their place. They got to like Doc because he was so jolly, they said, and they enjoyed his stories. He treated Mrs. Hardman for an old complaint in the small of her back and wouldn't take any money for it. They thought he was a fine gentleman. Then there came a day when they announced that they were going to St. Louis, where they had a son. They talked some of settling in St. Louis. Doc Marlowe told them they ought to buy a nice auto cheap and drive out, instead of going by train—it wouldn't cost much and they could see the country, give themselves a treat. Now, he knew where they could pick up just such a car.

Of course, he finally sold them the decrepit Cadillac—it had been stored away somewhere in the back of a garage whose owner kept it there for nothing because Doc had relieved his mother of a distress in the groins, as Doc explained it. I don't know just how the garage man doctored up the car, but he did. It actually chugged along pretty steadily when Doc took the Hardmans out for a trial spin. He told them he hated to part with it, but he finally let them have it for a hundred dollars. I knew, of course, and so did Doc, that it couldn't last many miles.

Doc got a letter from the Hardmans in St. Louis ten days later. They had had to abandon the old junk pile in West Jefferson, some fifteen miles out of Columbus. Doc read the letter aloud to me, peering over his glasses, his eyes twinkling, every now and then punctuating the lines with "Hay, boy!" and "Hay, boy-gie!" "I just want you to know, Dr. Marlowe," he read, "what I think of low-life swindlers like you [Hay, boy!] and that it will be a long day before I put my trust in a two-faced lyer and imposture again [Hay, boy-gie!]. The garrage man in W. Jefferson told us your old rattle-trap had been doctored up just to fool us. It was a low down dirty trick as no swine would play on a white man [Hay, boy!]." Far from being disturbed by the letter, Doc Marlowe was plainly amused. He took off his glasses, after he finished it and laughed, his hand to his brow and his eyes closed. I was pretty mad, because I had liked the Hardmans, and because they had liked him. Doc Marlowe put the letter carefully back into its envelope and tucked it away in his inside coat pocket, as if it were something precious. Then he picked up a pack of cards and began to lay out a solitaire hand. "Want to set in a little seven-up game, Jimmy?" he asked me. I was furious "Not with a cheater like you!" I shouted, and stamped out of the room, slamming the door. I could hear him chuckling to himself behind me.

The last time I saw Doc Marlowe was just a few days before he died. I didn't know anything about death, but I knew that he was dying when I saw him. His voice was very faint and his face was drawn; they told me he had a lot of pain. When I got ready to leave the room, he asked me to bring him a tin box that was on his bureau. I got it and handed it to him. He poked around in it for a while with unsteady fingers and finally found what he wanted. He handed it to me. It was a quarter, or rather it looked like a quarter, but it had heads on both sides. "Never let the other fella call the turn, Jimmy, my boy," said Doc, with a shadow of his old twinkle and the echo of his old chuckle. I still have the two-headed quarter. For a long time I didn't like to think about it, or about Doc Marlowe, but I do now.

21. Food Fun for the Menfolk

FIVE OR SIX WEEKS AGO, SOMEONE WHO SIGNED HIMSELF SIMPLY A Friend sent me a page torn from the Sunday magazine section of the *Herald Tribune*. "I thought this might interest you," he wrote. Unfortunately, he failed to mark the particular item he had in mind. On one side of the page was an article called "New Thoughts about Awnings," which, naturally, didn't interest me at all. I turned the page over and came to this announcement: "Why shouldn't you be among the prize winners in our reader-recipe contest for dishes made with plain or prepared gelatin?" The answer to that was so simple as to be silly, so I went on to another column and a recipe for "Plum Surprise." That couldn't have been what A Friend wanted me to see, for the least of my interests in this world, the least of anybody's interests, is Plum Surprise. Gradually, by this process of elimination, I came to an article called "Shower Parties, Up-to-Date!" (the exclamation point is the author's). This was without doubt what A Friend wished to bring to my attention. I read the article with mingled feelings of dismay and downright dread and then threw it away. But it haunted me for weeks. I realized finally that "Shower Parties, Up-to-Date!" presented one of those menaces which it is far better to face squarely than to try to ignore, so I dug it up again and you and I are now going to face it together.

If we all stand as one, we can put a stop to the ominous innovation in shower parties which the author of the article, Miss Elizabeth Harriman, so gaily suggests.

It is Miss Elizabeth Harriman's contention that *it is high time to invite the bridegroom and his men friends to shower parties for the bride!* (The italics and the exclamation point are mine.) "Nowadays," she says, flatly, "the groom insists

The Hostess Hands Each Guest, Including Joe, a Piece of Cardboard

on being included in the party." Without descending to invective, mud-slinging, or the lie direct, I can only say that you and I and Miss Harriman have never met a groom and, what is more, are never going to meet a groom who insists on being included in a shower party given for his bride. A groom would as soon wear a veil and carry a bouquet of lilies of the valley and baby's-breath as attended a shower party. Particularly the kind of shower party which Miss Harriman, with fiendish glee, goes on to invent right out of her own head. Let her start it off for you herself: "After supper—which should be simple—comes the 'shower,' and here's where we surprise the bride—and the groom—by not giving them a complete set of kitchen equipment. With a mischievous twinkle in our eye, we deposit in front of the happy couple a bushel basket, saying 'The grocer left this a little early for your new home, but you'd better open it now.'" I will take up the story of what is supposed to happen next myself, with a glint of cold horror in my eye.

It seems that the bushel basket is covered with a large piece of brown paper marked with the date of the forthcoming wedding. The very thought of a prospective bridegroom standing in a group of giggling women, with mischievous twinkles in their eyes, and looking at a bushel basket covered with brown paper bearing the date of his wedding is enough to convince anybody that Miss Harriman has got the wrong group of people together. But let us see what happens further (both according to Miss Harriman and according to me). In the basket, she says, are six brown-paper bags. The groom is made to pick up one of these, marked "What the Groom Gets." No groom in the United States would open a bag of that description—he is going through enough the way things are—but let us suppose that he does. Do you know what falls out of it, amid screams of laughter? A peach falls out of it. The bride now picks up a second brown-paper bag, labelled "What the Bride Gets." If you can't picture the look on the face of the groom at this point, I can. Well, out of this bag comes a box of salt marked "Genuine Old Salt." It seems that Miss Harriman has made the groom in this particular case "an ardent fisherman"—hence, Genuine Old Salt. Of course, that wouldn't work in the case of a groom who was not an ardent fisherman. All the guests would just stand there, with their mischievous twinkles turning to puzzled stares. If the groom is *not* an ardent fisherman, Miss Harriman suggests that the bride's bag contain "a gingerbread man cutter." You can hear the pleased roars of the groom and his men friends. "By George," they cry, "this is more fun than a barrel of monkeys!" Everybody is so interested that nobody wonders whether drinks are going to be served, or anything of that sort. There are four brown-paper bags yet to be opened, you see.

The bride now opens the first of these bags, marked simply "The Bride." From this emerge, amid the ecstatic squeals of the ladies, an old potato, a new potato, a borrowed rolling pin, and a blue plum. All the men stare blankly at this array and one of them begins to wonder where they keep the liquor in this house; but the girls explain about the contents of the bag. "Don't you see, Joe? It's 'something old and something new, something borrowed and something blue.'" "What's the potatoes for?" says Joe, gloomily (he is the man who was wondering where they keep the liquor). "I don't get it." "Well, Bert gets it," says the woman who has been explaining to Joe. Bert is a man whose guts Joe hates. "Let him have it," says Joe. This is one of his worst evenings, and there are still three brown-paper bags to be opened. The groom is now holding one of these, on which is printed "The Groom Is In the Kitchen Closet." There is a Bronx cheer from somewhere (probably from Harry Innis) and the groom grins redly; he wishes he were back in college. You and I know that the groom would simply put this bag back in the basket muttering something about it must be getting late, but Miss Harriman says he would open it. All right, he opens it. And pulls out a toy broom. At this point the groom's embarrassment and Joe's gloom are deeper than ever. "What's the idea?" Joe growls. "Stupid!" cries one of the ladies, gaily. "Don't you know 'Here comes the groom, stiff as a groom—stiff as a broom,' I mean?" "No," says Joe. He now moves directly on the pantry to see what there is in the way of drinks around the place. What he finds, in the icebox, is a Mason jar filled with cranberry juice. Joe instantly begins to look for his hat and overcoat, but the hostess captures him. There is more fun to come, she tells him—it is still *frightfully* early, only about eight-thirty.

The hostess leads Joe back to the bushel basket and pulls a fifth bag out of it, which she asks him to open; it is labelled "What the Guests Have." "What's the idea?" Joe grumbles, holding the bag as if it were a doily or a diaper. "Open it, silly!" squeal the excited girls, several of whom, however, are now squealing a little less excitedly than they have been. Joe finally opens the bag and pulls out a box of rice and a box of thyme marked "Good Thyme." "Thyme," mutters Joe, blankly, pronouncing the "h." He hands the boxes to the groom, who distractedly puts them back in the brown bag and puts the brown bag back in the bushel basket. One of the women hastily takes the bag out and opens it again, putting the rice and the thyme on a table. A slight chill falls over the party, on account of the groom's distraction and Joe's sullenness. There is a bad pause, not helped any by Harry Innis's wide yawn, but the hostess quickly hands the sixth and last brown bag to the bride, who extracts from it "a small jar of honey and a moon-shaped cooky-cutter." Joe takes the cooky-cutter from the bride; he is mildly interested for the first time. "What's this thing belong on?" he asks. Somebody takes it away from him. The groom glances at his wristwatch. It is not yet nine o'clock. "Isn't this fun, dear?" asks his bride. "Yeh," says the groom. "Yeh, sure. Swell." The bride realizes, with a quick intuition, that she is losing her hold on the groom. If she is a smart bride, she will be taken suddenly ill at this point and the groom will have to see her home (and Joe will have a chance to cry out with great concern, "Is there any whiskey in the house?"). But let us suppose that the bride is too dumb to realize why she is losing her hold on the groom. The party in this case goes right on. Miss Harriman has a lot more plans for it; she again has a mischievous twinkle in her eye.

The hostess—I shall just call her Miss Harriman—now hands each guest, including Joe, a piece of cardboard ruled off into twenty-five numbered squares (you can look up the article yourself). Each of the squares is large enough for a word to be written in it. Several of the men who have pencils swear they haven't, but Miss Harriman manages to dig up twenty-two pencils and two fountain pens from somewhere. Harry Innis puts his piece of cardboard on the arm of a davenport, stands up, and says, "Whatta you say we all run up to Tim's for a highball?" At this, Joe instantly puts on his overcoat, but one of the women makes him take it off, whispering harshly that he will break Miss Harriman's heart if he doesn't stay. "Aw," says Joe, and slumps into a chair. Mrs. Innis is quietly giving Harry a piece of her mind in a corner.

Miss Harriman now appears before everybody with an *enormous* piece of cardboard, also ruled off into twenty-five squares. Each square contains a dab of some kitchen staple or other: a dab of salt, a dab of pepper, a dab of sugar, a dab of flour, a dab of cayenne, a dab of sage, a dab of cinnamon, a dab of coffee, a dab of tea, a dab of dry mustard, a dab of grated cheese, a dab of baking powder, a dab of cocoa, and dabs of twelve other things. "The bride has her groceries all mixed up!" Miss Harriman sings out brightly. "You must all help her straighten them out! Everybody may look at the things on my cardboard and feel them, too, but nobody must dare taste! Then you write down in the corresponding squares on your own cardboard what you think the different things are!" Most of the men are now standing in a corner talking about the new Buick. One of them has folded his cardboard double and then folded that double and is absently tearing it into strips. Only Bert and two other men stick in the staples game; they identify the salt, sugar, pepper, coffee, and tea, and let it go at that. Ten of the twelve women present get all the answers right. The prize is a can of pepper and, not knowing whom to give it to, Miss Harriman just puts it on a table and claps her hands for attention. She announces that there is another food game to come. "Geezuss," says Joe.

Let Miss Harriman describe the next game in her own words. "In a large pan we gather together as many different vegetables and fruits as we can find—a bunch of carrots, a few beets, a turnip or two, potatoes white and sweet, parsley, lettuce, beans, oranges, grapefruit, pineapple, cherries, bananas— oh, anything. On a tray are placed string, toothpicks, paper towelling, waxed paper, pins, knives, scissors, melon-ball scoops, and any other kitchen implements. This game calls for partners, and as this is a food shower, we try to think of all the foods that seem to go together—Salt and Pepper; Liver and Bacon; Corned Beef and Cabbage; Cream and Sugar, etc. Half the ingredients are written on one color paper, the other on another color, and the guests match them for partners."

If, like Joe (who has drawn Liver and, for partner, a Miss Bacon whom he has been avoiding all evening), you haven't got the idea yet, let me explain. The guests are supposed to manufacture the effigies of brides out of all these materials. Whoever makes the funniest or most original bride wins. (There are a lot of gags at this point, the men guffawing over in their corner. Bill Pierson tells the one about the social worker and the colored woman.) Of this bride-making game Miss Harriman writes: "Loud guffaws and wild dashes to the supply table will result." (She is right about the loud guffaws.) "Imaginations will run riot and hidden talents will come to the fore." But meanwhile, under cover of the loud guffaws and the wild dashes, Joe, Harry Innis, and the groom have slipped out of the house and gone on up to Tim's. When the bride discovers that the groom has disappeared she is distraught, for she thinks she has lost him for good, and I would not be surprised if she has.

An appropriate prize for this contest is, according to Miss Harriman, "a bridal bouquet of scallions and radishes with streamers of waxed paper, presented as someone plays 'Here Comes the Bride.'" You can imagine how Joe would have loved that if he had stayed. But he and Harry Innis and the groom are on their fifth highball up at Tim's. "And, so our kitchen shower ends," writes Miss Harriman, happily, "with demands for another wedding as an excuse for more food fun." You have to admire the woman for whatever it is she has.

22. Goodbye, Mr. O. Charles Meyer!

I AM LEAVING IN A FEW DAYS THE APARTMENT I HAVE LIVED IN for almost a year, on the corner of Eighth Street and Fifth Avenue. Its living-room windows and my bedroom window look out over Eighth Street to the west. Eighth Street is so far below that I cannot make out its signs. The top of a building hides the Jefferson Market clock. All the roofs I see are the same roof; they are indistinguishable, one from another. There is only one thing I shall remember: a sign high up on a building in Eighth Street near Sixth Avenue which says in letters four feet tall, "O. Charles Meyer." Mr. Meyer is in the upholstering business. The sign tells you all about it. I see O. Charles Meyer the first thing every morning when I wake up, and during the day whenever I look out the window, and I go to bed knowing that he is out there, as sturdy and staunch as the little toy soldier. In the months that have gone by, O. Charles Meyer has taken on the semblance of a friend to me. His name is as familiar as the name of any friend I have.

I do not, of course, know O. Charles Meyer in the flesh, but I have a certainty of what he is like, a large, heavy man, elderly and kindly, with the peering eyes of a person who has spent his life puttering with the upholstery of chairs and sofas. In the old chairs and sofas that have been brought to him for reupholstering he has found scissors and penknives

and necklaces and unopened letters and hundreds of thousands
of dollars in bills which little old ladies have hidden away.
If this is not true, I don't want to be told so. O. Charles Meyer
is, after all, my own creation. "My O. Charles," I could say of
Mr. Meyer as Willa Cather said "My Antonia" of a certain

Turning up with a Green Plush Chair of His Own to Sit in

Miss Shimerda. I figure him as having a number of sons: O.
Freddy, O. Samuel, O. George, O. Charles, Jr., and—if it is
not too much to ask—O. Henry. I think there may have been
three daughters, O. Grace, O. Patience, and O. Charity, but
they all married upholsterers in beaver hats and went away,
many years ago. I do not want to know what the O. stands for.

I have a sentimental feeling about O. Charles Meyer and I
shall hate to leave him, but I am going to have to because my

lease is running out and some new tenants will be moving in. I have no other person to turn to of O. Charles Meyer's peculiar stature as an intimate. It will take me a long time to get used to not seeing him in the morning and all day long. One gets sentimentally attached to curious things in this city of steel and cement. In Connecticut, where I used to have a farm, I could look out the window of the room I worked in and see an apple tree, an ancient russet apple tree. I got to know each bend and twist of its branches. It was a friendly and familiar tree, but, like all ancient apple trees, it began to lose its branches; a branch fell off in every storm, so that the appearance of the old tree was always changing. O. Charles Meyer, on the other hand, has always remained the same. O. Charles Meyer is immutable. Eighth Street changes under him in its restless way, people move in and out of the apartments round about, but O. Charles Meyer goes on forever. In such permanence one finds a sense of peace and assurance.

If I ever have to have any upholstering work done, I would want to take it to O. Charles Meyer, but I would be afraid to. I would be afraid that some crisp clerk in the establishment might say to me, "O. Charles Meyer? Why, there is no O. Charles Meyer any longer. Would you like to talk to Mr. Hinkley? Or Mr. Bence?" Something would go out of my life that would make me miserable, if that happened. I would feel that I couldn't trust anything or anybody any more, if O. Charles Meyer let me down. And yet something constantly nags at me—I like to think it's curiosity and not distrust—something nags at me to call up O. Charles on the phone and do something about him. I feel that there is a certain roundness lacking in my association with him. I feel that whereas he has meant a lot to me, I have meant nothing at all to him. I hate to leave my apartment without making a gesture of some kind on his behalf. It has occurred to me to ask him to a cocktail party (I see him turning up with a green plush chair of his own to sit in). I have thought of phrasing my note to him something like this:

"Mr. O. Charles Meyer,

"Eighth Street,

"Dear Mr. Meyer: Will you come to a cocktail party at my apartment tomorrow from 5 to 7? If there is no such person as you, please do not reply." There is a chance here, of course, that Mr. Meyer—or Mr. Hinkley or Mr. Bence—might turn my note over to the police. It would be a nasty bit of evidence in case any suit should ever be filed against me to commit me to an institution. I can hear a lawyer making the most of it. "If it please the Court, I should like to submit in evidence, as State's Exhibit A, this note I hold in my hand. This is a note written by the defendant to one O. Charles Meyer, an upholsterer, inviting Mr. Meyer to a cocktail party. The defendant had never met this man Meyer in his life, as the note proves, and furthermore did not even know whether there *was* such a man. What is more, the note shows that the defendant did not even want to find *out* whether there was such a man. Now, the State contends quite simply . . ."

I suppose, everything considered, that I better drop my relationship with O. Charles Meyer right where it is. The chances are, however, that I will drop around the day before I leave, just to say goodbye and to tell him how much I will miss him, in which case will probably be committed before the summer is out. I'll try not to call on him. I'll try to let it go at this. Goodbye, Mr. O. Charles Meyer! Don't upholster any electric chairs!

23. What Are the Leftists Saying?

For a long time I have had the idea that it would be interesting to attempt to explain to an average worker what the leftist, or socially conscious, literary critics are trying to say. Since these critics are essentially concerned with the improvement of the worker's status, it seems fitting and proper that the worker should be educated in the meaning of their pronouncements. The critics themselves believe, of course, in the education of the worker, but they are divided into two schools about it: those who believe the worker should be taught beforehand why there must be a revolution, and those who believe that he should be taught afterward why there was one. This is but one of many two-school systems which divide the leftist intellectuals and keep them so busy in controversy that the worker is pretty much left out of things. It is my plan to escort a worker to a hypothetical, but typical, gathering of leftist literary critics and interpret for him, insofar as I can, what is being said there. The worker is likely to be so confused at first, and so neglected, that he will want to slip out and go to Minsky's; but it is important that he stay, and I hope that he has already taken a chair and removed his hat. I shall sit beside him and try to clarify what is going on.

Nothing, I must explain while we are waiting for the gentlemen to gather, is going to be easy. This is partly because it is a primary tenet of leftist criticism to avoid what is known as Oversimplification. This is a word our worker is going to encounter frequently at the gathering of critics and it is important that he understand what it means. Let me get at it by quoting a sentence from a recent review in *The Nation* by a socially conscious critic: "In so far as men assert and

The Others Are Not so Much Listening as Waiting for an Opening

counter-assert, you can draw an assertion from the comparison of their assertions." As it stands, that is not oversimplified, because no one can point to any exact or absolute meaning it has. Now I will oversimplify it. A says, "Babe Ruth is dead" (assertion). B says, "Babe Ruth is alive" (counter-assertion). C says, "You guys seem to disagree" (assertion drawn from comparison of assertions). Here I have brought the critic's sentence down to a definite meaning by providing a concrete instance. Leftist criticism does not believe in that, contending that all thought is in a state of motion, and that in every thought there exists simultaneously "being," "non-being," and "becoming," and that in the end every thought disappears by being absorbed into its opposite. I am afraid that I am over-simplifying again.

Let us get back to our meeting. About sixteen leftist literary critics have now gathered in the room. Several are talking and the others are not so much listening as waiting for an opening. Let us cock an ear toward Mr. Hubert Camberwell. Mr. Camberwell is saying, "Sinclair Lewis has dramatized the process of disintegration, as well as his own dilemma, in the outlines of his novels, in the progress of his characters, and sometimes, and most painfully, in the lapses of taste and precision that periodically weaken the structure of his prose." This is a typical leftist critic's sentence. It has a facile, portentous swing, it damns a prominent author to hell, and it covers a tremendous amount of ground. It also has an air of authority, and because of this the other critics will attack it. Up speaks a Mr. Scholzweig: "But you cannot, with lapses of any kind, *dramatize* a process, you can only *annotate* it." This is a minor criticism, at best, but it is the only one Mr. Scholzweig can think of, because he agrees in general with what has been said about Sinclair Lewis (whose books he has never been able to read). At this point Donald Crowley announces that as yet nobody has *defined* anything; that is, nobody has defined "lapses," "dramatize," "process," or "annotate." While a small, excited man in shell-rim glasses is asking him how he would define the word "definition" in a world of flux, let us listen to Mr. Herman Bernheim. Mr. Bernheim is muttering something about Camberwell's "methodology" and his failure to "implement" his argument. Now, "methodology," as the leftist intellectuals use it, means any given wrong method of approach to a subject. "To implement" means (1) to have at the tip of one's tongue everything that has been written by any leftist since Marx, for the purpose of denying it, and (2) to possess and make use of historical references that begin like this: "Because of the more solidly articulated structure of French society, the deep-seated sentiments and prejudices of the northern French, and the greater geographical and political accessibility of France to the propaganda of the counter-Reformation," etc., etc.

The critics have by this time got pretty far away from Camberwell's analysis of Sinclair Lewis, but this is the customary procedure when leftists begin refuting one another's statements, and is one phase of what is known as "dialectic." Dialectic, in this instance, means the process of discriminating one's own truth from the other person's error. This leads to "factionalism," another word our worker must be familiar with. Factionalism is that process of disputation by means of which the main point at issue is lost sight of. Now, the main point at issue here—namely, the analysis of Sinclair Lewis—becomes even more blurred by the fact that a critic named Kyle Forsythe, who has just come into the room, gets the erroneous notion that everybody is discussing Upton Sinclair. He begins, although it is not at all relevant, to talk about "escapism." Escapism means the activities of anyone who is not a leftist critic or writer. The discussion, to our worker, will now appear to get so far out of hand that we must bring him a Scotch-and-soda if we are to hold his interest much longer. He will probably want to know whether one leftist intellectual ever agrees with another, and, under cover of the loud talking, I shall explain the one form of agreement which these critics have. I call it the "that he—but when" form of agreement. Let us say that one leftist critic writes in a liberal weekly as follows: "I like poetry, but I don't like Tennyson." Another leftist critic will write often in the same issue and immediately following the first one's article: "That he likes poetry, we must concede Mr. Blank, but when he says that Tennyson is a great poet, we can only conclude that he does not like poetry at all." This is, of course, greatly oversimplified.

Midnight eventually arrives at our party and everybody begins "unmasking" everybody else's "ideology." To explain what unmasking an ideology means, I must give an example. Suppose that I were to say to one of the critics at this party, "My country, 'tis of thee, sweet land of liberty." He would unmask my ideology—that is expose the background of my illusion—by pointing out that I am the son of wealthy bourgeois parents who employed an English butler. This is not true, but my ideology would be unmasked, anyway. It is interesting to note that it takes only one leftist critic to expose anybody's ideology, and that every leftist critic unmasks ideologies in his own special way. In this sense, Marxist criticism is very similar to psychoanalysis. Ideology-unmasking is a great deal like dream interpretation and leads to just as many mystic results.

A general midnight unmasking of ideologies at a gathering of leftist literary critics is pretty exciting, and I hope that a second Scotch-and-soda will persuade our worker to stay. If he does, he will find out that when your ideology is unmasked, you can't do anything with it, because it has no "social currency." In other words, anything that you say or do will have no more validity than Confederate money.

The party now breaks up, without ill feeling, because the critics have all had such a good time at the unmasking. A leftist critic gets as much fun out of disputation, denial, and disparagement as a spaniel puppy gets out of a steak bone. Each one will leave, confident that he has put each of the others in his place and that they realize it. This is known as the "united front." On our way out, however, I must explain to the worker the meaning of an extremely important term in Marxist criticism; namely, "Dialectical Materialism." Dialectical Materialism, then, is based on two fundamental laws of dialectics: the law of the permeation of opposites, or polar unity, and the law of the negation of the negation, or development through opposites. This second proposition is the basic law of all processes of thought. I will first state the law itself and then support it with examples . . . Hey, worker! Wait for baby!

24. How to Write an Autobiography

THE COMMUNIST INTELLECTUALS KNOW A LOT MORE THAN I do, and while I am the first, or among the first, anyway, to admit it, I am also the first to explain why. For one thing, they keep all the letters they get from intellectual friends and use them in their writings; and, for another thing, they keep carbon copies of all the letters they write. Everybody gets off a few pretty good cracks, comments, and the like in his letters, but almost everybody forgets them after he sends them off. I suspect there is a type of author (both Communist and bourgeois) who, dashing off, in a letter, a sentence or a paragraph, or even a phrase, he thinks is pretty good, copies it down before he mails the letter. But the Communist intellectuals, as I say, keep carbon copies of the whole works. This seems to me unfair, for some reason; maybe I don't mean unfair, maybe I mean something else, but if I do, I mean something I don't like.

Take "An American Testament," published not long ago. It was written by one of America's brightest Communist intellectuals, Mr. Joseph Freeman. It runs, I have estimated, to 330,000 words. I can't go back through the book and find all the letters Mr. Freeman quotes, and I doubt if he could, but I can find some of them. On page 191, for instance, there is a paragraph beginning: " 'For me personally'—Irwin [Edman]

wrote me from Dresden in the fall of 1920—'the world these last few weeks has been almost romantically perfect. I have been moving, to quote your own phrase, through rich experiences, though not swiftly; not swiftly because the experiences have been too rich to hurry through.' " The letter, or the part of it that is quoted, runs to about three hundred words. It is followed by a thousand-word letter Mr. Freeman wrote to Mr. Edman in answer to his, and at the end of that Mr. Freeman writes: "To this long disquisition, Irwin replied from Venice three days later"—and there follow five hundred words of that. Then comes part of a long letter from Irwin in Rome. This is followed by a letter from Louis Smith, and that is followed by Mr. Freeman's answer, and *that* is followed by a letter from "Mac's sister-in-law Lillian," and then comes Mr. Freeman's answer to her, and then a long letter he wrote to Professor James Harvey Robinson, to which Professor Robinson did not reply (if he had, I know darn well the letter would have been printed, together with Mr. Freeman's answer to it). All these letters were written seventeen years ago, but there they are.

Now, whether or not these letters are interesting or important is beside the point I want to make, but I suppose it is only fair to give some idea of what they are like. Take the opening sentence of Mr. Freeman's thousand-word letter to Mr. Edman. He wrote: "It was my idealistic, religious, artistic bias which made me blind to pragmatism." That is the topic sentence of a letter which somehow does not sound like a letter to a friend at all. It sounds more like an essay written to save in a file and someday print in a book. You get the inescapable feeling that the original was sent to a friend in order to get a well-written essay in return, which also could be used in the book. That, of course, is one way to get a book together, and the fact that it is not my way is not so much because I don't like the studied and disingenuous tone of the whole thing as because I could never keep a carbon copy or a letter for fifteen or twenty years, the way Mr. Freeman can. If I keep a letter two weeks, I am doing fine. Then, too, my friends never write me long letters dealing with profound subjects. Their letters are usually hurried and to the point, and they sometimes deal with matters which I wouldn't want to have exposed in a book even after I was dead.

Mr. Irwin Edman and some of Mr. Freeman's other correspondents are well-known writers, and whereas I have got a few letters from well-known writers in my time, none of them would be usable in a book even if I could find them. Some of them are both illegible and illiterate, as if they had been written at a bar. Few of them say anything, really, that anybody would want to read, and none of them sounds as if it had been rewritten several times, the way Mr. Freeman's letters to his friends, and theirs to him, sound. Communist intellectuals are the most facile and articulate of all writers, and words come out of most of them like water from a faucet, so I can't say for sure the letters were rewritten; I just say they sound rewritten. (Rewriting a letter to a girl is all right, under certain circumstances, but that's as far as I will go.)

I happen to remember a letter one well-known writer sent to me some years ago, because it contained only one sentence. It read: "Will you please for God's sake come back with my shoes?" That's all; just that one sentence. And I wouldn't have got that if he had been able to get me on the phone. It seems that this author and myself and a couple of lecturers from Hollywood went to the author's apartment one night. Around five o'clock in the morning, the argument on idealism, religion, art, and pragmatism having rather worn me out, I took off my shoes and lay down on the author's bed. When I got up, I put on his shoes by mistake—not the ones he had on, of course, although I could have done that, but another pair, apparently his favorites. I noticed on my way home that I couldn't walk very well—my feet hurt—but I put it down to the argument. The next morning, however, I had a terrible time getting the shoes on. They were two sizes too small for me, but since I thought they were my own, I could only believe that my feet had swelled. I started to walk up Fifth Avenue, with the gait of a man who is stalking a bird across wet cement. It was pretty painful, and I finally had to take a cab. I suffered all day, but the next morning the author's letter came in asking me to bring back his shoes, and you can imagine my relief, both physical and mental. I had been on the point of going to a doctor. None of this really belongs in a book.

Such letters as I get from persons other than friends of mine are usually written with pen and ink, and often on blue or purple paper. These are almost impossible to make out, and I couldn't use them in a book even if I wanted to. I have one at hand now, for instance, which came just a day or two ago and hasn't been lost yet. I'll quote the first few lines the way I make them out (the letter is written in black India ink on aquamarine paper):

DEAR MR. THUMBER:

For agree blest you've been out of my perine parasites. The obline being in case you're interested, a girl whose name escapes me, but merits swell pecul, and I know you'd know who she is.

That's all I can get out of that. It appears to be signed Keriumiy Luud Roosool, or Kaasaat. Nothing, of course, could be done with it. Even when I can decipher all but a word or two of my correspondence (I never get *every* word), nothing much can be done with it. For instance, I got a post-card last January from a famous man in Washington, and although I practically mastered it, I don't see how I could ever work it into a book. I will quote it verbatim:

WASHINGTON, D. C.

JAN. 8, 1937

MR. JAMES THURBER—On reading some back numbers of N. Yorker came across article, "An Outline of Science." It is plain you know a thing or two about science, but—heh! heh! heh! heh!—[illegible word]. Especially speed of light & those terrible bloodhounds.

Yours Truly, ALBERT GAMBLE,

Hobo Scientist

(Originator of famous Fireball-Waterball Theory of Swimming Continents.)

I'm afraid I'm not going to be able to use any letters or other communications in my own 300,000-word testament, unless I make up some—and I didn't make up Mr. Gamble's—or sneak a few out of Mr. Freeman's book. He'd probably never miss them.

25. After the Steppe Cat, What?

THERE ARE MANY SIGNS WHICH INDICATE THAT OUR CIVILIZA-
tion is on the wane, and these are to be seen not only
in the economic, political, and military phenomena of our
dying day, which are portentously analyzed in every periodi-
cal one picks up, but also in a tiny phenomenon here, a small
paragraph there. Poets have a quick eye to detect these minute
portents of the approaching end. The clairvoyant Stephen
Vincent Benét was probably just one step ahead of actuality
when he wrote of observing a termite which held in its tiny
jaws a glittering crumb of steel. Morris Bishop, another seer
who views tomorrow clearly, has written of the time when in
the mothproof closet will dwell the moth.

It is all very interesting to indulge in polysyllabic discus-
sions of dialectical materialism and dialectical idealism, of
democracy and the totalitarian state, of Marxist hope and
capitalist illusion, but I am more interested in wondering
whether the fleck of dust that got in my eye yesterday may not
have been all that was left of a planet like ours which burned
out a million years ago, ten hundred billion miles away. Perhaps I was struck with that wonder because once in Carthage,
two thousand years ago, the gleam of a Roman shield got in
my eye or a speck of that sand which was to conquer the
very conquerors of one of the oldest and strongest civilizations

known to man. A bit of steel glittering here, a moth flutter-ing there, a handful of dust in the air: these are the signs of doom.

Perhaps some manifestations of the sort always accompany any politico-social collapse. Then again, who is there to say for sure that political and social collapse doesn't merely accom-pany such manifestations? Which reached Rome first, the

The Aardvark

Visigoth or the wolf? It is a momentous question, calling for a great amount of research, and I am sorry I haven't got space to pursue it. I have space for only a few random notes on this general theme, which may haply lead some scientist—or some poet—to a more exhaustive treatment of the subject.

Let us look, first, at a paragraph in the *New York Times*, not long ago, by its Berlin correspondent, Mr. Otto D. Tolischus.

This winter's extraordinary character is already arousing concern for this year's crops; and in addition, certain districts, especially Silesia, complain of a veritable plague of rats and mice. German agricultural quarters are now engaged in a hot public debate regarding charges that the many draining, land reclamation, and river regulation projects the National Socialist regime has undertaken are so interfering with the country's water economy as to turn Germany gradually into a steppe. There are assertions by experts that certain unmistakable steppe animals and plants are already beginning to make themselves at home in Germany.

Here we see how the Nazi land-reclamation engineers are beginning to make Germany into a steppe, exactly as the United States' land-*wasting* pioneers began to make this country into a Sahara. There would appear to be no way

The Bandicoot

out, in a time of world decay, no matter what you do. It proceeds by curious, inexorable laws of its own, this ending of a jaded civilization, that a new way of life may begin. Nature helps along the destruction by sending her rodents in hordes to gnaw at the very foundations of man's existence. Thus rats and mice appear in Silesia—and don't get one hundredth the attention that LaGuardia got when he gnawed only at German pride. And yet these rodents are a hundred times more important, for they will outlast LaGuardia—and

German pride, too—as the mollusks from which Tyrian dye was made have outlived Tyre and the Tyrians.

The desert into which America is turning is perhaps more familiar than the steppe into which Germany is changing. A steppe is a large tract of arid land characterized by xerophilous vegetation—that is, plant life that can stand the absence or scarcity of moisture. It is a primitive sort of land, flat and treeless, suitable for open warfare, fit for man and his activities in the last stages of a civilization. Among the "unmistakable steppe animals" that will eventually trot into Berlin is the steppe cat, a small wildcat. It has grayish-white fur, useful as camouflage in the open spaces, but it is interesting to note that

The Wombat

it also has blackish transverse bands, a coloration obviously developed by nature to serve as camouflage when it finally reaches the cities, where it can creep unnoticed between car tracks and behind picket fences.

Walter Lippman recently insisted in the *Atlantic Monthly*

that "Communism and fascism are not only much alike as systems of government; they are alike in the inwardness of their purpose." To which I feel impelled to add that the systems and purposes of man are all one to the steppe cat. And to the termite, the rat, the mouse, the grasshopper, the locust, the caterpillar, the weevil, the wombat, the rabbit, the aardvark, the bandicoot, the Scotch terrier, the cockroach, the coddling moth, and the Colorado potato beetle, to name just a few of the thousands of insects and animals that will go to town with the steppe cat when the Great Invasion begins.

In the olden days, of which Omar sang, it was the lion and the lizard that moved sleepily into the courtyard of the

The Steppe Cat

palace; they had no system and no purpose, so that man, rising again from the ashes of his ruined civilization, could easily oust them. The next and greatest invasion of the lower species will find, I think, all the living things, with a kind of planned economy, moving in on man, who has too long been keeping a hostile and fearful eye on his fellow man, to the exclusion of any interest in the steppe cat and the steppe cat's million allies. Pick up any large dictionary and turn the pages —you'll have to turn only one or two—till you come to the picture of a pest of some sort. In the majority of cases you will find under its name these descriptive phrases: "now widely distributed" and "often causing great damage." There is a bug that works at the foundation of houses; there is one that destroys each kind of tree; there is one that gets into tea and spices; there is one that specializes in the ruining of tobacco; there is even one, common to the Congo, that seeks to inhabit the human eye.

Working quietly through the ages, the insects and the rodents, at once specialists and collectivists, have prepared themselves, I believe, to take over the world. I see no reason to believe that they will not make a better job of it than man. One July day in 1863 a handful of troopers rode idly into a town called Gettysburg, in Pennsylvania. The inhabitants glanced at them and went about their business. There could be no war in that little town; the troopers would ride away. Two or three steppe cats are observed in Germany, and the fact is recorded briefly on page 8 of the *New York Times*.

Not long ago Dr. Earnest A. Hooton, Harvard professor of anthropology and President of the American Association of Physical Anthropologists, announced in a lecture that man is deteriorating—in behavior, in physique, and in intelligence. This was not news to those of us who have our ears to the steppe. I think it also quite probable that it was not news to the steppe cat. In the course of his talk Dr. Hooton pointed out that man has not added any new domestic animals to his collection since the time when animals were first put to use. He might have extended this observation to include the prophecy that one day the animals may begin, in their own way, to domesticate man, who, as Dr. Hooton said, is becoming ludicrous in body, ineffective in culture, and moronic in intelligence. In short, a set-up for animals, which are becoming less ludicrous, more cunning, and smarter every year.

Dr. Hooton also said that man is "not yet successful in his fight against micro-organisms, to any great extent." To which he might have added that, while man is peering into microscopes at micro-organisms, the steppe cat has slipped into Germany. It was not so long ago that the praying mantis came in a horde to look over New York City. You could find them reconnoitering high up on the Empire State Building. They peered into bedrooms and kitchens from window sills. They were all over the place. Then they quietly went away. The papers and the public treated it as a curious but unimportant phenomenon, that visit. I regard it as an extremely significant occurrence. Scouting planes in advance of the infantry, the tanks, and the bombers.

Where Carthage once stood in her glory and pride there rises a cluster of modern villas, forming a suburb of the modern city of Tunis. Thus has the greatness of a sovereign power diminished. To what new kind of metropolis may Tunis someday become a suburb? Look through your field glasses at the nearest steppe land—look close to the ground. There—see that grayish-white blur, with the blackish transverse bands?

26. Women Go On Forever

THE OUTLOOK FOR THE CONTINUANCE OF THE LIFE OF MAN ON this earth, in the style to which he has been accustomed, is, as everybody must surely know, not very bright. Socially, economically, physically and intellectually, Man is slowly going, I am reliably informed, to hell. His world is blowing over; his day is done. I have the word of a hundred scientists and psychologists for this sorry fact. You have but to pick up the nearest book or magazine—or the one right next to it—to read the disconcerting news.

There have been prophecies of doom, such as Oswald Spengler's; there have been diagnoses of the malady, such as Dr. Carrel's; there have been programs for its correction, such as Karl Marx's; there have been sociological formulas for its clarification, such as Pareto's; there have even been whole new cosmogonies proposed, such as H. G. Wells'. Each expert, in his fashion, has analyzed the decline of Mankind and most of them have prescribed remedies for the patient. But none of them, I believe, has detected the fact that although Man, as he is now traveling, is headed for extinction, Woman is not going with him. It is, I think, high time to abandon the loose generic term "Man," for it is no longer logically inclusive or scientifically exact. There is Man and there is Woman, and Woman is going her own way.

Scientists, statisticians, actuaries, all those men who place numbers above hunches, figures above feelings, facts above possibilities, the normal above the phenomenal, will tell you that the life span of the average man is, and will remain, approximately the same as the life span of the average woman. This is because, with their eyes on the average, they fail to discern the significant. The significant is never, to begin with, larger than a man's hand, and sometimes it is no larger than a hole in a dike—or a three-line item in the New York *Times*.

It was on January 14, 1937, that I clipped this bit of significance from the pages of that newspaper: "La Salle, Ont.—Cheerful, remarkably agile, Mrs. Felice Meloche celebrated her 104th birthday here yesterday. Mrs. Meloche sang for her guests the French song 'Alouette' without a quaver in her voice."

Since that day I have kept track of news items dealing with persons who have lived to be 100 years old or older, and the record is provocative. It contains the names of six men. Four of them were written about because they had died. The oldest of the six was 103. The record contains the names of 37 women. Twenty-four of the items, or about two-thirds, reported how the ladies celebrated their birthdays—by singing, dancing, riding in airplanes, playing kettledrums, running foot races, chinning themselves or entertaining their great-great-grandchildren. Let us look at the record for one week, the last week in March—a record that is confined, because of the short scope of my news sources, to greater New York and the region roundabout:

On March 25, Mrs. Amorette E. Fraser of Brooklyn celebrated her 101st birthday by taking a vigorous walk, riding in a taxi, standing for two hours to greet dozens of visitors, and denouncing the Roosevelt Administration. On March 28, Mrs. Emily S. Andrews, of Plainfield, New Jersey, celebrated her 101st birthday by entertaining 100 guests at tea—an event which she took in her stride. On March 29, the Burlington County Almshouse in New Jersey was destroyed by fire and among those saved was "Uncle Joe" Willow, aged 103. As reporters gathered around and were about to interview this remarkable ancient, who should emerge casually from the flames, fit as a fiddle and chipper as a lark, but "Aunt Mary" Asay, aged 114? When Joe Willow was ten years old and in the fourth grade, Mary Asay was 21—and probably married and running a big household. "The fire," said the story in the New York *Herald Tribune,* "was discovered by a 132-year-old-nurse"—no, I'm wrong there. It was discovered by a nurse in the 132-year-old east wing of the building. But anyway, here was Mary Asay, born when James Monroe was President, one of the numerous outstanding proofs of my theory that women are tending to become immortal, that the day will come when they will never die. They are flourishing on all sides of us, singing and dancing and denouncing the Administration, these deathless ladies, some of whom have outlived their husbands by periods ranging from 50 to 100 years.

The increasingly tenacious hold on life of the female of the human species begins, my researches show, at birth. I recently asked an eminent obstetrician whether, if a baby he was about to deliver were in foetal distress, he would prefer it to be a boy or a girl. Prefacing his hesitant answer with the cautious announcement that there are no scientific data to go by, he said he would prefer it to be a girl. Does any obstetrician, I asked him, believe for a moment that five *males* would have survived up there in Callander, Ontario, on that historic night? To which, since, again lacking data, he declined to reply, I replied for him; no. The birth of five females and their survival against incredible odds assumes the clear nature of a portent that only the Scientist is too blind to see. Man's day is indeed done; the epoch of Woman is upon us.

I should like in conclusion to call attention to figures I and

II which accompany this treatise and which you probably thought I had forgotten. They are, you will observe, absolutely identical faces, save that one (Fig. I) is male and the other (Fig. II) is female. Yet it is easy to discern in the male physiognomy the symptoms of that extinction which threatens his sex: an air of uncertainty, an expression of futility, a general absence of "hold," which are inescapable.

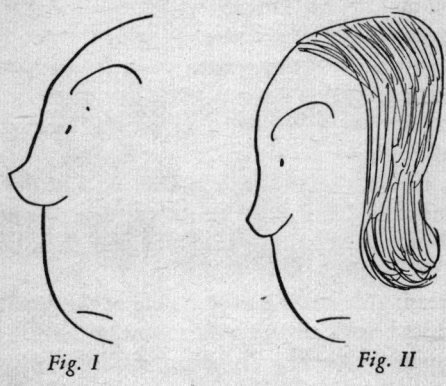

Fig. I   Fig. II

There is about the female, on the other hand, a hint of survival, a threat of perpetuation, a general "Here I am and here I always will be," which are equally unmistakable. The male is obviously not looking at anything; he is lost in the moody contemplation of an existence which is slipping away from him; already its outlines are far and vague. The female unquestionably has her eyes on an objective; you can feel the solid, sharp edges of her purpose.

It was, unless I've got my notes mixed up, our old friend Professor Ernest A. Hooton of Harvard who, in the course of a recent lecture on the physical and mental decline of Mankind, observed that "when women reach a certain age they seem to become immortal." I think that he and I have got hold of something. Just what good it will do us, being males, I do not know.

27. The Wood Duck

Mr. krepp, our vegetable man, had told us we might find some cider out the New Milford road a way—we would come to a sign saying "Morris Plains Farm" and that would be the place. So we got into the car and drove down the concrete New Milford road, which is black in the center with the dropped oil of a million cars. It's a main-trunk highway; you can go fifty miles an hour on it except where warning signs limit you to forty or, near towns, thirty-five, but nobody ever pays any attention to these signs. Even then, in November, dozens of cars flashed past us with a high, ominous whine, their tires roaring rubberly on the concrete. We found Morris Plains Farm without any trouble. There was a big white house to the left of the highway; only a few yards off the road a small barn had been made into a roadside stand, with a dirt driveway curving up to the front of it. A spare, red-cheeked man stood in the midst of baskets and barrels of red apples and glass jugs of red cider. He was waiting on a man and a woman. I turned into the driveway—and put the brakes on hard. I had seen, just in time, a duck.

It was a small, trim duck, and even I, who know nothing about wild fowl, knew that this was no barnyard duck, this was a wild duck. He was all alone. There was no other bird of any kind around, not even a chicken. He was immensely solitary. With none of the awkward waddling of a domestic duck, he kept walking busily around in the driveway, now and then billing up water from a dirty puddle in the middle of the drive. His obvious contentment, his apparently perfect adjustment to his surroundings, struck me as something of a marvel. I got out of the car and spoke about it to a man who had driven up behind me in a rattly sedan. He wore a leather jacket and high, hard boots, and I figured he would know what kind of duck this was. He did. "That's a wood duck," he said. "It dropped in here about two weeks ago, Len says, and's been here ever since."

The proprietor of the stand, in whose direction my informant had nodded as he spoke, helped his customers load a basket of apples into their car and walked over to us. The

duck stepped, with a little flutter of its wings, into the dirty puddle, took a small, unconcerned swim, and got out again, ruffling its feathers. "It's rather an odd place for a wood duck, isn't it?" asked my wife. Len grinned and nodded; we all watched the duck. "He's a banded duck," said Len. "There's a band on his leg. The state game commission sends out a lot of 'em. This'n lighted here two weeks ago—it was on a Saturday—and he's been around ever since." "It's funny he wouldn't be frightened away, with all the cars going by and all the people driving in," I said. Len chuckled. "He seems to like it here," he said. The duck wandered over to some sparse grass at the edge of the road, aimlessly, but with an air of settled satisfaction. "He's tame as anything," said Len. "I guess they get tame when them fellows band 'em." The man in the leather jacket said, " 'Course they haven't let you shoot wood duck for a long while and that might make 'em tame, too." "Still," said my wife (we forgot about the cider for the moment), "it's strange he would stay here, right on the road almost." "Sometimes," said Len, reflectively, "he goes round back o' the barn. But mostly he's here in the drive." "But don't they," she asked, "let them loose in the woods after they're banded? I mean, aren't they supposed to stock up the forests?" "I guess they're supposed to," said Len, chuckling again. "But 'pears this'n didn't want to."

An old Ford truck lurched into the driveway and two men in the seat hailed the proprietor. They were hunters, big, warmly dressed, heavily shod men. In the back of the truck was a large bird dog. He was an old pointer and he wore an expression of remote disdain for the world of roadside commerce. He took no notice of the duck. The two hunters said something to Len about cider, and I was just about to chime in with my order when the accident happened. A car went by the stand at fifty miles an hour, leaving something scurrying in its wake. It was the duck, turning over and over on the concrete. He turned over and over swiftly, but lifelessly, like a thrown feather duster, and then he lay still. "My God," I cried, "they've killed your duck, Len!" The accident gave me a quick feeling of anguished intimacy with the bereaved man. "Oh, now," he wailed. "Now, that's awful!" None of us for a moment moved. Then the two hunters walked toward the road, slowly, self-consciously, a little embarrassed in the face of this quick incongruous ending of a wild fowl's life in the middle of a concrete highway. The pointer stood up, looked after the hunters, raised his ears briefly, and then lay down again.

It was the man in the leather jacket finally who walked out to the duck and tried to pick it up. As he did so, the duck stood up. He looked about him like a person who has been abruptly wakened and doesn't know where he is. He didn't ruffle his feathers. "Oh, he isn't quite *dead!*" said my wife. I knew how she felt. We were going to have to see the duck die; somebody would have to kill him, finish him off. Len stood beside us. My wife took hold of his arm. The man in the leather jacket knelt down, stretched out a hand, and the duck moved slightly away. Just then, out from behind the barn, limped a setter dog, a lean white setter dog with black spots. His right back leg was useless and he kept it off the ground. He stopped when he saw the duck in the road and gave it a point, putting his head out, lifting his left front leg, maintaining a wavering, marvellous balance on two legs. He was like a drunken man drawing a bead with a gun. This new menace, this anticlimax, was too much. I think I yelled.

What happened next happened as fast as the automobile accident. The setter made his run, a limping, wobbly run, and he was in between the men and the bird before they saw him. The duck flew, got somehow off the ground a foot or two, and tumbled into the grass of the field across the road, the dog after him. It seemed crazy, but the duck could fly—a little, anyway. "Here, here," said Len, weakly. The hunters shouted, I shouted, my wife screamed, "He'll kill him! He'll *kill* him!" The duck flew a few yards again, the dog at his tail. The dog's third plunge brought his nose almost to the duck's tail, and then one of the hunters tackled the animal and pulled him down and knelt in the grass, holding him. We all breathed easier. My wife let go Len's arm.

Len started across the road after the duck, who was fluttering slowly, waveringly, but with a definite purpose, toward a wood that fringed the far side of the field. The bird was dazed, but a sure, atavistic urge was guiding him; he was going home. One of the hunters joined Len in his pursuit.

The other came back across the road, dragging the indignant setter; the man in the leather jacket walked beside them. We all watched Len and his companion reach the edge of the wood and stand there, looking; they had followed the duck through the grass slowly, so as not to alarm him; he had been alarmed enough. "He'll never come back," said my wife. Len and the hunter finally turned and came back through the grass. The duck had got away from them. We walked out to meet them at the edge of the concrete. Cars began to whiz by in both directions. I realized, with wonder, that all the time the duck, and the hunters, and the setter were milling around in the road, not one had passed. It was as if traffic had been held up so that our little drama could go on. "He couldn't o' been much hurt," said Len. "Likely just grazed and pulled along in the wind of the car. Them fellows don't look out for anything. It's a sin." My wife had a question for him. "Does your dog always chase the duck?" she asked. "Oh, that ain't my dog," said Len. "He just comes around." The hunter who had been holding the setter now let him go, and he slunk away. The pointer, I noticed, lay with his eyes closed. "But doesn't the duck mind the dog?" persisted my wife. "Oh, he minds him," said Len. "But the dog's never really hurt him none yet. There's always somebody around."

We drove away with a great deal to talk about (I almost forgot the cider). I explained the irony, I think I explained the profound symbolism, of a wild duck's becoming attached to a roadside stand. My wife strove simply to understand the duck's viewpoint. She didn't get anywhere. I knew even then, in the back of my mind, what would happen. We decided, after a cocktail, to drive back to the place and find out if the duck had returned. My wife hoped it wouldn't be there, on account of the life it led in the driveway; I hoped it wouldn't because I felt that would be, somehow, too pat an ending. Night was falling when we started off again for Morris Plains Farm. It was a five-mile drive and I had to put my bright lights on before we got there. The barn door was closed for the night. We didn't see the duck anywhere. The only thing to do was to go up to the house and inquire. I knocked on the door and a young man opened it. "Is—is the proprietor here?" I asked. He said no, he had gone to Waterbury. "We wanted to know," my wife said, "whether the duck came back." "What?" he asked, a little startled, I thought. Then, "Oh, the duck. I saw him around the driveway when my father drove off." He stared at us, waiting. I thanked him and started back to the car. My wife lingered, explaining, for a moment. "He thinks we're crazy," she said, when she got into the car. We drove on a little distance. "Well," I said, "he's back." "I'm glad he is, in a way," said my wife. "I hated to think of him all alone out there in the woods."

28. The Admiral on the Wheel

WHEN THE COLORED MAID STEPPED ON MY GLASSES THE other morning, it was the first time they had been broken since the late Thomas A. Edison's seventy-ninth birthday. I remember that day well, because I was working for a newspaper then and I had been assigned to go over to West Orange that morning and interview Mr. Edison. I got up early and, in reaching for my glasses under the bed (where I always put them), I found that one of my more sober and reflective Scotch terriers was quietly chewing them. Both tortoiseshell temples (the pieces that go over your ears) had been eaten and Jeannie was toying with the lenses in a sort of jaded way. It was in going over to Jersey that day, without my glasses, that I realized that the disadvantages of defective vision (bad eyesight) are at least partially compensated for by its peculiar advantages. Up to that time I had been in the habit of going to bed when my glasses were broken and lying there until they were fixed again. I had believed I could not go very far without them, not more than a block, anyway, on account of the danger of bumping into things, getting a headache, losing my way. None of those things happened, but a lot of others did. I saw the Cuban flag flying over a national bank, I saw a gay old lady with a gray parasol walk right through the side of a truck, I saw a cat roll across a street in a small striped barrel, I saw bridges rise lazily into the air, like balloons.

I suppose you have to have just the right proportion of sight to encounter such phenomena: I seem to remember that oculists have told me I have only two-fifths vision without what one of them referred to as "artificial compensation" (glasses). With three-fifths vision or better, I suppose the

Cuban flag would have been an American flag, the gay old lady a garbage man with a garbage can on his back, the cat a piece of butcher's paper blowing in the wind, the floating bridges smoke from tugs, hanging in the air. With perfect vision, one is extricably trapped in the workaday world, a prisoner of reality, as lost in the commonplace America of 1937 as Alexander Selkirk was lost on his lonely island. For the hawk-eyed person life has none of those soft edges which for me blur into fantasy; for such a person an electric welder is merely an electric welder, not a radiant fool setting off a sky-rocket by day. The kingdom of the partly blind is a little like

Oz, a little like Wonderland, a little like Poictesme. Anything you can think of, and a lot you never would think of, can happen there.

For three days after the maid, in cleaning the apartment, stepped on my glasses—I had not put them far enough under the bed—I worked at home and did not go uptown to have them fixed. It was in this period that I made the acquaintance of a remarkable Chesapeake spaniel. I looked out my window and after a moment spotted him, a noble, silent dog lying on a ledge above the entrance to a brownstone house in lower Fifth Avenue. He lay there, proud and austere, for three days and nights, sleepless, never eating, the perfect watchdog. No ordinary dog could have got up on the high ledge above the doorway, to begin with; no ordinary people would have owned such an animal. The ordinary people were the people who walked by the house and did not see the dog. Oh, I got my glasses fixed finally and I know that now the dog has gone, but I haven't looked to see what prosaic object occupies the spot where he so staunchly stood guard over one of the last of the old New York houses on Fifth Avenue; perhaps an unpainted flowerbox or a cleaning cloth dropped from an upper window by a careless menial. The moment of disenchantment would be too hard; I never look out that particular window any more.

Sometimes at night, even with my glasses on, I see strange and unbelievable sights, mainly when I am riding in an automobile which somebody else is driving (I never drive myself at night out of fear that I might turn up at the portals of some mystical monastery and never return). Only last summer I was riding with someone along a country road when suddenly I cried at him to look out. He slowed down and asked me sharply what was the matter. There is no worse experience than to have someone shout at you to look out for something you don't see. What this driver didn't see and I did see (two-fifths vision works a kind of magic in the night) was a little old admiral in full-dress uniform riding a bicycle at right angles to the car I was in. He might have been starlight behind a tree, or a billboard advertising Moxie; I don't know —we were quickly past the place he rode out of; but I would recognize him if I saw him again. His beard was blowing in the breeze and his hat was set at a rakish angle, like Admiral Beatty's. He was having a swell time. The gentleman who was driving the car has been, since that night, a trifle stiff and distant with me. I suppose you can hardly blame him.

To go back to my daylight experiences with the naked eye, it was me, in case you have heard the story, who once killed fifteen white chickens with small stones. The poor beggars never had a chance. This happened many years ago when I was living at Jay, New York. I had a vegetable garden some seventy feet behind the house, and the lady of the house had asked me to keep an eye on it in my spare moments and to chase away any chickens from neighboring farms that came pecking around. One morning, getting up from my typewriter, I wandered out behind the house and saw that a flock of white chickens had invaded the garden. I had, to be sure, misplaced my glasses for the moment, but I could still see well enough to let the chickens have it with ammunition from a pile of stones that I kept handy for the purpose. Before I could be stopped, I had riddled all the tomato plants in the garden, over the tops of which the lady of the house had, the twilight before, placed newspapers and paper bags to ward off the effects of frost. It was one of the darker experiences of my dimmer hours.

Some day, I suppose, when the clouds are heavy and the rain is coming down and the pressure of realities is too great,

I shall deliberately take my glasses off and go wandering out into the streets. I daresay I may never be heard of again (I have always believed it was Ambrose Bierce's vision and not his whim that caused him to wander into oblivion). I imagine I'll have a remarkable time, wherever I end up.